George Edward Weare

Cabot's Discovery of North America

George Edward Weare

Cabot's Discovery of North America

ISBN/EAN: 9783337321529

Printed in Europe, USA, Canada, Australia, Japan

Cover: Foto ©ninafisch / pixelio.de

More available books at **www.hansebooks.com**

CABOT'S DISCOVERY

OF

NORTH AMERICA

BY

G. E. WEARE
AUTHOR OF
"EDMUND BURKE'S CONNECTION WITH BRISTOL FROM
1774 TILL 1780" "COLLECTANEA RELATING TO
THE BRISTOL FRIARS' MINORS (GREY FRIARS)" ETC.

JOHN MACQUEEN
HASTINGS HOUSE, NORFOLK STREET
LONDON
1897

PREFACE

IT would take up considerable space to enumerate all the printed books, pamphlets, etc., I have consulted in the course of completing this work. I desire, however, to say that I have derived very considerable assistance from the several able works of Mr. Henry Harrisse; from Dr. Justin Winsor's *Narr. and Crit. History of America*, and his recent pamphlet on the Cabot controversies; from Professor John Fiske's work, *The Discovery of America*; Mr. H. F. Brownson's translation of Francesco Tarducci's book, a work which deals with, but leaves unsettled, several moot points in the history of John and of Sebastian Cabot; *The Journal of Columbus*, by Sir Clements R. Markham, K.C.B., the president of the Royal Geographical Society (to whom we are indebted for a further contribution to the Cabot literature contained in an address recently delivered at a meeting of the society over which he presides); the very valuable monograph by Dr. S. E. Dawson, F.R.G.S., of Ottawa, published in 1894, together with a sequel thereto published last year.; a contribution by Rev. Dr. Harvey, of St. John's, Newfoundland, published in *Collections of the Nova Scotia Historical Society, for the years* 1893-95.

Among those who have given me advice and assistance are—the Right Hon. Professor Max Müller, of Oxford; Sir Clements R. Markham, K.C.B., who has spared me much of his valuable time in interchanging ideas as to the doubtful points in the history of the two voyages of 1497 and 1498; Dr. R. Garnett, C.B., of the British Museum; Dr. S. E. Dawson, of Ottawa, the most erudite of Canadian historians; Dr. Moses Harvey, of Newfoundland; Messrs. William George and John Latimer, both of Bristol, the two best authorities on all matters of historical interest pertaining to Bristol, from both of whom I have received valuable help; Mr. F. W. Coleman, the librarian of the Weston-super-Mare Free Library, who has kindly assisted me in the revision of the "Introduction"; Miss E. M. Walford, of London; Mr. C. W. Moule, Fellow and Librarian of Corpus Christi College, Cambridge; Mr. Miller Christy, of Chelmsford; Mr. E. E. Baker, F.S.A., of Weston-super-Mare; Mr. Lorin A. Lathrop, the American Consul at Bristol; and Mr. Frank George, of Park Street, Bristol.

If I shall succeed in making plain to a few of my readers the facts relating to the important Cabotian discovery; if I shall succeed in making a permanent addition—however slight it may be—to the ever-increasing common stock of reliable information, I shall regard my labours, which have occupied a considerable time, as not having been quite barren of result.

G. E. WEARE.

WESTON-SUPER-MARE,
May 1897.

CONTENTS

INTRODUCTION . . . . *pp.* 1–30

CHAPTER I

The current belief (in the fifteenth century) in the existence of islands in the Atlantic Ocean called "St Brandon," "Brasil," "The Seven Cities," etc.—Allusions to the Expedition from Bristol (twelve years before Columbus embarked upon his first voyage) in quest of the mythical islands—The ancient belief in the existence of "The Fortunate Islands" and "The Isles of the Blest"—References to the origin, etc., of "Brasil" and the other mythical islands—Brandon Hill, Bristol, formerly known as St. Brandon Hill, with a hermitage or chapel thereon—References to William Wyrcestre, a fifteenth-century Chronicler, his family, etc.—Wyrcestre's notes as to Brandon Hill, the Expedition in search of "Brasil" in 1480, in a ship belonging to John Jay and another—Pedro de Ayala's reference to the Expedition from Bristol in search of the island of Brasil and the Seven Cities *pp.* 31–59

CHAPTER II

References to the Papal Bull granted in the year 1493, which purported to divide all undiscovered lands between the Spanish and the Portuguese—Translation of the Papal Bull—The successful voyage of John Cabot in the *Matthew*, of Bristol, in the year 1497—Cabot's discovery of the continent of North America—The planting of the English flag on the continent by Cabot—The importance of Cabot's discovery—John Cabot's character—Tarducci's opinion of Cabot's adventure—Cabot's theory as to "the land of the Grand Khan"—References to Cabot's description of the land found by him—To whom should the credit of the discovery of America be given ?—References to Columbus, Toscanelli, Prince Henry of Portugal—Rev. M. Harvey's references to the voyages of the Portuguese down the African coast—References to the struggle for the supremacy of the Mediterranean—The Italian Renaissance and its effect upon the European States—The citizens of Bristol and John Cabot's discovery . *pp.* 60-93

CHAPTER III

The petition of John Cabot and his three sons to King Henry VII.— A transcript of the Letters-patent *ipsissimis verbis* from the original—A translation of the Letters-patent—References to the character of King Henry VII.—Concessions obtained for the merchants, whom the King ultimately fleeced—The up-break of exclusive trading begun in this reign—Cabot's plans probably understood and appreciated by the King—References to Christopher Columbus and his brother Bartholomew—Hakluyt's reference to the offer by Christopher Columbus to the King in the year 1488— Cabot's connection with Bristol—References to William Canynges, of Bristol, merchant—Canynges's connection with the Church of St. Mary Redcliff, Bristol—The Jay brasses in St. Mary Redcliff Church—The Will of John Jay—References to the whale's rib which is fixed to the wall of St. Mary Redcliff Church—The despatch of Ruy Gonzales de Puebla, the Spanish Ambassador, to their Catholic Majesties, in which he refers to the arrival of Cabot—Puebla calls Cabot a Genoese—Professor John Fiske's description of the sailing of the *Matthew* from the Bristol Channel—Mr. Sandford Fleming's reference thereto—Note as to the sailing of the *Matthew* in Barrett's *History of Bristol*—Ditto in a MS. Chronicle formerly in the possession of the Fust family; certain excerpts taken therefrom, being in the possession of Mr. W. George, of Bristol . . . . *pp.* 94-122

CHAPTER IV

Dr. M. Harvey's notes as to the sailing of the *Matthew*—Confirmation of the date of the return of the *Matthew*—John Cabot's journey to Westminster to apprise the King of his discovery— The King gives him £10—References to the voyage by Ambassadors and others—Cabot's negotiations with the King—The King grants Cabot an annuity of £20 per annum—Copy of the

CONTENTS ix

document relating to Cabot's annuity—Copy of another document relating to the annuity—References to the Collectors of the King's Customs at Bristol—References to the documents relating to the voyages of 1497 and 1498, which have been found in the archives of foreign countries—Copy letter written by Lorenzo Pasqualigo —Copy despatch from Raimondo de Soncino—Copy of the second despatch of Raimondo de Soncino—Dr. S. E. Dawson's allusion to Soncino's despatches—Notes as to the second Cabotian voyage, and the documents relating thereto—Entries of payments by the King to Thirkill, Bradley, and Carter—Copy of John Cabot's petition for the grant of Letters-patent—Copy (in English) of the Letters-patent to John Cabot from the roll of the Privy Seals— Copy (in Latin) of the same Letters-patent—Extract from a despatch from Dr. Puebla—Copy despatch from Pedro de Ayala— Extract from an anonymous Chronicle—References to the fate of Cabot and his Expedition—Tarducci's references to John Cabot . . . . *pp.* 123-166

CHAPTER V

Entries made by foreign Historians and Chroniclers as to the discovery of the continent of North America—The account given by Pietro Martire (Peter Martyr) of Anghiera—References to Richard Eden, the translator and author—The facts relating to the dispute as to the birthplace of Sebastian Cabot, and as to the comparative agency of John and Sebastian Cabot in the work of discovery— The words used by Marc-Antonio Contarini—The accounts of the discovery given by Galvão, Gomara, and Ramusio respectively— Peter Martyr's statement that some Spaniards had thrown doubt on the generally accepted statement that Sebastian Cabot was the discoverer of the region called Baccalaos—Statement made by the Drapers Company as to Sebastian Cabot . . *pp.* 167-209

CHAPTER VI

Proposals by Sebastian Cabot to King Henry VIII. for an Expedition to "the newe found Iland"—References to Sebastian Cabot's intrigues with Venice—The circumnavigation of the Globe by the Expedition fitted out by Magellan—The Correspondence relating to Sebastian's intrigue with the Council of Ten of Venice— Sebastian's offer to enter the English service accepted in the year

x   CONTENTS

1547—Sebastian returns to England—Grant of an annuity to
Sebastian—The intrigues of Sebastian in the year 1550 with the
Council of Ten of Venice . . . . . *pp.* 210-243

CHAPTER VII

Mr. Harrisse's references to the belief that Sebastian Cabot was the
discoverer of the north continent of America—Richard Hakluyt's
first publication in the year 1582—References to Hakluyt and his
works—References to a Chronicle in the Cottonian MSS. in the
British Museum, to the Fabyan MS. Chronicle, and to the work of
John Stow—Hakluyt's references to Sebastian Cabot—Notes by
Harrisse and Tarducci—Richard Biddle's work published in 1831—
Discovery of the so-called Sebastian Cabot's planisphere—References
to the inscriptions on the planisphere—Notes by Major, Harrisse,
d'Avezac, Kohl, Winsor, as to the map and its inscriptions—
Summary of the important questions raised in the course of the
discussion as to the genuineness of the map . . *pp.* 244-277

CHAPTER VIII

As to the landfall of John Cabot in 1497—Description of La Cosa's
Map constructed in the year 1500—Dr. Dawson's remarks as
to the identification of Cape Race with Cavo de Ynglaterra—
Report of the Canadian Committee as to the landfall—Mr. Henry
Harrisse's theory—Dr. S. E. Dawson's theory—Sir Clements
Markham's theory—The fate of John Cabot's Expedition of 1498
—The Cantino Map—The Quater-centenary Celebration in 1897
of John Cabot's great achievement . . . *pp.* 278-303

APPENDIX A—Plato's Story of the Lost Island of Atlantis *pp.* 305-326

APPENDIX B—The Latin Text of the Bull of Pope Alexander VI.,
dated the 4th day of May 1493 . . . . *pp.* 327-332

APPENDIX C—Account of the Collectors of the Bristol Customs
pp. 333-336

INDEX   .   *pp.* 337-343

LIST OF ILLUSTRATIONS

	PAGES
CABOT DESCRIBING HIS DISCOVERY TO KING HENRY VII. [*After an old engraving. Conjectural.*]	*Frontispiece*
BEHEM'S TERRESTRIAL GLOBE (PART OF)	28–29
BRANDON HILL, WITH A VIEW OF THE AVON (BRISTOL) RIVER (*a section of an ancient map of Bristol*)	56–57
TOSCANELLI'S MAP	80–81
ST. MARY REDCLIFF CHURCH, BRISTOL (NORTH VIEW) [*This Illustration is taken from a block kindly lent by Messrs.* MACK & Co. *of Bristol.*]	106–107
THE JAY BRASSES IN ST. MARY REDCLIFF CHURCH	108–109
THE PENN MEMORIAL IN ST. MARY REDCLIFF CHURCH	110–111
OLD BRISTOL BRIDGE (*showing the Chapel of the Assumption of the B.V. Mary built across the Bridge, and "St. Nicholas's Gate," one of the city gates, with the Chancel of the Church of St. Nicholas over the gateway*)	132–133
THE NORTH AMERICAN PORTION OF THE SO-CALLED CABOT MAPPEMONDE OF 1544	266–267
THE "MATTHEW" OF BRISTOL—REPRESENTED BY A SHIP OF THE PERIOD—SAILING NEAR CAPE RACE	278–279
JUAN DE LA COSA'S MAP (A.D. 1500)	292–293
THE CANTINO MAP (A.D. 1502)	300–301

INTRODUCTION

IF we desire to trace the history of the science and practice of navigation from the outset, it is necessary to go back to Phœnician and Egyptian sources. But, unfortunately, the paucity of authentic knowledge as to the Phœnician navigations leaves us no alternative but to pass on to some of the important events associated with the ancient Egyptians.

Among the important events in Egyptian navigation may be mentioned a large expedition which the Queen of Egypt (*circa* 1600 B.C.) equipped to the land known as Punt, of which there is a long and very interesting account given on the walls of the temple at Deir-el-Bahari. They seem to have got a little beyond Cape Guardafui. We are thus enabled to give some of the details of this early voyage of discovery. It is recorded that the queen was incited to undertake the expedition to "the unknown Balsam Land of Punt" by the oracle of the chief Theban god, Amon. This, however, was a pious fiction so far as it purports—either directly or by inference—to be a revelation from the god as to the existence of a land hitherto unknown to the Egyptians. It seems clear that the early Egyptians had become acquainted with the distant "land of spices." There had been previous expeditions, which had resulted in their obtaining the spices used in the making of incense for the temples, and the places whither they went in those early times were known as Ophir[1] and Punt.[2] "The Ophir" was probably the coast of Somali, while Punt seems to have been the name given to the south and west coasts of Arabia. Queen Hatshepsu's fleet consisted of a number of vessels which were apparently of sufficient strength and construction to undergo what must have been at that period a hazardous voyage. It is recorded that the vessels were manned by able seamen, probably Phœnicians.[3] The expedition ultimately reached its destination. It is also recorded that they landed on the coast of "the incense mountain," which appeared to them to have been cut into terraces, in the vicinity of Cape Guardafui, the "Arômata Akron" of the Greek historians. The ships were filled for the return voyage with a most extraordinary collection of the products of this "divine earth," and included "thirty-one incense trees, well packed in tubs, [which] were dragged on board by the natives," also "different nut woods of the divine land, with heaps of the resin of incense . . . with ebony,

---

[1] Columbus died in the full belief that the lands he had discovered were portions of Asia. He, thinking Toscanelli's map to be correct, came to the conclusion that the island afterwards known as Hispaniola was Ophir! And even in the year 1525 we find that Sebastian Cabot held a belief that by sailing in the westward waters a way would be found to "las islas de Tarsis e Ofir al Catayo oriental—the islands of Tarsis and Ophir in Eastern Cathay."

[2] The first expedition to Punt, the "Holy Land," was sent by Se-aukh-Ka-Ra about 2500 B.C., under Hannu, who has left an account of it.

[3] Phœnician is only a translation of Kefa, or Kêphene, the people of the Palm Land, the name by which they were known to the ancient Egyptians.

objects in ivory inlaid with much gold from the land of the Amoo, with sweet woods, Khesit wood, with Ahem incense, with 'holy resin,' and paint for the eyes, with dog-headed apes, with long-tailed monkeys and greyhounds, with leopard skins, and with natives of the country, together with their children." The arrival of the expedition in Thebes appears to have created great excitement, and the celebration of such an important event seems to have been carried out on a scale of great magnificence. There is very little doubt that the early voyages of the Egyptians were carried out under the guidance of Phœnician sailors, who were considerably in advance of the Egyptians in the art of navigation. The Eastern provinces of the Egyptian Empire were inhabited by foreigners, and it was due to the intercourse with the people of Char, who were descendants of the Phœnicians, that the Egyptians were indebted for much of their knowledge. According to Herodotus, Sesostris (Rameses II.) fitted out ships of war on the Red Sea, and was the first who went beyond the straits into the Indian Ocean. Diodorus says they amounted to no fewer than 400. Some of the vessels had twenty-two oars on a side.

Herodotus has given particulars of an Egyptian voyage which proves that the supposed discovery of the Cape of Good Hope by de Gama, the Portuguese explorer, had been anticipated by about 2100 years—"As for Libya[1] [Africa], we know it to be washed on all sides by the sea, except where it is attached to Asia. This discovery was first made by Necôs, the Egyptian king, who, on desisting from the canal which he had begun between the

[1] Book IV. 42.

Nile and the Arabian Gulf, sent to sea a number of ships *manned by Phœnicians*, with orders to make for the Pillars of Hercules,[1] and return to Egypt through them and by the Mediterranean. The Phœnicians took their departure from Egypt by way of the Erythræan Sea, and so sailed into the Southern Ocean. When autumn came they went ashore, wherever they might happen to be, and, having sown a tract of land with corn, waited until the grain was fit to cut. Having reaped it, they again set sail; and thus it came to pass that two whole years went by, and it was not till the third year that they doubled the Pillars of Hercules, and made good their voyage home. On their return they declared—I, for my part [says Herodotus], do not believe them, but perhaps others may—that in sailing round Libya, they had the sun upon their right hand."

In this way (says Herodotus) was the extent of Libya first discovered. There are records which go far to prove beyond doubt that the Phœnicians sent by Necôs were not the only circumnavigators of Africa (Pliny, II. 67; and Arrian). Necôs, however, has been given the credit of discovering the Cape and the form of Africa *twenty-one centuries before Diaz and Vasco de Gama* (Sir G. Wilkinson's Notes). Hanno, the Phœnician, sailed from Carthage about 500 B.C., and got as

---

[1] Sir Gardner Wilkinson in a note says: "We may infer, from Necôs ordering the Phœnicians to come round by the 'Pillars of Hercules,' *that the form of Africa was already known,* and that this was *not* the first expedition which had gone round it. The fact of their seeing the sun rise on their right as they returned northwards, which Herodotus doubted, is the *very proof of their having gone round the Cape* and completed the circuit."

far south as the mouths of the Senegal and the Gambia. About the same time Himiles reached the Court of Britain (Plin.). Pytheas of Massilia, about 334 B.C., coasted N.-W. Europe. Polybius sailed along the West Coast of Africa. The Carthaginians also claimed (on the authority of Herodotus, Book IV. 43) that an expedition under Sataspes, son of Teaspes, sailed from Egypt, and having passed the Straits [of Gibraltar], doubled the Libyan [African] headland known as Cape Soloeis [the modern Cape Spartel], and proceeded southward. Following this course for many months over a vast stretch of sea, and finding that more water than he had crossed still lay ever before him, he put about and came back to Egypt. Herodotus was of opinion that Darius was the discoverer of the greater part of Asia. Wishing to know where the Indus emptied itself into the sea, he sent a number of men to sail down the river. It appears that they sailed down the stream in an easterly direction to the sea. Here they turned westward, and after a voyage of thirty months reached the place from which Necôs, the Egyptian king, sent the Phœnicians to sail round Libya [Africa].

"But," says Herodotus, "the boundaries of Europe are quite unknown, and there is not a man who can say whether any sea girds it round either or on the north or on the east." . . . "For my part, I cannot conceive why three names, and women's names especially, should have been given to a tract which is in reality one, nor why the Egyptian Nile and the Colchian Phasis . . . should have been fixed upon for the boundary lines; nor can I even say who gave the three tracts their names, or whence they took the epithets. According to the Greeks in general, Libya [Africa] was so called after a certain Libya, a native woman, and Asia after the wife of Prometheus. . . . As for Europe, no one can say whether it is surrounded by the sea or not, neither is it known whence the name of Europe was derived, nor who gave it name, unless we say that Europe was so called after the Tyrian Europé, and before her time was nameless. But it is certain that Europé was an Asiatic, and never even set foot on the lands which the Greeks now call Europe, only sailing from Phœnicia to Crete, and from Crete to Lycia."

The remarks of Herodotus as to the three names go to show that there was no certainty as to their origin. Andron of Halicarnassus made Libya, like Asia and Europé, a daughter of Oceanus (Fr. I.). Others derived the three names from three men, Europus, Asius, and Libyus (Eustath. ad Dionys. *Perieg.* 270). Sir G. Wilkinson says: "The name of Europe is evidently taken from the Semitic word *ereb* (the Arabic *gharb*), the 'western' land sought for and colonised from Phœnicia."

. . . . .

Eighteen centuries before Columbus, Aristotle appears to have come to the conclusion that the coasts of Spain were not very far distant from those of India. This was apparently an original idea of Aristotle, and was a deduction, based, it is true, upon an error of calculation, from his firm and unshaken supposition as to the sphericity of the earth. The knowledge of geography acquired by Aristotle ultimately produced a great revolution in the general ideas with regard to the surface of the globe. Aristotle says:

"As to the figure of the earth, it must necessarily be spherical.[1] . . . And, moreover, from the visible phenomena, for if it were not so the eclipses of the moon would not have such sections as they have. For in the configurations in the course of a month, the deficient part takes all different shapes,—it is straight, and concave, and convex; but in eclipses it always has the line of division convex, wherefore, since the moon is eclipsed in consequence of the interposition of the earth, the periphery of the earth must be the cause of this by having a spherical form. And again, from the appearance of the stars, it is clear not only that the earth is round, but that its size is not very great; for when we go a little distance to the south or to the north, the circle of the horizon becomes palpably different, so that the stars overhead undergo a great change, and are not the same to those that travel to the north and to the south. For some stars are seen in Egypt and at Cyprus, but are not seen in the countries north of them; and the stars that in the north are visible, while they make a complete circuit there [that is, in Egypt and at Cyprus], undergo a setting. So that from this it is manifest, not only that the form of the earth is round. . . . Wherefore we may judge that those persons who connect the region in the neighbourhood of the Pillars of Hercules with that toward India, *and who assert in this way the sea is one*, do not assert things very improbable."

It seems more than probable that the mind of Columbus was sensibly influenced by the ideas of

[1] The mathematicians who try to calculate the measure of the circumference make it amount to 400,000 stadia; whence we infer that the earth is not only spherical, but that it is not large compared with the magnitude of the other stars.—*De Coelo*, lib. II. cap. xiv.

Aristotle. Columbus was in possession of a book known as the *Imago Mundi* which contains references to the views of Aristotle. In a letter written by Columbus while he was in Hispaniola in 1498, and sent to Ferdinand and Isabella, he quotes the views of Aristotle (*Navarrette*, tom. i. p. 261). Ferdinand Columbus distinctly and emphatically points out that the sentence in Aristotle which states "that there is but a narrow sea between the western points of Spain and the eastern border of India" had exercised a considerable influence upon his father.

. . . .

Strabo, the geographer, who wrote about nineteen centuries ago, was possessed of the same idea which led Columbus towards his great discovery, and gave to the American islands the name of the West Indies. He (Strabo) argues that it is in accordance with natural philosophy to reckon the greatest dimension of the habitable earth from east to west, and that it ought to occupy a greater length from east to west than its breadth from north to south. "The temperate zone, which," says he, "we have already designated as the longest zone, is that which the mathematicians denominate a continuous circle returning upon itself. So that if the extent of the Atlantic Ocean were not an obstacle,[1] we might

[1] The Atlantic Ocean was the Sea of Darkness (Mare Tenebrosum), or the Sea of the Dead (Mare Mortuum). It was the Bahr-al-Zulmat of the Arabs. In its waters, according to popular superstition, lived fearful monsters which followed ships and with their sucker arms, which they were able to extend to the top-mast of a ship, drew the sailors and the ship under. The superstitions of the mariners, although founded upon popular oral traditions, were derived—at least in part— from geographical absurdities which were depicted upon maps made by or under the authority of the ecclesiastics of various periods. The

easily go by sea from Iberia[1] to India, still keeping in the same parallel; the remaining portion of which parallel, measured as above in stadia, occupies more than a third of the whole circle, since the parallel drawn through Athens, on which we have taken the distances from India to Iberia, does not contain in the whole 200,000 stadia."[2]

Strabo also expressed a belief that if it were not for the vastness of the Atlantic Ocean it would be possible to find an ocean path from Iberia to India, and that "in the same temperate zone as we inhabit, and especially the parallel passing through Thinæ and traversing the Atlantic, there may exist two inhabited countries, and perhaps even more than two."

. . . .

old charts contained representations of frightful looking creatures, who were supposed to reside in places situated either in the depths of the ocean or at some distant oceanic region in the western waters from whence it would not be possible for any human being to return. The sailors of the period immediately preceding Columbus—and perhaps we ought to include many of the contemporary and subsequent generations of those who ploughed the waves—believed that at a certain point in the westward waters they would descend into Cimmerian waters—into the homes of the Kraken, which were believed to be sea monsters of such a size that they were regarded as floating islands! Even Columbus, although he had abandoned many of the old superstitions, fully believed that the world was pear-shaped, and that towards the point which he delineated in the form of the stalk there existed the earthly paradise; in some other part he believed there was chaos or Erebus. When the early *voyageurs* reached the vast oceanic fields of thickly grown weeds—the Sargossa Sea or waters—they believed at first that they had arrived at the abode of the fearful monsters of the deep, and they fully expected to see the uncanny forms emerging from the entangled vegetation. When Columbus set sail in 1498, on his third voyage of discovery, the sailors, on their approach to within five degrees of the equator, were reminded, by the effect of the stifling glow of the atmosphere, of an old fable of a torrid zone made uninhabitable by the parching heat of an immediately direct sun.

[1] Spain.
[2] The *Geography of Strabo*, vol. i. p. 101, Bohn's edition.

Quite recently there has been revived a belief in the lost island of Atlantis mentioned by Plato. Some think Atlantis a synonym for America, while others suggest that it represents an island which in the distant past had an actual existence in a part of the Atlantic Ocean near to "the Pillars of Hercules," that is, the Straits of Gibraltar. A book which relates to this matter, *Atlantis: The Antediluvian World*, written by Ignatius Donnelly, and containing 490 pages, has passed through no fewer than twenty-four editions. Inasmuch as at the period which immediately preceded the discovery of the "new world," every allusion by the ancient writers to the Atlantic Ocean beyond the Pillars of Hercules was eagerly discussed, it may be thought not quite irrelevant to reproduce Plato's allusions, and they will appear in Appendix A. Anyone requiring information as to the line of thought taken by Mr. Donnelly should read his work. Various opinions are held as to the value of the material which Plato had at his disposal when he wrote. Some critics contend that the whole story was concocted by Plato, and a learned professor speaks of it as "a noble lie"! It appears, if we may rely upon Plato's statement, that Solon visited Egypt[1] nearly 600 years B.C., and the priests of that country informed him, among other matters, of a tradition to the effect that in ancient times there existed a peopled island known as the Atlantic Island. "Beyond the strait [*i.e.* Gibraltar], which you in your language call the Pillars of Hercules, was an island larger than Libya [Africa]

[1] It was popularly, and perhaps not erroneously, believed that the Egyptian priests were the custodians of much esoteric information, which they transmitted to their successors. This belief would have materially assisted towards an acceptation of Plato's revelation.

and Asia put together." We learn from Plato,[1] who states that he derived his information from Solon's writings,[2] that in the beginning the gods divided the whole earth into large and small portions, and that "Poseidon [Neptune] received as his portion the Atlantic Island and begat children by a mortal woman and placed them on a part of the island." We are also told—and in matters of this kind the details are not devoid of interest—that Poseidon begat ten male children and that he divided the island into ten portions, giving each child a portion over which he was to rule as a king. The eldest, who was made a principal king, or head ruler over the others, he called Atlas, after whom was named the Atlantic Island and the Atlantic Ocean. The Egyptian priests also told Solon that "nine thousand years ago" a war was declared between the inhabitants of the land "outside the Pillars of Hercules" and the people living within it.

The disappearance of the Atlantic Island with its inhabitants is explained as follows :—

"But in a later age, by extraordinary earthquakes and deluges bringing destruction in a single day and night,[3] . . . the Atlantic Island was plunged be-

[1] Plato, who was probably born about 430 B.C., died about the year 348 B.C.
[2] Plato's descent from Solon is said to have been through the female line. He asserted that the writings were formerly in the possession of his grandfather.
[3] It was an early belief of the Hebrews—probably borrowed from either Persian or Egyptian sources—that there had been a destruction of men as a punishment for their wickedness. Thus, in Genesis, we find that Yahveh repented His alleged act of the creation of man, and said, "I will exterminate man, whom I have created, from the surface of the ground." The Egyptian priests, in certain secret records, alleged that the god Râ, on a certain occasion, had summoned certain other gods to consult with him as to the conduct of the men whom he

neath the sea and concealed from view; therefore that sea is, at present, neither passable nor to be traced out, being blocked up with a great depth of mud made by the sunken island." It is, of course, somewhat difficult to assert that Plato's narrations have at the bottom no truth whatever; at the same time, persons acquainted to any extent with the ancient writers must know that the geological facts as to the floors and elevations of the sea which are now known to us were not at Plato's disposal. It is possible that Phœnician or other sailors may have got as far into the Atlantic as the region of marine vegetation known as the Sargossa Sea, which it has been estimated extends over an area six times as large as France. This area of water is covered with a mass of gulf seaweed which is growing upon the surface, and to mariners of Plato's period, if by any chance they ever ventured so far, it might have been accepted as evidence that there existed a mass of slime which would render the ocean impassable. A slight knowledge of the works of ancient writers will prove that they were given to romance in their descriptions of far-off regions, and more especially when they wrote of persons or of events appertaining to localities whose existence savoured of the mythical, or to lands which were so far distant that the truth or otherwise could not be ascertained.[1]

. . . .

had begotten, and, addressing himself to the eldest of the gods, said, "Thou, of whom I am sprung, and you ancient gods, behold the men who have been begotten by me! They speak words against me. Tell me what you would do in this crisis. Behold, I have waited, and I have not destroyed them before having heard your counsel." (A chapter of the so-called sacred books of Tahout.)

[1] Before leaving the story of Poseidon, or Neptune, it may be here mentioned that from time to time coins of the very earliest times have

We have given some of the ancient ideas as to the Atlantic Ocean. It is now proposed to make reference to certain matters which influenced the citizens of the maritime republics, particularly those of Venice and Genoa, in their desire to find a sea route to the lands of the Grand Khan, and which ultimately ended in the conception that it would be possible to reach the rich Asiatic kingdom by sailing towards the west in the unknown waters of the Atlantic Ocean.

The rumours and conversational descriptions as to the vast wealth—the gold, the precious stones, the spices, and other valuable productions—of "the Golden East" seem to have made an impression at a very early period upon the imaginative Venetians,

been discovered in various parts of the Bristol River. The immense number of coins found, together with the great age of many of them, have suggested to many minds the possibility that they came into the river, not by accident, but by design. Many persons believe, rightly or wrongly, that in ancient times there existed a custom among the sailors of casting a coin into the river either at the commencement or at the termination of a voyage. Rev. Father Grant, S.J., formerly of Bristol, during the time he remained in the city, made a very considerable collection of coins brought to him by men who from time to time were employed in the river, and from casual finds made by men and boys at the culvert in the Bristol harbour, where the dredging machines deposit the mud. Having regard to the unusual variety of these coins, and to the fact that so many of them belong to maritime nations, it certainly seems difficult to believe that they originally got into the river as the result of accident. Father Grant seems inclined to conclude that the presence of the coins is due to a survival of a custom which existed in olden times of propitiating Neptune. The silly story of a certain person having been thrown into the sea, and afterwards found in a whale's belly, is considered by many to have had its origin in the ancient idea of the necessity of propitiating the spirit of the storm by some offering, whether of human life or otherwise. Father Grant, in the course of a lecture given by him in the year 1883, says: "Everything about the sea and sailors has a character of unchangeableness. When heathenism was abolished, the Church could not at once abolish old habits. . . . The feasts of Neptune were on the 23rd and 24th June. . . . I cannot help thinking that the custom of two thousand years ago and more, of throwing money to

to whom, in common with the other maritime States, the enterprise and the activity of the Phœnicians had descended. They were dazzled by the stories, probably combinations of fact and fiction, of the pomp and profusion at the Courts of Eastern potentates (more particularly that of the Great Kaan or Grand Caan, otherwise the "Grand Khan"), which had been gathered in the course of their intercourse with the people of Constantinople and with the travellers from far-off lands who came thither for the purposes of trading. But the difficulties connected with the long and tedious journeys to those distant territories were insuperable, so far as they would allow of a profitable intercourse. Still, the obvious fact that those who should be the first to establish direct

Neptune for a good fortune, may have survived until even the days of 'The Merchant Venturers' of this country. You may proscribe and abolish an Act, you cannot so easily eradicate a national habit. The people will have their customs in spite of Acts of Parliament, and in spite even of the Christian Church. . . . Neptune comes as a sailor dressed up as Neptune when vessels cross the line, and levies 'blackmail' in a manner that would do honour to 'el Barbiere de Seviglia.'" Mr. A. T. Martin, F.S.A., of Bristol, in the course of a paper read by him, November 22, 1894, as to a large number of coins found in the mud dredged up in the Bristol River, which were then in the possession of Mr. M'Currick, our docks engineer, says: "These coins are by no means the only ones that have been found in this way, as others have already passed into different hands. It will be noticed that the period covered by this list extends from the earliest to the present times, and that it includes examples of the coinage of various foreign countries, and affords a striking testimony to the antiquity and importance of the trade of our ancient city. The number and variety of the coins which have been from time to time found in our harbour is somewhat remarkable, and may possibly be accounted for by a habit, which I am told still prevails among sailors, of propitiating the Fates by throwing a coin into the water at the beginning of the voyage. But whether these coins are offerings to Neptune, or whether their presence in the river is due only to the proverbial carelessness of sailors, we must at anyrate thank our kindly river naid, which has preserved them all these years and returned them to us again full of interest and importance."

commercial relationships with the Tartarian countries would succeed in obtaining an enormous profit, caused the Venetians and others to endeavour to ascertain whether it would be possible to establish a quicker or more continuous caravan service, combined with greater facilities for the necessary carriage by water, at those points where water-carriage became a necessity.

Going back to the eleventh century, we find that Venice had gained a high position among the nations of the world, owing to the wealth that had accrued to her from the traffic with those remote Eastern parts, with which for a long period, and only by indirect means, her citizens had been brought into communication. After the conquest of Constantinople and the Greek provinces by the united forces of the French and the Venetians in the early part of the thirteenth century, a very large share of the conquered territory came under the control and influence of the Republic of Venice. Prior to that conquest, Constantinople was superior to Venice in the world of commerce, and the desire to humiliate a rival was an important factor in the proceedings which led to the conquest, a record of which exploit may be seen by every visitor to Venice who glances at the four exquisite horses that are to be seen on the façade of the magnificent Church of St. Mark.[1] As a consequence of the victory, Venice was represented at Constantinople by a magistrate or regent, and between the two places a very thriving and lucrative trade was established. And as a further consequence,

[1] As it will appear hereafter that John Cabot placed the banner of St. Mark on the land found by him, it is perhaps desirable to mention that St. Mark was the patron saint of Venice.

an increasing trade was carried on between Constantinople and the distant eastern territories, *vià* Egypt and Syria, the greater share of the profits falling into Venetian hands. From this period may be traced that keen rivalry which subsequently ended in a racial struggle for maritime supremacy between Venice and Genoa. This struggle eventually became so fierce that it was no longer safe for the trading vessels of either of the two republics to proceed to sea without a convoy.

Amongst the first to exhibit a curiosity to visit the Courts of the Tartarian potentates were two Venetians named Maffio Polo, a bachelor, and his brother, Nicolo, a married man. The Polos were a family of considerable importance in Venice. The father's name was Andrea Polo da S. Felice, and the family was believed to be of Dalmatian extraction. About the year 1254 (some say 1255) they set out upon a journey, and proceeded at first to Constantinople for the purpose of disposing of a large stock of merchandise which they took with them. As the wife of Nicolo was *enceinte* she was left behind. It will be seen hereafter why this fact is here mentioned. At Constantinople, after disposing of their goods, they obtained information as to the existence of certain markets for the sale of some very valuable articles, which prompted them to proceed at first to the residence of Barkah, the brother or the son of Baatu, who was related to Jengiz-Khan, whose places of residence were Saraï and Bolghar, well known to the geographers of the Middle Ages.

At this period occasional visits had been made by traders to the Courts of some of the princes of the race of Jengiz. Subsequently, after leaving the residence of Barkah, they journeyed via Bokhara to the countries under the rule of the Grand Khan. They were favourably received by that great potentate, and after a long visit they got back to Venice in or about the year 1269, having been absent about fourteen or fifteen years. Upon their arrival, Nicolo Polo found that his wife had died after giving birth to a son, to whom she had given the name of Marco. In the year 1271 the two brothers, accompanied by Marco, the son of Nicolo, set forward for the purpose of paying another visit to the Grand Khan. After a long and tedious journey the travellers reached their destination. The Khan received them with great honour, and paying considerable attention to young Marco, he made him an officer of his household. " In this situation Marco Polo had an opportunity of displaying his abilities; he adopted the dress and customs of the country, and made himself master of the four principal languages then in use, which were probably the Mongol, the Turkish, the Manchu of eastern Tartary, and the Chinese. By his talents and the variety of his accomplishments, he soon acquired a great degree of influence at Court, and was employed on missions to the most distant provinces of the empire."[1] To cut a long but very interesting story short, it is necessary to relate that the Poli remained so long away that they were thought to be dead, and therefore it is not surprising to learn that, upon their return to their native city in the year 1295, after an absence of about twenty-four years, they experienced some difficulty in convincing some of their relatives and friends of their identity.

The next point of interest in the story is the

[1] *Geography of the Middle Ages: Travels of Marco Polo.*

capture of Marco Polo by the Genoese in a naval engagement in the year 1296.[1] "From the scene of action he was conveyed to a prison in Genoa, where, his personal qualities and his surprising history becoming soon known, he was visited by all the principal inhabitants, who did everything in their power to soften the rigours of his captivity; treating him with kindness as a friend, and liberally supplying him with everything necessary for his subsistence and accommodation. His rare adventures were, as in his own country, the subject of general curiosity, and the frequent necessity he was under of repeating the same story unavoidably became irksome to him. He was, in consequence, at length induced to follow the advice of those who recommended his committing it to writing." (*The Travels of Marco Polo, the Venetian.* The translation of Marsden revised.) It is related that "he was called on continually . . . to *describe the Court of the Grand Khan.*" With the assistance of Marco Polo's notes, which had been sent from Venice, and from his verbal communications, an account of his travels were written down (so it is said) by Rusticien de Pise, " a well-known medical writer, who made a compilation in French of the romances of the cycle of

[1] In this decisive victory no fewer than sixty-five Venetian ships were burned, and eighteen, with seven thousand prisoners, captured. Among the latter was the Venetian admiral, Dandolo, who committed suicide by dashing his head against the side of his vessel. These battles were carried on with so much determination and energy, that it would not be wrong to say that each defeat served only to increase the energies of the defeated. As a consequence, the ships of each gradually became of larger frame and of more complicated gear, which necessitated greater skill and ingenuity in their navigation. It was in this and other ways that the seamanlike qualities of the men of the two republics *became gradually developed until they became national characteristics.*

CABOT'S DISCOVERY OF NORTH AMERICA 19

King Arthur." *The Travels of Marco Polo* are said to have been written, and the manuscript circulated, in 1298.[1] For the purposes of this work the references to the book of Marco Polo are given just for what they are worth. This is neither the time nor the place to criticise Polo's book; many of his statements may have been made from hearsay, and from information of an unreliable kind; his book may be founded partly on fact and partly on fiction; it may contain arrant nonsense, gross exaggerations, and highly-coloured statements. It is certain, however, that it was one of the principal causes which excited the curiosity of Europeans, and eventually led to a general desire to find a sea-route to the countries (including the territories of the Grand Khan) described by Marco Polo.

A writer tells us that "the finest of all the results due to the influence of Marco Polo is that of having stirred Columbus to the discovery of the new world. Columbus, jealous of Polo's laurels, spent his life in preparing to get to that Zipangu (Cipangu or Japan) of which the Venetian traveller had told such great things; his desire was to reach China by sailing westward, and in his way he fell in with America."[2]

Another writer says: "Never before had the people of Europe heard of such extraordinary wealth and unlimited resources as existed in the far-off countries visited by Marco Polo. His novel descriptions of stately, gold-covered palaces, of the royal magnificence of the entertainments of the Grand Khan, of the intoxicating fragrance of an endless

[1] *The Travels of Marco Polo, the Venetian.* The translation of Marsden revised.
[2] *Il des Sciences Mathśm*, etc., ii. 150.

profusion of rare flowers, of luscious fruits and sweet spicery, of heavily-laden argosies of valuable merchandise floating on noble rivers, and of vast collections of gold, silver, and precious stones, were read with the most exaggerated conceptions of their reality."

Referring again to Polo's descriptions of the far-off territories which he had visited, we are told, "He was the first traveller to trace a route across the whole longitude of Asia, naming and describing kingdom after kingdom which he had seen with his own eyes; the flowering plateaux and wild gorges of Badakh-Shan, the jade-bearing rivers of Khotan, the Mongolian steppes. . . . The first traveller to reveal China in all its wealth and vastness,—its mighty rivers, its huge cities, its rich manufactures, its swarming population, the inconceivably vast fleets that quickened its seas and its inland waters; to tell us of the nations on its borders, with all their eccentricities of manner and worship; of Tibet, with its sordid devotees; of Burma, with its golden pagodas and their tinkling crowns; . . . of India the Great, not as a dream-land of Alexandrian fables, but as a country seen and partially explored, with its virtuous Brahmins, its obscene ascetics, its diamonds, and the strange tales of their acquisition."[1]

In a description of the Khan's palace in or near to the city of Chandu, Polo's readers were told that it was a very fine marble palace, the rooms of which were all gilt, and painted with figures of men and beasts and birds, and with a variety of trees and flowers, all executed with such exquisite art that you regard them with delight and astonishment.

[1] Yule's *The Book of Ser Marco Polo*, Introd. p. cxxxi.

The palace enclosure was described to be "a compass of sixteen miles." There was a second palace built of cane, of which he (Polo) gave a description. "It is gilt all over. . . . It is stayed on gilt and lacquered columns, on each of which is a dragon all gilt, the tail of which is attached to the column, whilst the head supports the architrave, and the claws are stretched out right and left to support the architrave." The Great Khan was possessed of a stud of twenty thousand white horses and mares, "and all pure white without a speck." The Khan had four wives, each of whom enjoyed the title of empress. . . . "And each has a special court of her own, very grand and ample; no one of them having fewer than three hundred fair and charming damsels. They have also many pages and eunuchs, and a number of other attendants of both sexes. . . . When the emperor desires the society of one of these four consorts, he will sometimes send for the lady to his apartment, and sometimes visit her at her own. He has also a great number of concubines, and I will tell you how he obtains them. You must know that there is a tribe of Tartars called Ungrat who are noted for their beauty. Now, every year a hundred of the most beautiful maidens of this tribe are sent to the Great Khan, who commits them to the charge of certain elderly ladies dwelling in his palace. And these old ladies make the girls sleep with them, in order to ascertain if they have sweet breath and do not snore, and are sound in all their limbs. Then such of them as are of approved beauty, and are good and sound in all respects, are appointed to attend on the emperor by turns. Thus six of these damsels take their turn for three

days and nights, and wait on him when he is in his
chamber. . . . At the end of the three days and
nights they are relieved by other six. And so
throughout the year there are reliefs of maidens
by six and six, changing every three days and
nights." . . .

"Of the children by his lawful wives," Polo says,
"there are seven who are kings of vast realms or
provinces, and govern them well, being all able and
gallant men, as might be expected. For the Great
Khan their sire is, I tell you, the wisest and most
accomplished man, the greatest captain, the best to
govern men and rule an empire, as well as the most
valiant that ever has existed among all the tribes
of Tartars." . . . "You must know that for three
months of the year, to wit—December, January, and
February, the Great Khan resides in the capital
city of Cathay. . . . In that city stands his great
palace, and now I will tell you what it is like. It
is enclosed all round by a great wall forming a
square, each side of which is a mile in length; that
is to say, the whole compass thereof is four miles.
This you may depend on; it is also very thick, and
a good ten paces in height, whitewashed and loop-
holed all round. At each angle of the wall there is
a very fine and rich palace, in which the war-harness
of the emperor is kept, such as bows and quivers,
saddles and bridles, and bowstrings, and everything
needful for an army. Also midway between every
two of these corner palaces there is another of the
like, so that, taking the whole compass of the
enclosure, you find eight vast palaces stored with
the Great Lord's harness of war. And you must
understand that each palace is assigned to only one

kind of article; thus one is stored with bows, a second with saddles, a third with bridles, and so on in succession right round. The great wall has five gates on its southern face, the middle one being the great gate, which is never opened on any occasion except when the Great Khan himself goes forth or enters. . . . You must know that it is the greatest palace that ever was. . . . The roof is very lofty, and the walls of the palace are all covered with gold and silver. They are also adorned with representations of dragons [sculptured and gilt], beasts and birds, knights and idols, and sundry other subjects. And on the ceiling, too, you see nothing but gold and silver and painting. On each of the four sides there is a great marble staircase leading to the top of the marble wall. . . . The building is altogether so vast, so rich, and so beautiful, that no man on earth could design anything superior to it. The outside of the roof also is all covered with vermilion, and yellow, and green, and blue, and other hues, which are fixed with a varnish so fine and exquisite that they shine like crystal, and lend a resplendent lustre to the palace as seen for a great way round. . . . On the interior side of the palace are large buildings with halls and chambers, . . . in which reside the ladies and concubines. There he occupies himself at his own convenience, and no one else has access.

. . . . . .

" Of the City and great Haven of Zayton.

"Now, when you quit Fuju and cross the river, you travel for five days south-east through a fine country, meeting with a constant succession of flourishing cities, towns, and villages, rich in every product. You travel by mountains, and valleys, and plains, and in some places by great forests in which are many of the trees that give camphor. There is plenty of game on the road, both of bird and beast. The people are all traders and craftsmen, subjects of the Great Kaan. ... When you have accomplished those five days' journey, you arrive at the very great and noble city of Zayton. ... At this city, you must know, is the Haven of Zayton, frequented by all the ships of India, which bring thither spicery and all other kinds of costly wares. It is the port also that is frequented by all the merchants of Manzi,[1] for hither is imported the most astonishing quantity of goods, and of precious stones and pearls, and from this they are distributed all over Manzi. And I assure you, that for one shipload of pepper that goes to Alexandria or elsewhere, destined for Christendom, there come a hundred such, ay, and more too, to this Haven of Zayton; for it is one of the two greatest havens in the world for commerce."[2]

. . . . . .

But the most important reference, so far as these references and descriptions of places have a bearing upon the discovery of the new world, is that which relates to the island of Cipango, or Chipangu, otherwise Zipangu.

He says: "Chipangu[3] is an island towards the east in the high seas, 1500 miles distant from the Continent; and a very great island it is. The people are white, civilised, and well-flavoured. They are idolaters, and are dependent on nobody.

[1] *Infra*, p. 82. [2] See the letter of Toscanelli, *infra*, p. 81.
[3] Japan, *infra*, p. 82.

And I can tell you, the quantity of gold they have is endless; for they find it in their own islands, and the king does not allow it to be exported. Moreover, few merchants visit the country, because it is so far from the mainland, and thus it comes to pass that their gold is abundant beyond all measure. I will tell you a wonderful thing about the palace of the lord of that island. You must know that he hath a great palace, which is entirely roofed with fine gold, just as our churches are roofed with lead, insomuch that it would be scarcely possible to estimate its value. Moreover, all the pavement of the palace, and the floors of its chambers, are entirely of gold, in plates like slabs of stones a good two fingers thick; and the windows also are of gold, so that altogether the richness of this palace is past all bounds and all belief. They have also pearls in abundance, which are of a rose colour, but fine, big, and round, and quite as valuable as the white ones. They have also quantities of other precious stones."

There are descriptions of other kingdoms and other islands in which references are made to their numerous natural productions. Concerning one island, he declares that they find "rubies, and sapphires, and topazes, and amethysts, and many other stones of price. And the king of this island possesses a ruby which is the finest and biggest in the world. It is about a palm in length, and as thick as a man's arm; to look at, it is the most resplendent object on earth; it is quite free from flaw, and as red as fire. Its value is so great that a price for it in money could hardly be named at all. You must know that the Great Kaan sent an

embassy and begged the king [of the island], as
a favour greatly desired by him, to sell him this
ruby, offering to give for it the ransom of a city,
or, in fact, what the king would. But the king
replied that on no account whatever would he sell
it, for it had come to him from his ancestors." In
a description of a kingdom called Locac, which he
says was situated 500 miles beyond the island
of Sondur, he mentions that "the *brazil*[1]
which we make use of grows in great plenty; and
they also have gold in incredible quantity."

    In the interval of three-quarters of a century
since Marco Polo's work was made known, other
inquisitive explorers had made their way to Cathay.
One of these explorers was Friar Odericus, of the
order of Minorites, who, it is said, visited Hindustan,
Sumatra, Java, Cochin China, the Chinese Empire,
and Thibet. The success of Marco Polo's work,
coupled with the information given by subsequent
travellers, served to stimulate the desire for a
greater knowlege of, and closer acquaintance with,
the rich Asiatic territories. In the *Journal of
Friar Odericus* additional stories, suitable for the
popular fancies, as to the precious stones, pearls,
ivory, marvellous palaces, and extraordinary wealth
and luxury, were circulated. The journal of Odericus was drawn upon, to some extent, at anyrate,
for the construction of a book of a most extraordinary description, which was entitled *The
voiage and travayle of Sir John Maundeville,
Knight*. There is very little doubt that the descriptions of places and of people contained in the

[1] *Infra*, pp. 42, 43, 149.

book were cribbed from the works of others, and added to from the writer's facile brain. The work alleges that "Sir John Maundeville," the supposed author, was born at St. Albans, and that he set forth on his peregrinations in 1332, and spent no fewer than thirty-four years in wandering through the East. It is believed that this book, which is regarded as one of the most successful instances of plagiarism ever recorded, was written by an Englishman named Burgoyne, who had been compelled to leave England for some political offence. Burgoyne died at Liege about 1370.

This book must have been well circulated, and in all probability was as well, if not better known than that of Marco Polo. It was by means of such publications, some of which abound with the most extraordinary and fascinating descriptions of the wealth of the Indies, together with exaggerated stories of an extraordinary character as to the persons and animals which the travellers had either met with or heard about, that men's minds were gradually laid hold of, and furnished with an ever-increasing desire to find a more expeditious route to the lands of the Grand Khan.

In course of time the works of the classical writers were ransacked for information or guidance as to the possibility of reaching the Indies by water. In addition to the passages which were to be found in Aristotle, Strabo, and others, Roger Bacon, a learned English Franciscan, or Gray friar, had made a collection of quotations from which he appears to have formed a belief that it would be possible to reach the eastern shore of Asia by sailing westward into the Atlantic Ocean, and that those shores would be found at no very great distance from Spain. In the early part of the fourteenth century the *Imago Mundi* was compiled by Pierre d'Ailly, popularly known as Petrus Alliacus, the latinised form of his name. A printed copy of this work, which contains all Bacon's arguments and deductions, is yet preserved in the Biblioteca Columbina, and it contains a number of marginal manuscript notes in the handwriting of Columbus. This was Columbus's own copy of the work.

It will thus be seen that Columbus was well acquainted with the ideas of the ancients with regard to an oceanic passage, by way of the Western Ocean, to the Oriental lands. Subsequently the idea that it would be possible to find Eastern lands by sailing towards the westward in the Atlantic, took a permanent hold in the minds of many persons. Before Columbus had conceived that the difficulties and superstitious ideas as to the "Sea of Darkness" might be got rid of, considerable progress had been made in navigation, and the astrolabe had received many improvements. The first attempts to find a sea-route to the lands of the Grand Khan were made in accordance with a growing belief that the circumnavigation of Africa was possible, and that India might be reached by following the African coast. Prince Henry of Portugal, in whose early days the sailors had only the physical features of the land to guide them, had devoted himself to nautical studies, with the result that in course of time the various African capes were passed, and ultimately the science of navigation received such an impetus that the rounding of the Cape of Good Hope came within the range of practical ideas.

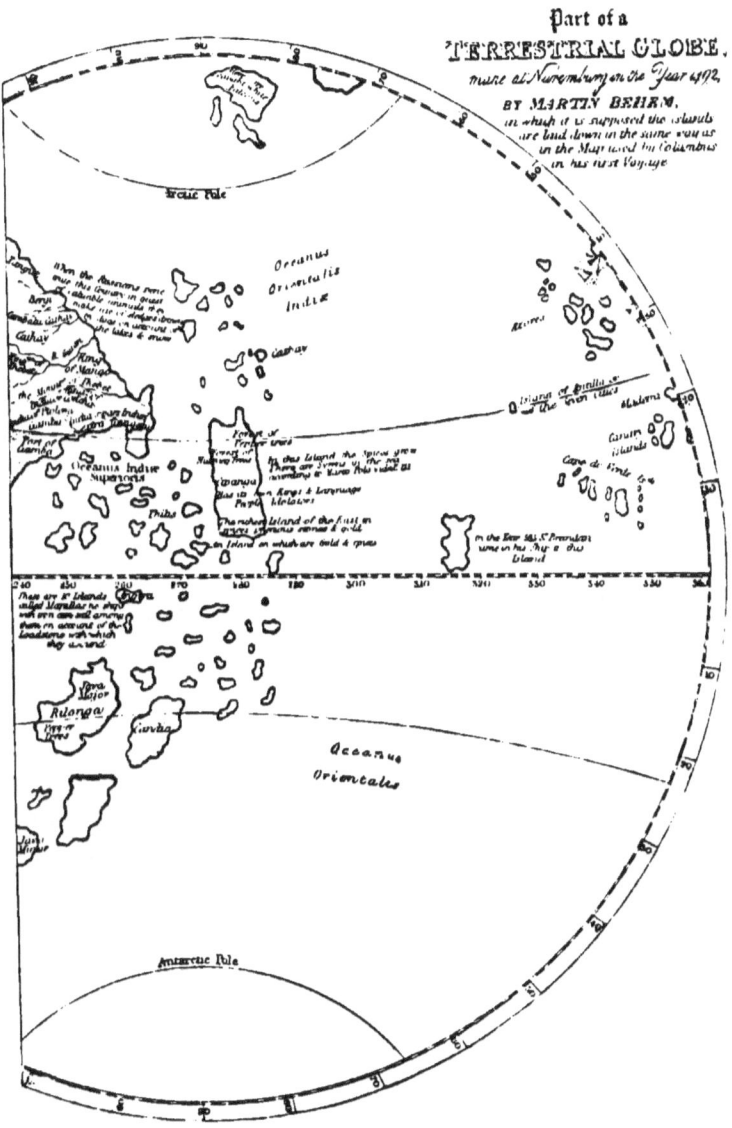

There are reasons for believing that Columbus's idea of finding the lands of the Grand Khan was strengthened, about the year 1471, by the discovery that the Guinea coast extended south of the equator. In the year 1474 the advice of the celebrated astronomer, Paul Toscanelli, was sought, and the preparation of the map or sailing-chart by Toscanelli seems to have supplied the necessary equipment for Columbus's daring and successful attempt in the year 1492 to explore the Western Ocean. A copy of Toscanelli's sailing-chart will be found at page 80. In the year 1492 Martin Behem, or Behaim, made a terrestrial globe which, as will be seen by a comparison with Toscanelli's sailing-chart, was founded upon Toscanelli's ideas.

It has been well said, that from the East streams the light focussed into science by the West ("Ex Oriente lux, ex Occidente lex"). From Eastern sources came the incentive for the desire to reach the mysterious Ophir. From contact with Constantinople and its commerce, the Italian States received their knowledge of the stores of Eastern wealth. And from these Italian States came the men whose undaunted courage was due to that knowledge of their superiority which strengthens men for great enterprises. They were well aware that they had no rivals in maritime experience. At the opportune moment there arose a genius who was anxious to satisfy the cravings of men quickened for discovery. Prince Henry of Portugal was well aware of the superiority of the seamen of the Italian States, and he took into his employ a number of Venetians, Genoese, and Florentines. The prince died in 1463, at his favourite retreat at Sagres on

Cape Vincent, without the satisfaction of seeing the circumnavigation of Africa. In the Italian republics it began to dawn upon the merchants and traders that the monopoly of their commercial intercourse with the East, which was the source of their supremacy as well as of their opulence, was now in real danger. And in the whirligig of events which then, as now, formed food for the cynic and the scoffer, it was perceived that the maritime republics were being drawn upon for the materials which would, in all probability, be the means of transferring their maritime supremacy to the growing power of the Western nations.

And eventually Christopher Columbus, a Genoese, and John Cabot, " another Genoese, like Columbus," were the men whom fate had selected for those enterprises which eventually destroyed the supremacy of the Italian republics.

CHAPTER I

In the fifteenth century, as the outgrowth of numerous traditions which appeared at intervals in various forms, and were frequently the subjects of new variations, an idea had become fixed in the minds of all sorts and conditions of men in several of the kingdoms of Europe, that certain islands known as St. Brandon, otherwise "St. Brandan," or "St. Brendan," or "St. Brendon," or island of "San Boranden"; "Brasil," otherwise "Brazil," or "O'Brasile"; "Antillia," or "Antilia," otherwise "The Seven Cities," or "The Island of the Seven Cities,"—that these and other islands,[1] some with and some without

[1] One of the phantom islands, which was called Satanaxio, or Satanatio, was supposed to be an island connected with the hand of Satan. The origin of the belief has been attributed to an ancient Italian legend, to the effect that in a part of India a great hand rose every day from the sea and carried off a certain number of persons to the depths of the ocean. The Arabians have, so it is said, a similar tradition. In all probability the story permeated through Europe from some Eastern source.

In the Ptolemy map of 1482, published at Ulme, in the Sexta Tabula Asiæ, there appears an island of Demons, "Insula Demonum." Later on this island was found a place in the newly-discovered American Waters. Biddle, in his Memoir, pp. 250, 251, says: "Ortellius, on whose map the 'Insula Demonum' figures with St. Brandon, etc., places it not very far from Hudson Strait. Ramusio, in his text, would give it a local habitation about half-way between that strait and Newfoundland, but in constructing the map which accompanies his third volume he seems to have thought a great

names, had an actual existence in the Atlantic Ocean. Some of these traditions may be traced back to a distant period of time. They were believed in alike by princes and paupers, philosophers and fools, landsmen and seamen, map makers and chart constructors, practical men and romantic women. Exaggerated unrealities had taken firm hold of the popular mind. It was possessed by a dream that these visionary Hesperian islands were situated in a delightful tropical region of perpetual summer;[1] that they were lands which contained untold gold, precious stones, and sparkling gems; elysian fields, cool and refreshing groves, streams and fountains of water[2] which conferred perennial youth and vigour; precious trees, aromatic perfumes and spices, gracious beauties and exquisite felicities—a blissful mundane paradise!

gulf a much fitter place, and it therefore occupies a conspicuous station in the 'Golfo Quadrado,' or St. Lawrence. It is about five times as large as Newfoundland, from which it is divided by a narrow strait. On it demons are seen, as well flying as on foot, with nothing to protect them from a climate, so little suited to their former habits, but a pair of wings and a ridiculously short tail; yet they are made, poor devils! to appear happy, and even sportive."

[1] "Where falls not hail, or rain, or any snow,
Nor ever wind blows loudly; but lies
Deep-meadow'd, happy, fair with orchard lawns
And bowery hollows crown'd with summer sea."

[2] According to a popular tradition as to the "Garden of the Hesperides," there existed a fountain of perpetual youth the waters of which restored to bloom and vigour all who bathed therein, be they ever so old or wrinkled.

It was the supposed existence of an island which contained a fountain, *by bathing in the waters of which* perpetual youth would be acquired, that prompted Juan Ponce de Leon, a Spanish cavalier, to set out in search of the imaginary island, with the result that he made what was then supposed to be the discovery, but which in reality was the re-discovery of a portion of territory to which he (Juan Ponce de Leon) gave the name of Florida, because it was discovered at the time of the floral feast of the Roman Catholic Church (Pascua Florida).

Herein may probably be discerned a trace of the influence which Marco Polo's revelations had exercised on the credulity of Europeans. He states that near to Khatai, "bounded by the Eastern Ocean," there existed a happy and blissful land "where strange men and women, who migrate thither, cease to grow old." The credulity of the period affords an object-lesson as to the great influence which the development of a whimsical story — by additions of details and by reiterations—may have upon the popular mind. No truth was ever received with the avidity with which statements as to "islands" in the West were swallowed. Peter Martyr, the historian, says: "There is an island . . . on which is a never-failing spring of running water, of such marvellous efficacy that when the water is drunk, perhaps with some attention to diet, it makes old people young again!"[1] And he adds, "not only all the common people, but also the educated and the wealthy believe it to be true."[2]

It will hereafter appear that the men of Bristol placed so much confidence in the current stories regarding these islands, that in the year 1480 (twelve years before Columbus embarked upon his first voyage for the purpose of finding the lands of the "Great Khan") an expedition went out from Bristol in quest of "the island of Brasylle,"[3] and

---

[1] The mythical Prester John knew of a fountain, the source of which "is hardly three days' journey from Paradise, from which Adam was expelled. If any man drinks thrice of this spring, he will from that day feel no infirmity, and he will, as long as he lives, appear of the age of thirty."
[2] *De orbo novo decades*, dec. ii. cap. x.
[3] *Infra*, pp. 58, 59.

that between 1480 and 1497 at least seven expeditions left Bristol, at the risk and expense of townsmen, "in search of the island of Brasil and the seven cities."[1] Although these voyages have not commanded much attention, it cannot be denied that the outcome of such chimerical enterprise was an event than which, in the history of the world, there is none of greater interest to the human family. Poetic fancies and legendary lore suddenly became actual facts. The shores of a mysterious land, and a landscape of thrilling and absorbing interest, were presented to the gaze of those who had embarked upon a search for the phantom isles. The discovery of the continent of North America was the direct consequence of the persistent efforts of the townsmen of Bristol to find certain "islands" which, although actually named and marked in maps, had no real existence. Visions of Eldorado, of fabulous summer islands, and of delectable delights—and a new continent of vast extent was ultimately revealed! It was the unveiling of a fairy scene on the stage of the world.

It is necessary to state a few facts to explain the illusions which obtained with regard to the phantom isles. In the *Geography of Strabo*,[2] the author, writing with reference to Homer, says: "He portrays the happiness of the people of the West, and the salubrity of their climate, having no doubt heard of the abundance of Iberia,[3] which had attracted the arms of Hercules, afterwards of the Phœnicians, who acquired there an extended rule,

[1] *Infra*, pp. 58, 59.   [2] Bohn's edition, vol. i. p. 3.
[3] Spain. Gosselin remarks that in his opinion Strabo frequently attributes to Homer much information of which the great poet was entirely ignorant.

and finally of the Romans. There the airs of zephyr breathe, there the poet feigned the fields of Elysium, when he tells us Menelaus was sent thither by the gods—

> 'Thee the gods
> Have destined to the blest Elysian isles,
> Earth's utmost boundaries. Rhadamanthus there
> For ever reigns, and there the human kind
> Enjoy the easiest life; no snow is there,
> No biting winter, and no drenching shower,
> But zephyr always gently from the sea
> Breathes on them, to refresh the happy race.'[1]

The Isles of the Blest are on the extreme west of Maurusia, near where its shore runs parallel to the opposite coast of Spain; and it is clear he considered these regions also blest from the contiguity to the islands." Strabo was born B.C., and there is evidence that he was in existence during the first two decades of the Christian era, consequently we now know that the belief in the existence of the Isles of the Blest, which are synonymous with the Fortunate Islands referred to by other historians, existed as far back as nineteen centuries ago.[2] Strabo's "Isles of the Blest" were probably the Canary Islands.[3]

---

[1] "But the immortals will send you to the Elysian plain, and the boundaries of the earth, where is auburn-haired Rhadamanthus; there of a truth is the most easy life for men. There is nor snow, nor long winter, nor even a shower, but every day the ocean sends forth the gently blowing breezes of the west wind to refresh men."—*Odyssey*, iv. 563.

[2] The Arabians held a belief in the existence of "Fortunate Islands," and they were known to them by the name of *Chaledat*, or the *Perpetual Islands*.

[3] Washington Irving states that expeditions would launch from the Canaries to explore this land of promise. "For a time its sun-gilt peaks and long shadowy promontories would remain distinctly visible, but in proportion as the voyagers approached, peak and promontory would gradually fade away until nothing would remain but blue sky above and deep blue water below."

In due course the mythical attributes of the Isles of the Blest were extended to the Azores, and when those islands became well known, the happy islands became located still farther westward in the great and unknown sea.

Down to a comparatively late period the Roman geographers had no precise knowledge of the islands in the Atlantic. Sertorius, during his exile in Spain, seems to have heard of two very fertile islands, in all probability two of the Canaries. About twenty years later Statius Sebosus made inquiries as to these islands. Pliny says: "Beyond the *Fortunate Islands* there are others." There are reasons for believing that some of the ancient geographers regarded the most easterly of the group of the Canaries as the Hesperides, or Fortunate Isles.

Humboldt[1] refers to a very ancient belief: "A fanciful idea, raised up in the imagination, of Elysium the Islands of the Blessed, which were situated in the extreme limits of the ocean, and were warmed by the vicinity of the setting sun. It was supposed that in the farthest distance all the charms of life and the most precious productions of the earth existed. The ideal country, the geographical fable of Elysium, was moved farther westward, beyond the Pillars of Hercules, as soon as the acquaintance of the Greeks became more extended. The real knowledge of geography, and the earliest discoveries of the Phœnicians, concerning the dates of which no certain notice has been transmitted to us, probably did not give origin to those fables of the Blessed Islands, but the fables have been interpreted in this way since. The geographical dis-

[1] *Kosmos*, vol. ii. p. 160.

covery has only given substance to the picture of the fancy, and furnished, as it were, a support for it." The old and floating traditions most probably date back to the time of the Egyptians. In the days of the Pharaohs the priests taught that the greatest perfection of happiness, after leaving a mundane sphere of existence in which toil and worry were the chief factors in the lives of men, would consist "in tilling the Elysian fields of the subterranean god Osiris, in feeding and herding his cattle, and navigating the breezy water of the other world in slender skiffs." But blended with these traditions were visions of actual magnificence seen by travellers in the East, together with Eastern beliefs in a sensual paradise in a garden odorous with scented blossoms and perfumed surroundings, affluent in luscious fruit and luxurious repose. The fabled Elysian plains became in course of time a paradise, in which blooming nymphs and perennial youth, and an odour-laden and buoyant atmosphere, were believed to be in actual existence. It was not an "over-world,"—an imaginary heaven beyond the clouds,—but a place of pure unalloyed happiness situated somewhere beyond the sea-horizon of the Western waters.

During the Middle Ages, again, there existed a well-established belief as to the reality of certain islands known as the Hesperides, otherwise the Fortunate Islands. In *Curious Myths of the Middle Ages*,[1] it is stated that "the ancients had a floating tradition relative to a vast continent called Atlantis, in the far West, where lay Kronos asleep, guarded by Briarieus; a land of rivers and woods and soft

[1] P. 524.

airs, occupying in their thoughts the position assumed in Christian belief by the earthly paradise. The fathers of the Church waged war against this object of popular mythology, for scripture plainly indicated the position of the 'garden of Eden' (Gen. ii. 8), but notwithstanding their attempts to drive the Western paradise from the minds of men, it held its ground, and was believed in throughout the Middle Ages."[1]

The Chinese look towards the West for their paradise, and among the nations professing the religion of Buddha the same idea holds. Many myths have passed from India and the East to Europe, and there is very little doubt that the belief in the existence of a land of peace, tranquillity, and happiness came originally from the East. It was, in all probability, due to some Eastern myth that the ancient geographers placed the Elysian Field of Homer, and the Happy Isles of Hesiod, in the Western Ocean.

In Dr. Justin Winsor's work[2] the author says: "Among the islands which prefigured the Azores[3] on fourteenth-century maps appears 'I. de Brazi' on the Medicean portulano of 1351. . . . On the Pezigani map of 1367 appear three islands with this name, Insula de Bracir, or Bracie, two not far from

[1] Columbus, who fully believed that the land he had discovered was a remote part of Asia, indicated his belief in an earthly paradise in the following words:—"The saintly theologians were right when they fixed the site of the terrestrial paradise in the extreme Orient, because it is a most temperate clime; and the lands which I have just discovered are the limits of the Orient."
[2] *Narr. and Crit. Hist.*, vol. i. p. 49.
[3] The Azores are over 800 miles west of Portugal; they lie in an oblique line, north-west and south-east, between 36° 50' and 39° 50' north latitude, and 24° 30' and 31° 20' west longitude. They were named *Açores* in consequence of the vast number of Goshawks found upon them by the discoverers of the islands.

the Azores, and one off the south or south-east end of Ireland. On the Catalan map[1] of 1375 is an Insula de Brazil in the southern part of the so-called Azores group, and an I. de Brazil applied to a group of small islands enclosed in a heavy black ring west of Ireland." In a translation of *Old Celtic Romances*, by P. W. Joyce, we meet with allusions to ancient stories which tell of "a beautiful country under the sea. In some romantic writings it is called Tir-fa-Tonn, the land beneath the wave; sometimes it is O'Brasil, that dim land which appears over the waters once in seven years. This very old Celtic tradition is obviously the same as the legend of the continent of Atlantis mentioned by Plato."

Macpherson, in his introduction to the *History of Great Britain*, points out that the belief in the existence of the Isle of the Blest was prevalent among the Keltic peoples. An old-time tradition relates that in the dim past there lived in Skerr a Druid of renown who sat with his face to the west of the shore, his eye following the declining sun, blaming the careless billows which tumbled between him and the distant Isle of Green. One day, as he sat musing on a rock, a storm arose on the sea; a cloud, under whose squally skirts the foaming waters tossed, rushed suddenly into the bay, and from its dark womb emerged a boat with white sails bent to the wind, and banks of gleaming oars on either side. But it was apparently destitute of mariners.[2] An

[1] This map embodies a large quantity of geographical information derived from statements in Marco Polo's book.
[2] Procopius has left a very curious relation as to how, in the remote past, the souls of the deceased inhabitants of the coast of the land, over against a certain island called Brittia, were carried to their final rest-

unusual terror seized on the aged Druid; he heard a voice call, "Arise, and see *the Green Isle of those who have passed away.*" After sailing on the ocean for seven days, he saw the Isle of the Departed basking in golden light. Its hills sloped green and tufted with beauteous trees to the shore, the mountain-tops were enveloped in bright and transparent clouds, from which gushed limpid streams which, wandering down the steep hillsides with pleasant harp-like murmur, emptied themselves into the twinkling blue bays. The valleys were open and free to the ocean; trees loaded with leaves, which scarcely waved to the light breeze, were scattered on the green declivities and rising ground; all was calm and bright; the pure sun of autumn shone from his blue sky on the fields; he hastened not to the West for repose, nor was he seen to rise in the East, but hung as a golden lamp ever illuminating the Fortunate Isle. There, in radiant halls, dwelt the spirits of the departed, ever blooming and beautiful, ever laughing and gay.

The legendary lore of the Celts teems with ideal personifications of natural phenomena. The brimming rivers were "Mothers bringing food and abundance of riches. The whirling eddy concealed a demon, the lake was ruled by a lonely queen, and every well and grotto in the forest was haunted by its fairy nymph. They saw the palaces of Morgan la Faye in the mirage and the coloured clouds at sunset, and believed that on the 'blue verge of the sea' were the shores of the Land of Youth, of

ing-place. This myth states that a boat arrived at Brittia at night, that voices were heard announcing its arrival, but that the rowers of the boat were invisible to the islanders.

O'Brasil the Island of the Blest, and of the 'green isles of the flood,' which vanished at the fisherman's approach. The earthly paradise was always on the sea-horizon; it was set by different tribes in Somerset, in the Isle of Man, and in fabulous countries off the Irish coast. The inhabitants of these homes of summer were a divine race of the pure Celtic type. . . . The Irish O'Brasil, 'the Isle of the Blest,' was drawn in some of the mediæval maps as a country lying to the west of Ireland. Its inhabitants were thus described by the fairy messenger who carried away an Irish queen—

> 'O Béfinn! wilt thou go with me
> To a wonderful land which is mine?
> The hair there is as the blossom of water flags,
> Of the colour of snow is the fair body.
> There will be neither grief nor care;
> White the teeth, and black the brows:
> Pleasant to the eye is the number of the hosts,
> With the hue of the foxglove on every cheek.'[1]

"A murmuring rill flows from a spring in the midst of the island, and thence drink the spirits and obtain life with the draught. Joy, song, and minstrelsy reign in that blessed region."[2]

Although the union of the old and new world, which was consummated by the fifteenth-century voyages, gradually dispelled many illusions which had been cherished by poets and imaginative chroniclers, the belief in the existence of O'Brazile died very hard. It is said that it yet exists in distant places in the west of Ireland. At the present day the inhabitants of the Arran Islands,

[1] Elton's *Origins of English History*, pp. 282, 283; O'Curry, *Mann. Anc. Irish.*
[2] *Mém. de l'Acad. Celtique*, v. p. 202.

on the western coast of Ireland,[1] who are descended from the Northmen, believe that from time to time they see the shore of a happy island rise above the waves; and they say that Ireland was formerly united to that land, until, for the sins of its inhabitants, the greater part of it was engulfed in the ocean.[2]

Jeremy Taylor, in the year 1667, refers to this island. The allusion to it appears in his introduction to his *Dissuasive from Popery*, as follows:—
"And I will not be asking any more odd questions, as why, . . . having so clearly demonstrated his religion by grounds firm as the land of Delos or O'Brasile, he should now be content to argue his cause at the bar of probability" (vol. vi. p. 318, Eden's edition). In 1674 was published in London *The Western Wonder, or O'Brazeel*, giving an account, somewhat in the style of De Foe, of a visit to the island. There was also published a pamphlet with the title, "O. Brazile; or the Enchanted Island: being a perfect relation of the discovery and wonderful Disenchantment of an Island in the North of Ireland, etc. London, 1675." With regard to the derivation of the name, "Brazil does not appear in the epic literature of Ireland, relating to the ocean voyages of 540 and 560, but it seems to belong to the same class of legends. The name is derived by Celtic scholars from *breas*, large, and *i*, island" (Winsor, vol. i. p. 49). "The name of Brazil[3] has had a curious history. Etymologists

---

[1] Reilly, *Trans. Roy. Irish Acad.*, xv.
[2] This is a probable survival of the story of Plato's lost Atlantis.
[3] In Marco Polo's book (Yule, vol. ii. chap. vii.), under the heading, "Wherein the Isles of Sondur and Condur are spoken of; and the Kingdom of Locae," *e.g.*, we find the following:—"In this country the *brazil* which we make use of grows in great plenty." In chapter xi.,

refer it to the colour of braise or hot coals, and its first application was to the dye-wood from the far East" (Yule's *Book of Ser Marco Polo*, vol. ii. p. 316). "The word brazil is found in our literature as early as the reign of Edward I." (Talbot, *English Etymologies*, p. 451). French, braise; Portuguese, braza, live coals; English, brasier. The vast country known as Brazil (South America) was "so called from the discovery on its shores of a dye-wood which produced the Brazil-colour, or colour of glowing coals" (*Etymological Illustrations*, by Isaac Taylor, M.A.).

"The Isle of Seven Cities," otherwise Antillia,[1] appears in several early maps. Toscanelli's map shows his belief in the existence of this island, and Toscanelli himself, in writing to Columbus with explanations of the map or chart which he had made out as a guide of "a shorter route to the places of spices by ocean navigation," speaks as follows:—
"That city [Quinsay] is in the province of Mangi, or near the province of Cathay, in which land is the royal residence. *But from the island of Antilia, which you know*, to the very splendid island of Cipango,[2] there are ten spaces.[3] For that island

in speaking of the people of the kingdom of Lambri and Tansur, we are told: "They also have plenty of brazil. . . . This they sow, and when it is grown to the size of a small shoot they take it up and transplant it; then they let it grow for three years, after which they tear it up by the root. You must know that Messer Marco Polo aforesaid brought some seed of the brazil, such as they sow, to Venice with him, and had it sown there, but never a thing came up. And I fancy it was because the climate was too cold."

[1] The word "Antilia," or "Antillia," is the origin of the name Antilles, which, since the first decade of the sixteenth century, has been applied to the West India or American Islands.

[2] Japan. This and other names of places were taken by Toscanelli from Marco Polo's book.

[3] Each space on Toscanelli's map was supposed to contain two hundred and fifty miles.

abounds in gold, pearls, and precious stones, and they cover the temples and palaces with solid gold." The most ancient tradition as to the Isle of Seven Cities, otherwise Antillia, informs us that certain refugees sailed from Spain, on the occasion of the conquest of the Spanish peninsula by the Moors, in the early part of the eighth century, and after a long voyage in the "Sea of Darkness" they discovered the island. They were accompanied "by an archbishop and six bishops, each of whom built him a town." (A variant of this story declares that the ecclesiastics were "seven bishops"; another variant declares that there were "two archbishops and five bishops.") One of the legends states that when the refugees landed, the bishops burned the ships which had conveyed the party to the island, in order to prevent the desertion of their followers. The island, in the current belief of the period, "abounded with gold, with magnificent houses and temples, and high towers that shone at a distance." Ruych's map contains a legend that "Antilia was discovered by the last of the Gothic kings of Spain, who took refuge on the island after his defeat by the Moors." The various ephemeral stories, which were passed from mouth to mouth by enthusiastic believers, created among men of all grades an anxiety to obtain some particulars as to this scene of dazzling splendour. Traditions of early unsuccessful attempts were current; on the other hand, it was a popular belief that this island, like that of "St. Brandan," had been found by a number of persons, who, when they once landed on it, were compelled for ever after to remain there. The visionary land invariably faded before research, yet the belief in its existence never ceased.

The inhabitants of Madeira and Puerto Santo were for centuries under the impression that they could see at certain times, and in clear weather, land appearing in the western horizon, and ever in the same direction. This belief is said to have continued until a comparatively recent period; indeed, some people say it yet exists in a few of the credulous inhabitants.

References to "Antilla" and "the Island of the Seven Cities" appear in *Historie del S. D. Fernando Colombo.* The work of Ferdinand Columbus is regarded by students of American history as one of great value. He tells us that his father fully expected to meet with, " before he came to India, a very convenient island or continent, from which he might pursue with more advantage his main design. This hope was grounded upon the statements of many wise men and philosophers, who believed that the greatest part of this terraqueous globe was land, or that there was more land than water, and, if this were true, he assumed that between the coast of Spain and the limits of India, then known, there existed many islands and a considerable extent of mainland. . . . A pilot of the King of Portugal, named Martin Vicente, told him that, being at one time four hundred and fifty leagues westward of Cape St. Vincent, he found and picked up in the sea a piece of wood ingeniously carved, but not with iron, which led him to believe, as the wind had been blowing from the west for several days, that the piece of wood had drifted from some island lying toward the west. Then one Pedro Correa, who had married the sister of the admiral's wife, told him that at the island of Porto Santo[1] he had seen

[1] Situated to the north-west of Madeira.

another piece of wood, brought by the same winds, as nicely carved as the piece already mentioned, and that canes had been found there so thick that each joint would hold more than four quarts of wine, which reports, he said, he communicated to the King of Portugal while talking to him about these matters. The pieces of cane were shown to him. There being no place in our parts where such cane grew, he inferred it to be true that the wind had brought the cane from some neighbouring islands or else from India. For Ptolemy, in the first book of his geography, in the seventeenth chapter, says there is such cane in the eastern parts of India. And some of the people living on the islands, particularly on the Azores, told him that the west wind blew for a long time, the sea drifted some pieces of pine-wood upon these islands, particularly on the islands Gratiosa and Fayal, there being no pine-wood in all these parts, and that the sea cast upon the island of Flores, another of the Azores, the bodies of two dead men, who were very broad faced and different in appearance from Christians. At Cape Verd and thereabouts, they said they once saw some covered canoes or boats, which, the people believed, were driven there by stress of weather while the persons in them were going from one island to another. Nor were these the only grounds he then had which seemed reasonable, for there were those who told him that they had seen some islands in the Western Ocean. . . . These persons he did not believe, because he discovered from their own words and statements that they had not sailed one hundred leagues to the westward. . . . He says, moreover, that in the year 1484 a man came to Portugal from the island of Madeira to beg a caravel of the king to discover a country which he affirmed he saw every year, and always after the same manner, he agreeing with others who said they had seen the island from the Azores. On this account the Portuguese placed some islands thereabouts on the charts and maps made at that time; and also because Aristotle, in his book of wonderful things, affirms that it was reported that some Carthaginian merchants had sailed over the Atlantic Ocean to a most fruitful island. . . . This island the Portuguese inserted in their maps, calling it Antilla; and though they did not give it the same situation designated by Aristotle, yet none placed it more than two hundred leagues due west from the Canaries and the Azores. Some believe it to be the Island of the Seven Cities, peopled by the Portuguese at the time that Spain was conquered by the Moors, in 714,—at which time, they say, seven bishops with their people embarked and sailed to this island, where each of them built a city; and in order that none of their people might think of returning to Spain, they burnt the ships, tackle, and all things necessary for sailing. . . . It was also said that in the time of Prince Henry of Portugal, a Portuguese ship was driven by stress of weather to this island of Antilla, where the men went on shore, and were conducted by the islanders to their church, to learn whether or not they were Christians and acquainted with the Roman ceremonies. After perceiving that they were, the people of the island importuned them to remain till their king came, who was then absent, and who would be delighted to see them, and would give them many presents. . . . But the master and the seamen were afraid of being detained, suspecting these people did not wish to be discovered, and might for this reason burn their ship. On this account they returned to Portugal, hoping to be rewarded by the prince for what they had done. He reproved them severely, and bid them return at once to the island, but the master, through fear, ran away from Portugal with the ship and men. It is reported that while the seamen were at church on the island, the ship-boys gathered sand for the cook-room, the third part of which they found to be pure gold. . . . Seneca, in his fourth book, tells us that Thucydides speaks of an island called Atlantica, which in the time of the Peloponnesian war was entirely, or the greater part of it, submerged; whereof Plato also makes mention in his *Timæus.*"

It is said that in 1431 Prince Henry of Portugal sent Goncalo Cabral in search of certain islands which were marked on a map brought from Italy (Lisboa, lib. iv. cap. i. p. 97). A belief existed in Portugal that in 1447 a Portuguese ship was driven by stress of weather "to the Island of the Seven Cities" (*De Originibus Americanis*, p. 77); and, according to Columbus, an adventurer named Vogado succeeded in discovering two oceanic islands (Christopher Columbus, i. p. 315).

In the early part of the fifteenth century, according to a tradition, a pilot arrived at Lisbon, and stated that he had landed upon an island in the Atlantic Ocean "which he had found peopled with Christians and adorned with noble cities." The sequel of this story is exceedingly romantic in its details. Don Fernando de Alma, a young Portuguese cavalier, came to the conclusion that the pilot had discovered the Island of the Seven Cities. With the consent of the king he fitted out two vessels, and started upon a voyage of discovery. After encountering some difficulties, the caravel, with Don Fernando on board, after a storm, lay perfectly becalmed off the mouth of a river, "on the banks of which, about a league off, was descried a noble city, with lofty walls and towers and a protecting castle." Don Fernando was welcomed to the Island of the Seven Cities by the Grand Chamberlain. He spent an agreeable time on shore, and at night he returned in the State barge of the Grand Chamberlain. "The barge sailed out to sea, but no caravel was to be seen. The oarsmen rowed on,—their monotonous chant had a lulling effect. A drowsy influence crept over Don Fernando; objects swam before his eyes, and he lost consciousness. On his recovery he found himself in a strange cabin, surrounded by strangers. Where was he? On board a Portuguese ship bound for Lisbon. How had he come there? He had been taken senseless from a wreck drifting about the ocean. The vessel arrived in the Tagus, and anchored before the famous capital. Don Fernando sprang joyfully on shore, and hastened to his ancestral mansion. A strange porter opened the door, who knew nothing of him or of his family; no people of the name had inhabited the house for many a year. He sought the house of his betrothed, the Donna Serafina. He beheld her on the balcony; then he raised his arms towards her with an exclamation of rapture. She cast upon him a look of indignation, and hastily retired. He rang at the door; as it was opened by the porter, he rushed past, sought the well-known chamber, and threw himself at the feet of Serafina. She started back with affright, and took refuge in the arms of a youthful cavalier.

"What mean you, señor?" cried the latter.

"What right have you to ask that question?" demanded Don Fernando fiercely.

"The right of an affianced suitor!"

"O Serafina! is this your fidelity?" cried he in a tone of agony.

"Serafina! What mean you by Serafina, señor? This lady's name is Maria."

"What!" cried Don Fernando; "is not this Serafina Alvarez, the original of yon portrait which smiles on me from the wall?"

"Holy Virgin!" cried the young lady, casting her eyes upon the portrait,—"he is talking of my great-grandmother!"[1]

In the *Decades of the New World* (Eden's translations, Arber's edition, Birmingham, 1885, p. 287), in the course of some allusions to the noble enterprise of Antoni di Mendeza, Viceroy of Mexico, the narrator says: "And I remember that when I was in Flanders, in the Emperor's Court, I saw his letter written in the year 1541, and dated from Mexico; wherein was declared how towards the north-west he had found the kingdom of Sette Citta, (that is) Seven Cities, . . . and how beyond the said kingdom, yet farther toward the northwest, Capitain Francesco Vasques . . . came to the seaside, where he found certain ships; . . . he understood that these ships could be of none other country than of Cathay." This is a fair example of the universal belief in the existence of the Island of the Seven Cities, and of the

[1] *Curious Myths of the Middle Ages*, p. 543.

possibility of reaching India by a "North-West passage."

"There was a tradition afloat in Europe, that on the occasion of the conquest of the Spanish peninsula by the Arabs in the eighth century, a certain bishop of Lisbon, with a goodly company of followers, took refuge upon an island, or group of islands, far out on the Sea of Darkness, and founded seven cities there. . . . Its seven cities were curiously transferred into the very heart of the American continent. Among the Nahuatl tribes there was a legend of Chicomoztoc, or the Seven Caves, from which at some period in the past their ancestors issued. As soon as the Spaniards got hold of this legend they contrived to mix up these seven caves with their seven cities. They were supposed to be somewhere to the northward, and when Cabeza de Vaca and his comrades had disclosed the existence of such a vast territory north of Mexico, it was resolved to search for the seven cities in that direction. The work was entrusted to Fray Marcos, . . . a Franciscan monk. He was attended on the journey by the negro Estevánico and a few Pima Indians, who had been educated at Mexico. At Matape, an Indian village in Senora, they heard definite news of a country situated thirty days' march to the northward, where there were seven large cities. . . . The name of the first of these cities was said to be Cibola. And from that time forth this became a common name for the group, and we hear much of the seven cities of Cibola. These were the seven pueblos of Zuñi, in New Mexico, of which six were still inhabited at the end of the sixteenth century. . . . Estevánico travelled some miles in advance of Fray Marcos.

When he arrived at the first of the cities of Cibola, flaunting the turquoises and the handsome Indian girls, with whom he had been presented in the course of his journey,—much to the disgust of the Franciscan friar,—the elders and chiefs of the pueblo would not grant him admittance. He was lodged in a small house outside the enclosure, and was cautiously catechised. When he announced himself as the envoy and forerunner of a white man, sent by a mighty prince beyond the sky to instruct them in heavenly things, the Zuñi elders were struck with a sense of incongruity. How could black represent white, or be the envoy and forerunner of white? To the metaphysics of the middle status of barbarism the question wore a very uncanny look, and to the common sense of the middle status of barbarism the self-complacent Estevánico appeared to be simply a spy from some chieftain or tribe that wanted to conquer the Zuñis. . . . While the elders were debating whether they should do reverence to him as a wizard, or butcher him as a spy, he stole out of his lodging and sought safety in flight; and this act, being promptly detected, robbed him of all dignity, and sealed his fate. A hue-and-cry went after him, and an arrow soon found its way to his heart. The news of this catastrophe checked the advance of Fray Marcos. His Indian comrades were discouraged, and the most he could do was to keep them with him while he climbed a hill, whence he could get a Pisgah sight of the glories of Cibola. After he had accomplished this, the party returned with all possible haste to Culiacan, and arrived there in August 1539, after an absence of five months" (*The Discovery of America*, by J. Fiske, vol. ii. pp. 502-507).

It is scarcely possible to resist the conclusion that the belief in the existence of "the Seven Cities" was founded upon some primitive Eastern myth. In the Hindoo system, Priyauratta divided the earth into seven dwipas, or islands. It was believed at first that it was his intention to divide his possessions among his ten sons, but three retired from the world. "In the accounts which the writings of the Hindoos give of the Indian Seas, the tendency to dispose everything *according to the symmetry of a religious system*[1] prevails over the simplicity of truth." There is a tra-nate, or group of three islands, composed respectively of gold, silver, and iron. Co-existing with these, there is a mysterious assemblage of seven islands; and when Jambolo stated that the Indian islands were seven in number, he only repeated the language of the natives; for the expression *Yail Laneas*, or the seven lances, is still in use at the present day. It is obvious that these legends were all understood literally by the Greek geographers, and particularly by Ptolemy, who derived an unusually large share of information from India, and was careful to turn every atom to account. Accordingly, we find in his map a *Heptanesia nesos*, or *Septuple island*, which it is impossible to assign to any known position (*Mythic Geography of the Hindoos*, chap. x. p. 149). Marcellus distinctly states that there existed in early times seven islands (the *dwipas*) in the Atlantic Ocean, together with three others (the *tri-cutadri*) of an immense magnitude, sacred to Pluto, to Ammon, and to Neptune.

. . . .

[1] This is a reference to the two mystic numbers three and seven.

As to the island which, under the name of "San Brandon," appears in the so-called Cabot map of 1544, we find it solemnly recorded in all the glory of print that St. Brendon, otherwise St. Brandon, an Irish abbot of the sixth century,[1] had been told that an island existed far out in the ocean which was the land promised to the saints, the "Island of Paradise." St. Brendon, of Clofort, known as St. Brendon the Navigator, so the story goes, set sail with seventy-five monks, and spent seven years on the water, and eventually found the island he was in search of, and others. A variant of the story further records, as a fact, that in the course of their wanderings upon the ocean they landed upon what they fully believed to be an island, upon which they celebrated Easter, but the "island" turned out to be the back of a huge fish. This really genuine fish story has been traced back to a very early period.[2] St. Brandon's voyage was undertaken, so it is said, in consequence of a statement made to him by a monk, to the effect that he had sailed due east from Ireland, and had come at last to Paradise, which was an island full of joy and mirth, and the earth as bright as the sun, and it was a glorious sight, and the half year he was there slipped by as a few moments. *On his (the monk's) return to the abbey his garments were still fragrant with the odours of Paradise.* Brandon, on his arrival at the island, is said to have traversed it for the space of forty days without meeting anyone, till he came to a broad river, on the banks of which stood a young man, who told him that this stream

---

[1] He is commemorated on May 10.
[2] There are reasons for the belief that the story of Brandon is derived from that of Sindbad the Sailor.

divided the world in twain, and that none living might cross it.[1] The mythical island of St. Brandon is found in various positions on the early maps; it disappeared from one position only to reappear in another. The Toscanelli map, which was in existence in 1474, and from which Columbus drew an inspiration, shows an island marked "St. Brandon," and the island is also shown on Martin Behaim's globe, 1492.[2] The Spaniards had a legend that their Rodrigo retreated to this island, and the Portuguese believed it to be the retreat of their Don Sebastian. Many stories were told as to the island having been reached by various persons, none of whom were ever allowed to return therefrom.

Matthew Arnold, in right of poetic licence, takes the saint on a northern voyage—

> "Saint Brandon sails the northern main;
> The brotherhood of saints are glad.
> He greets them once, he sails again;
> So late!—Such storms!—The saint is mad!
>
> He heard, across the howling seas,
> Chime convent bells on wintry nights;
> He saw on spray-swept Hebrides
> Twinkle the monastery lights;
>
> But north, still north, Saint Brandon steer'd—
> And now no bells, no convents more!
> The hurtling Polar lights are near'd,
> The sea without a human shore.

---

[1] This part of the story is probably derived from the ancient fable relating to Charon, the ferryman, who, according to the fable, transported the shades in a boat over the Styx. In order to reward the ferryman, the ancients used to put a piece of money in the mouths of the dead.

[2] Both Toscanelli's map and Behaim's globe contain an island marked "Antilia," and Toscanelli's map also represents "Brazil" as an island lying at some distance in the Atlantic beyond a portion of the coast of Ireland. Behaim's ideas were founded upon Toscanelli's map.

> At last—(it was the Christmas night,
> Stars shone after a day of storm)—
> He sees float past an iceberg white,
> And on it—Christ! a living form.
>
> That furtive mien, that scowling eye,
> Of hair that red and tufted fell—
> It is—oh, where shall Brandon fly?—
> The traitor Judas, out of hell!"

. . . .

Brandon Hill is 250 feet above the level of Bristol; from the summit a grand panoramic view of the city and its surroundings may be obtained. It derives its name from "St. Brendan," who, on his return to Ireland, according to tradition, sailed for Britain with a large company of disciples. There was a hermit's cell or chapel on the top of Brandon Hill. Dallaway[1] says that the Irish mariners resorted to this chapel upon their reaching the port of Bristol. William Worcestre, a fifteenth-century chronicler, describes the chapel, which was dedicated to St. Brandon ("Sancti Brandani"),—and the hill was described as "Mons Sancti Brandani." Worcestre says: "The height of the hill of St. Brandon's chapel, as the hermit of that chapel told me, is supposed by sailors and well-judging men to be higher than any spire either of Redcliff or any other church by eighteen fathom of height, and each fathom measures six feet." ["Altitudo montis capellæ Sancti Brandani dicitur, ut heremita ibidem michi retulit, quod nautæ et discreti homines dicunt esse alciorem alicujus pinaculi sive ecclesiæ de Radclyff quam aliarum ecclesiarum per spacium altitudinis 18 brachiorum anglice a vathym, et quodlibet brachium continet 6 pedes."] (*Itiner-*

[1] Dallaway's *Antiquities of Bristol*, p. 46.

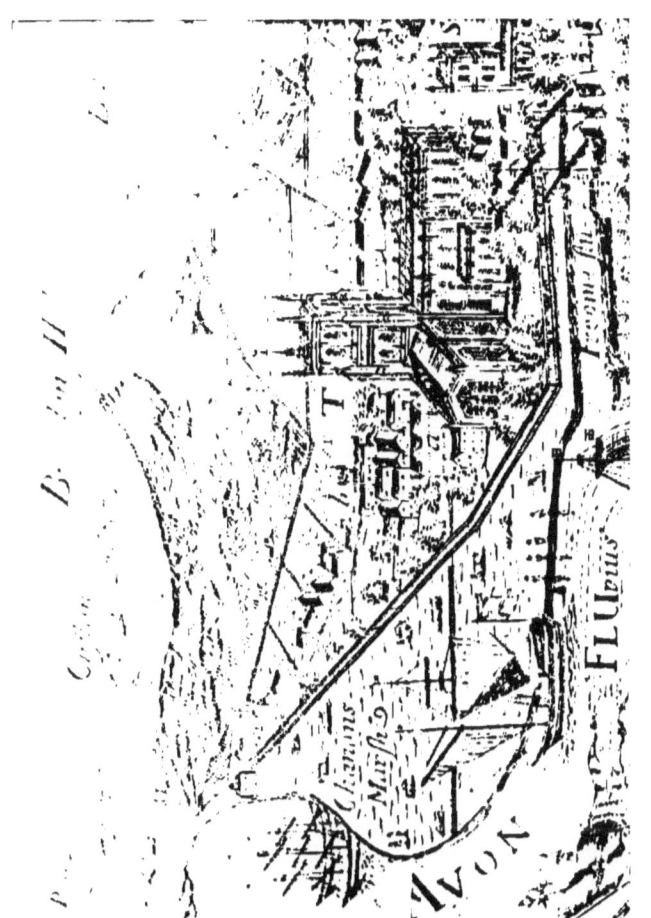

BRANDON HILL, WITH A VIEW OF THE AVON (BRISTOL) RIVER
[A Section of an Ancient Map of Bristol.]

arium Willelmi de Worcestre,[1] Nasmith's edition, p. 241.)

In the register of William of Wickham, Bishop of Winchester, is the following particular of the chapel of St. Brendan: "Ibidem 14 die Augusti 1403 dominas concessit, etc., he granted to all benefactors to the chapel of St. Brendan nigh Bristol, and to Reginald Taillor, the poor hermit of it, forty days of indulgence by his letters for one year only to continue"; by which it appears there was an

[1] William Wircestre, or Worcestre, popularly, but erroneously, known as "William of Worcester," who, as it will presently appear, was the chronicler of the first English attempt to sail in search of the island, was the son of a person of the same name, who was a worthy burgess of Bristol, and engaged in trade. He was born at a house in a very ancient street, called St. James's Back, in 1415. His mother was Elizabeth Botoner, of an opulent family settled in Coventry. After having passed four years as a student of Hart Hall, in Oxford, he became a retainer to Sir John Falstaff, of Caistre Castle, in Norfolk, and, in process of time, his secretary, physician, and finally was appointed one of his executors. It appears that Wyrcestre occasionally assumed the designation of W. Botoner, otherwise Wyrcestre, preferring his mother's name to that of his father. In the decline of life he established himself in Bristol, having a house and garden near St. Philip's churchyard gate. His chief amusement in his old age was most minutely to survey his native town by paces and measurements, committing the result of such investigation daily to his note-book. ... He died about the year 1484 (Dallaway's *Antiquities of Bristow*). The Worcestre family was for a long period connected with the ancient parish of St. James in Bristol. In the will of John Pedewell, burgess, proved in the year 1385, who desired to be buried in the cemetery of the parish church of St. James of Bristol, we find that "William Worcestre" was appointed one of the executors, and Richard, the prior of St. James, overseer of the will. In the will of Henry Calf, burgess, proved in 1394, the testator appointed Richard "Wircestre," prior of St. James of Bristol, to be overseer. John Fluyt, burgess, who died in 1398, desired to be buried in the parish of St. James of Bristol, in the chapel of the Blessed Mary there, and he appointed "Sir Richard Wircestre, prior of St. James of Bristol," one of the overseers of his will. By his will, dated October 20, 1420, William Worcestre expressed a wish to be buried in the east corner of St. James's cemetery at Bristol, beside Sir Richard, formerly parish chaplain of that church.

hermitage here, with a chapel dedicated to St. Brendan, an Irish saint. In the year 1351, Lucy de Newchirche repeatedly offered to the Bishop of Worcester, and desired leave to be shut up in the hermitage of St. Brendan of Bristol, and to quit the world, which, after due inquiry into her conduct and purity of life and necessary virtues for it, was granted her : as we find by the deed (E. Registris Wygorniæ, Thoresby, f. 21*a*. Barrett's *History of Bristol*, pp. 60, 61).

Dr. George Sigerson, the author of *Irish Literature, its Origin*, etc., says that the [mythical] voyage of St. Brendan "was influential in the discovery of America." He also says : "As you sail into Bristol, you must pass under a high hill which is known to this day as St. Brendan Hill. There was a little chapel of St. Brendan on its summit, because of the reverence which all seamen, whether Norse, Saxon, or Celt, professed for the sailor saint."

It was in Bristol ships, and at the risk and expense of Bristol men, that the first practical attempt was made to sail from England in quest of the unknown lands which, according to ancient writers and contemporary cosmographers, existed in the Western Sea.

"In 1480, on July 15th, the ship [of] . . . and John Jay, junior,[1] of the burthen of 80 tons . . . began a voyage from the port of Bristol . . . in search of *the island of Brasylle*, to the west of Ireland. . . . Thlyde,[2] the most scientific mariner in all England being the pilot, that news came to Bristol . . . on the 18th September, that the ships

---

[1] Probably a ship called *Trinite* (*infra*, p. 109). Wyrcestre, the chronicler, had a sister, Joan, who was married to John Jay.

[2] Mr. Harrisse is of opinion that "Thlyde" is the equivalent of Thomas Lloyde ; Professor Fiske puts after "Thlyde"—"[*i.e.* Th. Lyde = Lloyd]."

cruised about the sea for about nine months[1] without finding the island, but in consequence of tempests they returned to a port in Ireland for the repose of the ships and the mariners." ["1480 die 15 julii, navis . . . et Joh[ann]is Jay junioris ponderis 80 doliorum inceperunt viagium apud portum Bristolliæ de Kyngrode[2] usque ad insulam de Brasylle in occidentali parte Hiberniæ, Sulcando maria per . . . et [?] Thlyde est magister navis scientificus marinarius tocius Angliæ; et nova venerunt Bristolliæ die lunæ 18 die septembris, quod dicta navis velaverunt maria per circa 9 menses, nec invenerunt insulam, sed per tempestas maris reversi sunt usque portum . . . in Hibernia pro reposicione navis et marinariorum"] (Wyrcestre MS. in library of Corpus Christi College, Cambridge, No. 210, p. 195).

The following information as to certain voyages from Bristol, for the purpose of discovering unknown islands, is contained in a despatch, dated London, 25th July 1498, from Don Pedro de Ayala to Ferdinand and Isabella:—

"The people of Bristol have, for the last seven years, sent out every year, two, three, or four light ships (caravels), in search of the island of Brasil and the seven cities." ["Los de Bristol ha siete años que cada año an armado dos, tres, cuatro caravelas para ir a buscar la isla del Brasil y las siete ciudades."][3]

---

[1] It seems almost certain that "nine months" should read "nine weeks," which corresponds with the dates "July" and "September."

[2] Kingroad is outside the river Avon, but the boundary of the county of Bristol includes the waters called Kingroad.

[3] Sir Clements Markham, who inclines to the opinion that other voyages took place of which no record was made, says: "It is clear that numerous voyages of discovery were despatched while the Portuguese were still creeping along the African coast, and long before Cabota appeared on the scene."

CHAPTER II

IF any of the voyages from Bristol, prior to the year 1493,[1] in search of the imaginary islands had resulted in the discovery of land, whether continent or island, it would in all probability have necessitated an application by King Henry VII. to the pope for the grant of a papal bull, because we may readily imagine that the cautious monarch, from motives alike of prudence and of policy, would have applied for a bull or dispensation to enable him to hold such newly-discovered territory against all persons whomsoever; in other words, he would most certainly have availed himself of the papal authority for the purpose of strengthening and confirming his title. We may not be strictly defining the pope's position at this period, according to the canons of the Church, when we say that he claimed power over the lands of all persons other than Christians; however, it is clear that some of the Catholic monarchs of Europe formally conceded to His Holiness the right to authorise them to take possession of all the lands of the "heathen and infidels," and to hold such lands against all other potentates. It was clearly in a deferential spirit of submission to the authority, or alleged authority, of the papal chair that first

---

[1] The date of the papal bull by which all undiscovered lands were divided between Portugal and Spain.

Portugal, and subsequently Spain, applied for a bull, with the result that the pope divided about one half of the globe between these two countries. The claim of the Church over the lands of the "heathen and heretics" was founded upon, if not actually derived from, an edict concocted at Rome about the middle of the eighth century, under the title, "Edictum domini Constantini Imp., apud pseudo-Isidorus Decretalia." This forgery, which purported to be a donation from Constantine to Pope Sylvester I., was sometimes considered to be of doubtful origin, but a vast majority of Catholics accepted it as a genuine production. Speaking broadly, the ecclesiastical authorities claimed that the pope had certain powers over the whole of the world.[1] The popes claimed what was tantamount to universal allegiance. Dom Henrique of Portugal, surnamed the Navigator, seeing that important discoveries were at hand, and knowing that, however exaggerated some of Marco Polo's statements might prove, there were lands in the far East to which he might find a sea-route, and bring thence treasures untold, applied to the pope, in or about the year 1441, for a concession in perpetuity to the Portuguese crown of all lands to be discovered between Cape Bojador and the Indies, inclusive; representing, at the same time, that his principal object was the conversion of the natives of those lands to the Christian faith. It must not be hastily accepted as a fact, that this representation was merely used as a device to obtain a safe charter and enable the Portuguese to hold their discoveries

[1] Columbus fully believed that all persons who would not accept the teachings of the Roman Catholic priests were not entitled to any natural rights, and that almost any steps might be resorted to for the purpose of compelling persons to accept those teachings.

against all comers. It may be urged that Dom Henrique was conscientious in his desire to plant the Christian faith in those far-off regions. "There was, however, another side to this question. The profits to be obtained from the trade with Africa, consisting principally of negro slaves and gold, was such that it not only, by appealing to the avidity of the Portuguese, induced them to acquiesce in Dom Henrique's schemes of discovery,—which they had previously opposed on account of their cost,—but it filled all Europe with a desire to embark under the flag of the Portuguese, in order to share in the benefits of this trade. A company of merchants at Lagos obtained from the prince, in 1443, a charter for the exclusive right of trading with the Moors. . . . But instead of trading with the Moors, they made a hostile attack upon them, slew many, and brought off one hundred and fifty-five captives."[1] Subsequently Pope Nicholas v. granted to the King of Portugal an exclusive right to all the lands that he might discover between Cape Non, on the west coast of Africa, and the continent of India.

After the return of Columbus from his first voyage, the Spanish sovereigns applied to the pope for a charter to hold the newly-discovered islands, which they believed to be a part of the Indies. Pope Alexander vi., on the 4th of May 1493, granted a bull, by virtue of his apostolical and pontifical power, by which he established a line of limitation, running from the north to the south pole, distant one hundred leagues west of the Azores and the Cape Verd Islands, giving to Spain all the

[1] *The Portuguese in India*, by F. C. Danvers.

territory, mainland or islands, which she had discovered, or might discover, to the west thereof, and which had not been taken possession of by any Christian monarch *at any time preceding Christmas* 1492. To the Portuguese, in like manner, and subject to the same proviso, the pope granted all the territory which lay to the east of the line of limitation. Thus the lands of the Portuguese became the East Indies.

Some dissatisfaction having been occasioned as to the line of division, the celebrated meeting of the commissioners of Spain and of Portugal took place at Tordesillas, in Spain, in 1494, and an agreement was arrived at, known as the "Treaty of Tordesillas," by which the line of demarcation should be shifted to such a position that it should pass, north and south, three hundred and seventy leagues west of the Cape Verd Islands,—all to the west of that limitation to belong to Spain, and all to the east to Portugal.[1] For obvious reasons, it was agreed that the new line should not apply to islands or firm lands which might have been discovered before the 20th June 1494. A further agreement was come to that the treaty agreed upon between the two nations should be submitted to the pope for confirmation.[2]

[1] All these proceedings afforded a direct and wonderful impetus towards the acceleration of the knowledge of the sciences to which navigation owes so much. It not only caused permanent and useful additions to be made to nautical astronomy, but it induced a closer study of the phenomena of nature and of terrestrial magnetism. The study of the results of the pope's line of demarcation most certainly led to an acquisition of knowledge as to the proper basis for getting at the longitude, etc., which, speaking comparatively, was not yet properly understood.

[2] The papal bull which confirmed the treaty was not issued until the 24th June 1506.

[TRANSLATION OF THE PAPAL BULL]

"Alexander Bishop, the servant of the servants of God :—To our most dear beloved son in Christ, King Ferdinand, And to our dear beloved daughter in Christ, Elizabeth, Queen of Castile, Legion, Aragon, Sicily and Granada, most noble Princes, Greeting and Apostolical benediction.

"Among other works acceptable to the divine majesty and according to our hearts desire, this certainly is the chief, that the Catholic faith and Christian religion, especially in this our time, may in all places be exalted, amplified and enlarged, whereby the health of souls may be procured, and the barbarous nations subdued and brought to the same. And therefore, whereas by the favour of God's clemency (although not with equal deserts) we are called to this holy seat of Peter, and understanding you to be true Catholic princes, as we have ever known you, and as your noble and worthy deeds have declared in manner to the whole world, in that with all your study, diligence, and industry, you have spared no travels, charges, or perils, adventuring even the shedding of your own blood, with applying your whole minds and endeavours hereunto, as your noble expeditions achieved in recovering the kingdom of Granada from the tyranny of the Saracens in these our days, do plainly declare your deeds with great glory of the divine name. For the which, as we think you worthy, so ought we of our own free will favourably to grant all things whereby you may daily with more fervent minds, to the honour of God and the enlarging of the Christian empire, prosecute your devout and laudable purpose most acceptable to the immortal God. We are credibly informed that, whereas of late you were determined to seek and find certain islands and main lands far remote and unknown (and not heretofore found by any other), to the intent to bring the inhabitants of the same to our Redeemer, and to profess the Catholic faith, you have hitherto been much occupied in the expugnation and recovery of the kingdom of Granada, by reason whereof you could not bring your said laudable purpose to the end desired. Nevertheless, as it hath pleased Almighty God, the aforesaid kingdom being recovered, willing to accomplish your said desire, you have, not without labour, perils, and charges, appointed our well-beloved son, Christopher Columbus (a man well commended as most worthy and apt for so great a matter), well furnished with men and ships and other necessaries, to seek (by the sea where hitherto no man hath sailed) such main lands and islands far remote and hitherto unknown. Who (by God's help), making diligent search in the ocean sea, have found certain remote islands and main lands which were not heretofore found by any other. In the which, as is said, many nations inhabit, living peaceably and going naked, not accustomed to eat flesh. And as far as your messengers can conjecture, the nations inhabiting the aforesaid lands and islands, believe that there is one God creature in heaven: and seem apt to be brought to the embracing of the Catholic faith and to be imbued with good manners: by reason whereof, we may hope that if they be well instructed, they may easily be induced to receive the name of our Saviour Jesus Christ. We are further advertised that the before-named Christopher hath now built and erected a fortress with good munition in one of the aforesaid principal islands, in the which he hath placed a garrison of certain of the Christian men that went thither with him: as well to the intent to defend the same, as also to search other islands and main lands far remote and yet unknown. We also understand, that in these lands and islands lately found, is great plenty of gold and spices, with divers and many other precious things of sundry kinds and qualities. Therefore all things diligently considered (especially the amplifying and enlarging of the Catholic faith, as it behoveth Catholic princes following the examples of your noble progenitors of famous memory), whereas you are determined by the favour of Almighty God to subdue and bring to the Catholic faith the inhabitants of the aforesaid lands and islands. We greatly commend this your godly and laudable purpose in our Lord, and desirous to have the same brought to a due end, and the name of our Saviour to be known in these parts, do exhort you in our Lord, and by the receiving of your holy baptism, whereby you are bound to Apostolical obedience, and earnestly require you by the bowels of mercy of our Lord Jesus Christ, that when you intend for the zeal of the Catholic faith to prosecute the said expedition to reduce the people of the aforesaid lands and islands to the Christian religion, you shall spare no labours at any time, or be deterred with any perils, concerning firm hope and confidence that the omnipotent God will give good success to your godly attempts. And that being authorised by the privilege of the Apostolical grace, you may the more freely and boldly take upon you the enterprise

of so great a matter, we of our own motion, and not
either at your request or at the instant petition of
any other person, but of our own mere liberality and
certain science, and by the fulness of Apostolical
power, do give, grant, and assign to you, your heirs
and successors, all the main lands and islands found
or to be found, discovered or to be discovered, toward the west and south, drawing a line from the
Arctic pole to the Antarctic pole, that is, from the
north to the south, Containing in this donation,
whatsoever main lands or islands are found or to be
found toward India, or toward any other part whatsoever it be, being distant from, or without the
aforesaid line drawn a hundred leagues toward the
west and south from any of the islands which are
commonly called De los Azores and Cape Verde. All
the islands therefore, and main lands, found and to
be found, discovered and to be discovered, from the
said line toward the west and south, such as have
not actually been heretofore possessed by any other
Christian King or Prince, until the day of the
nativity of our Lord Jesus Christ last past, from the
which beginneth this present year, being the year of
our Lord M.CCCC.LXXXXIII., whensoever any shall be
found by your messengers and captains, We by the
authority of Almighty God granted unto us in Saint
Peter, and by the office which we bear on the earth
in the stead of Jesus Christ, do for ever by the
tenour of these presents, give, grant, and assign
unto you, your heirs and successors (the Kings of
Castile and Legion), all these lands and islands,
with their dominions, territories, cities, castles,
towers, places, and villages, with all the right and
jurisdiction thereunto pertaining: constituting, as-

signing, and deputing you, your heirs and successors, the lords thereof, with full and free power, authority, and jurisdiction. Decreeing, nevertheless, by this our donation, grant, and assignation, that from no Christian Prince, who actually hath possessed the aforesaid islands and main lands unto the day of the nativity of our Lord aforesaid, their right obtained to be understood hereby to be taken away, or that it ought to be taken away. Furthermore we command you, in virtue of holy obedience (as you have promised, and as we doubt not you will do upon mere devotion and princely magnanimity), to send to the said main lands and islands, honest, virtuous, and learned men, such as fear God and are able to instruct the inhabitants in the Catholic faith and good manners, applying all their possible diligence in the premises. We furthermore inhibit all manner of persons, of what state, degree, order, or condition soever they be, although of Imperial and regal dignity, *under the pain of the sentence of excommunication which they shall incur if they do to the contrary*, that they in no case presume, without special licence of you, your heirs and successors, to travel for merchandise or for any other cause, to the said lands or islands, found or to be found, discovered or to be discovered, towards the west and south, drawing a line from the Arctic pole to the Antarctic pole, whether the main lands and islands found and to be found, be situate toward India or toward any other part, being distant from the line drawn a hundred leagues toward the west from any of the islands commonly called De los Azores and Cape Verde : Notwithstanding constitutions, decrees, and Apostolical ordinances whatsoever they are to the contrary: In Him from whom empires, dominions, and all good things do proceed: Trusting that Almighty God directing your enterprises, if you follow your godly and laudable attempts, your labours and travels herein shall in a short time obtain a happy end with felicity and glory of all Christian people. But forasmuch as it should be a thing of great difficulty for these letters to be carried to all such places as should be expedient, we will, and of like motion and knowledge do decree that whithersoever the same shall be sent, or wheresoever they shall be received with the subscription of a common notary thereunto required, with the seal of any person constituted in ecclesiastical dignity, or such as are authorised by the ecclesiastical court, the same faith and credit to be given thereunto in judgment or elsewhere, as should be exhibited to these presents.

"It shall therefore be lawful for no man to infringe or rashly to act contrary to this letter of our commendation, exhortation, request, donation, grant, assignation, constitution, deputation, decree, commandment, inhibition, and determination. And if any shall presume to attempt the same, he ought to know that he shall thereby incur the indignation of Almighty God and his holy apostles Peter and Paul.

"Given at Rome, at Saint Peter's: In the year of the incarnation of our Lord M.CCCC.LXXXXIII. The fourth day of the nones of May, the first year of our pontificate." [1]

In the year 1497 John Cabot (Giovanni Caboto),

[1] The Latin text will be found in Appendix B.

who was probably of Genoese origin,[1] but had become a naturalised Venetian[2] after fifteen years' residence in Venice, sailed from Bristol on a voyage of discovery, under the direct authority of Henry the Seventh of England.[3] He had eighteen persons on board (most, if not all, of whom were men of Bristol),[4] and he succeeded in discovering the continent of North America, upon which he planted the flag of England.[5] [He thus took possession of the land he had discovered on behalf of the English Crown, and in total disregard of the papal partition between

---

[1] There are no authentic proofs extant, so far as can be ascertained at present, as to John Cabot's birthplace. He is described by a contemporary writer as "another Genoese like Columbus." There are reasons for inclining to the belief, but no proof exists, that he married a Venetian woman.

[2] The following copy of the entry in the Venetian archives gives the date of John Cabot's grant of citizenship:—

"1476, die 28 Martii,—Quod fiat privilegium civilitatis de intus et extra Ioani Caboto per habitationem annorum xv., iuxta consuetum.

        De parte   149
        De non   0
        Non sinceri 0."

"1476, 28th day of March,—That a privilege of citizenship within and without be entered in favour of John Caboto, as usual, in consequence of a residence of fifteen years.

        Ayes   149
        Noes   0
        Neutrals 0."

[3] *Infra*, pp. 97, 98.   [4] *Infra.* pp. 148, 149.

[5] John Cabot also set up the flag of St. Mark, the patron saint of Venice (*infra*, p. 141). The citizenship [of Venice] was of two kinds, viz.: de intus and de extra, relating respectively to privileges within and without the dominions of the republic. These two sorts of privileges were frequently combined in the same individual, who was then a citizen de intus et extra. And as the citizenship de extra comprised the enjoyment of all the commercial rights which Venice possessed in foreign lands, together with the privilege of sailing under the flag of St. Mark, dependent after 1472, so far as naturalised citizens were concerned, only on giving security to the State, applicants who were traders or seamen naturally sought to complete their naturalisation by becoming citizens de extra as well as de intus, and for their protection and development colonies were at first planted.

Portugal and Spain, the terms of which had been altered by the Treaty of Tordesillas. This voyage was undoubtedly the foundation of an empire, and is properly regarded as the derivation of the English title to the continent of North America, and the basis of the English claim against the pretensions of Spain founded upon the papal bull. In the words of Mr. Lathrop, the American consul at Bristol, this was "the event which pre-empted North America for the English-speaking race, and probably settled for all time the question whether the Anglo-Saxon or the Spaniard should be the possessor of that great continent." Out of this achievement by John Cabot came the colonisation of portions of the territory by Englishmen. The Rev. M. Harvey[1] says: "England established her claims to the sovereignty of a large portion of these northern lands. The fish wealth of the surrounding seas soon attracted her fishermen."

"The Cabot charter,[2] and the voyages made pursuant to it, were always regarded as the root of England's title to her American possessions. Charters of a similar kind had been from time to time granted by the Portuguese Crown. . . . Columbus's discoveries were as yet limited to the chain of islands separating the Carribean Sea from the Atlantic. . . . His [Cabot's] title to be considered the first pioneer of English colonisation is indisputable, and it is equally certain that the title of the English Crown to the shores which he is generally understood to have reached has never been successfully questioned."[3]

From the deck of the *Matthew*, of Bristol, was

---

[1] The Rev. M. Harvey's paper on the Cabot voyages, *Coll. Nova Scotia Hist. Soc.*, vol. ix. p. 20.
[2] *Infra*, p. 97.   [3] *Times* newspaper, March 5, 1896.

first espied the littoral of a vast continent, destined in the future to become a home of freedom for millions of the human race. But the veil was but partially withdrawn, the picture only half-revealed. The series of scenes which would show the ancient races inhabiting the continent, their modes of life, their customs, their warfare, their surroundings—these were reserved for the enraptured gaze of those who followed in the wake of Cabot and his brave and daring co-adventurers. Many years were destined to elapse ere even small portions of the North American continent yielded up their secrets to the view of the curious explorer. No record has been left of what took place on board when the magic moment arrived and the vistas of the long-wished-for shores were revealed. As yet more and more of the littoral and of the landscape gradually opened to their view, as the little vessel silently closed in the distance between her and the waters of the coast, as further developments of the natural scenery became more distinctly visible to their anxious eyes,—we are only faintly able to conceive the impressions of the beholders, and words can only feebly translate their emotions. Were their dreams of the pleasant Western lands satisfied by the realities which they saw before them? Little is told of what they did. They went ashore, and realised that the land was inhabited from seeing certain snares which had been laid to catch animals,[1] then they went back and embarked on their vessel. Not fear, but prudence, perhaps, caused their speedy return,—a prudent desire to make known

[1] *Infra*, p. 140. They merely secured an insignificant proof, in the shape of a snare, or snares, that there were men somewhere in the neighbourhood, whom the sight of the vessel may have scared away.

the discovery in Bristol. Whatever there was to be disclosed to view by an inland exploration was left for the future. The irony of fate destined generations to elapse ere the importance of the discovery should be fully comprehended, either in its substantial reality or its fruitful possibility; it was not realised until long afterward that the planting of the flag of England upon that coast was the event from which should be evolved the whole future history of Northern America.

There is little doubt that John Cabot was one of those skilful and courageous mariners who, at a critical period of geographical awakening, when men's minds were bursting through the shackles that had fettered them for ages, went forth from Italy, well skilled in navigation and cosmography, to seek the chance of perilous adventures. The following statement, which suggests that in it we have one incentive, at least, of his enterprise, would seem to indicate that Cabot was formerly a merchant or a trader.

"And he [Cabot] says he was once at Mecca, where, from remote countries, spices are carried by caravans; and that those carrying them, being asked where those spices grew, said they did not know, but that they came with other merchandise from remote countries to their home by other caravans, and that the same information was repeated by those who brought the spices in turn to them. And he argues that if the Oriental people tell to those of the south that these things are brought from places remote from them, and thus from hand to hand, presupposing the rotundity of the earth, it follows that the last carry to the northern, toward the west."[1]

[1] *Infra*, p. 150.

Here we have abundant testimony that he was a man capable of working out a problem on original, though mistaken, lines of thought, and that he had been engaged in trying to discover how to reach the lands and islands from which the spices came. And between the lines we may gather, as his reference to "the territory of the Grand Khan"[1] seems plainly to indicate, that he, an Italian of the Renaissance, had been influenced by either Marco Polo's book[2] or Toscanelli's map, or by the ideas and the speculations as to the trans-Atlantic lands which were then prevalent in Italy.[3] Although the men of the Italian republics who went forth to other countries, for the purpose of engaging in voyages of discovery, were acquainted with many of the notions as to the "Sea of Darkness" contained in ancient writings and contemporary maps, all their thoughts were bent upon the hope of a new oceanic path, by means of which the rich territories of the "Grand Khan" might be reached. Francesco Tarducci says: "To know Cabot's intention we must settle the order of his ideas in regard to the expedition he was undertaking. This is easy enough, for the history of Christopher Columbus . . . is an exact mirror of what everybody thought. . . . Columbus left Spain with the expectation of reaching the territory of the Grand Khan; he had touched land . . . with the conviction that he had come to the land of the Grand Khan; he had returned to Europe with the announcement, never doubted by him or anyone else, that he had arrived at the land of the Grand

---

[1] *Infra*, pp. 138-140.   [2] Introd. 16-27.
[3] Toscanelli's inspirations for his map were drawn from several sources, including Ptolemy's geographical notions, Marco Polo's book, and the gossiping stories of Eastern travellers.

Khan. Could John Cabot think differently? Certainly not. Sailing, then, on an expedition of discovery beyond the Atlantic for the account of England, he did and could only look to reaching also the land of the Grand Khan, which at that time was the ultimate term of the desires and hopes of discoverers and traders."

It is almost a certainty, therefore, that the townsmen of Bristol should have added to their mythical belief in the "islands of the West," the notions which John Cabot had brought with him from Italy, namely, that it could be possible to find the rich countries of the East—"the lands of the Grand Khan"—by sailing across the Western Ocean. It may be that John Cabot did not altogether accept, on his arrival in England, the well-circulated stories as to the islands of St. Brandon, of Brasil, of the Seven Cities; yet neither is it probable that the enthusiastic and imaginative Italian should wholly reject the popular belief, seeing, besides, that the islands were marked upon the maps. It may be readily believed that these current stories would have been the means of increasing his faith in the success of his project, and of inflaming his desire to embark upon his perilous enterprise. |Be it always remembered that his belief, that Cathay existed in the West, came from what to him was a source of knowledge almost inspired, and had bred in him the conviction that he should find Cipango in the course of his westward exploration.|| The fact, then, is that the fabled islands were still in existence in the popular fancy, and to this had been added the hazy kind of belief that they were synonymous with some of the islands or places described by Marco Polo. A contemporary writer tells us that Cabot, "who went with a ship from Bristol to search for a new island, is returned, and says that seven hundred leagues from here [England] he discovered firm land (terra firma), the territory of the Grand Khan.[1] It was also believed that he had "discovered the Seven Cities."[2] "And they say that the land is fertile and temperate, and think that the red-wood (el brasilio) grows there."[3] "But Mr. John (Messer Joanne) has his thoughts directed to a greater undertaking, for he thinks of going . . . along the coast toward the east until he is opposite the island called Cipango [Japan], . . . where he believes all the spices of the world grow, and where there are also gems ; . . . he hopes to make London a greater place for spices than Alexandria."[4] When Columbus discovered Cuba, he came to the conclusion that it was Cipango [Japan]. And doubtless it was with some pardonable exultation in his own superior perspicacity, and in the full belief that his discovery of "Cipango" was the result of a well-worked-out theory of his own, that he announced his intention to sail to Quinsay, one of the principal places of the Grand Khan, for the purpose of handing *to that long defunct potentate* a letter of introduction addressed to him by their Catholic Majesties (Ferdinand and Isabella). The very earliest opportunity was to be taken to impart the highly interesting news to the Grand Khan that he (Columbus) had taken possession of a portion of his territory on behalf of their Catholic Majesties of Spain ! " Alas ! poor Columbus, —unconscious prince of discoverers,—groping here in

[1] *Infra*, p. 140. [2] *Infra*, p. 144.
[3] *Infra*, p. 149. [4] *Infra*, p. 150.

Cuban waters for a way to a city *on the other side of the globe,* and to a sovereign *whose race had more than a century since* been driven from the throne, and expelled from the very soil of Cathay."[1]

It would be unjust to the memory of John Cabot to suggest, in the absence of proof, that he had merely copied the ideas of Columbus. All the evidence upon which we can place reliance goes to show that he had formed an opinion quite independent of Columbus, though possibly following the same line of thought. Both Columbus and Cabot saw fanciful resemblances between the lands sighted by them and the countries described by Marco Polo; both expressed an intention, after finding land, to embark upon a fresh voyage in the direction, whither, as they erroneously supposed, the "Grand Khan" would be found; both fully believed that they were merely engaged in elaborating the knowledge of the world as it was then known,—in other words, it was a fixed idea of both that the lands discovered by them were parts of Asia. When men have been long possessed by a conviction that they have arrived at a truthful solution of a theory, it so wholly engrosses their thoughts that they are frequently unable to see anything but that which tends to support their preconceived views of the matter.[1]

[1] *Discovery of America,* by John Fiske, vol. i. p. 434. Professor Fiske tells his readers that Columbus interpreted the statements of the natives in such a way that he believed not only that Cuba was part of the Asiatic continent, but that there was a king in the neighbourhood who was at war with the Grand Khan! Columbus "sent two messengers to seek this refractory potentate. . . . These envoys found pleasant villages, with large houses, surrounded with fields of such unknown vegetables as maize, potatoes, and tobacco; they saw men and women smoking cigars, and little dreamed that in that fragrant and soothing herb there was a richer source of revenue than the spices of the East."—*Ibid.* p. 435.

In the circumstances immediately preceding the discoveries, whether of Columbus or of Cabot, not a single authentic fact, not an ambiguous phrase, not even a crude idea, has been revealed from which to find an indication that either Columbus or Cabot went in search of anything other than their ideal; in an endeavour to find Cathay and Cipango and "the lands of the Grand Khan," so brilliantly presented to their imagination by the book of Marco Polo, they came to "a new heaven and a new earth." But neither Columbus nor Cabot comprehended the importance of their discoveries, and they both died, as far as we can find, without realising that they had met with an unknown continent.

Having regard to this, and at the same time bearing in mind the previous attempts of the men of Bristol to find ideal islands of the West, we may fairly put the question—To whom is due the credit of the great discovery? The real truth is that in this matter, as in others, no single person is entitled to the whole credit of the discovery. We should render to Columbus the just, the unqualified praise that is his due. It is impossible to minimise his great work, accomplished as it was amidst so many discouragements, and in spite of the difficulties thrown in his way by the common enemies of all new theories. The story which relates his sufferings and persecutions will never perish. Columbus had to pay the usual penalties for being ahead of his period. He had to encounter the ignorance and indifference of the masses, the machinations of the priestcraft,[1] and the duplicity of the king's advisers;

[1] They contended that there could be no possibility of the return of the ships if Columbus should sail for any long distance in a direct

his funds became exhausted, his creditors seized his belongings, including his maps and charts, and his liberty was threatened. At the same time, neither our admiration for his indomitable courage nor our sympathy for his misfortunes should make us forget the services which were rendered to Columbus by Toscanelli.[1] Washington Irving, the great historian of Columbus's voyages, remarks: " Columbus derived great support . . . from a letter which he received, in 1474, from Toscanelli, a learned Florentine, who was considered one of the ablest cosmographers of the day. This letter was made up from the narrative of Marco Polo. . . . The work of Marco Polo is deserving of . . . particular mention, from being a key to many of the ideas and speculations of Columbus."

The following extract from Toscanelli's letter speaks for itself: "Paul,[2] the physicist, to Christopher Columbus, greeting. I perceived your great line towards the West. They contended that, on account of the roundness of the earth, they would go downward, and that it would not be possible to return. They quoted from the teachings of Augustine, Bishop of Hippo, who says : " But as to the fable that there are antipodes — that is to say, men on the opposite side of the earth, where the sun rises when it sets to us—men who walk with their feet opposite ours, that is on no ground creditable ; . . . it is too absurd to say that some men might have taken ships and traversed the whole wide ocean, and crossed from this side of the world to the other, and that thus even the inhabitants at that distant region are descended from the first man."

[1] Paolo Toscanelli was so greatly distinguished as an astronomer that Behaim's teacher, Regiomontanus, dedicated to him, in 1463, his work, *De Quadratura Circuli*, directed against the Cardinal Nicolaus de Cusa. He constructed the great gnomon in the church of Santa Maria Novella at Florence, and died in 1482, at the age of eighty-five, without having lived long enough to enjoy the pleasure of learning the discovery of the Cape of Good Hope by Diaz, and of the tropical part of the new continent by Columbus.—Humboldt, *Cosmos*, Otte's trans., vol. ii. p. 644.

[2] Paolo [Toscanelli].

and noble desire to go to the place where the spices grow; wherefore in reply to a letter of yours, I send you a copy of another letter, which I wrote *a few days ago* to a friend of mine, a gentleman of the household of the most gracious King of Portugal before the wars of Castile, in reply to another, which by command of his Highness he wrote me concerning that matter: and I send you another sailing-chart, similar to the one I sent him, by which your demands will be satisfied. The copy of that letter of mine is as follows:—' Paul, the physicist, to Fernando Martinez, canon, at Lisbon, greetings. I was glad to hear of your intimacy and favour with your most noble and illustrious King. I have formerly spoken with you about a shorter route to the places of spices by ocean navigation than that which you are pursuing by Guinea. The most gracious King now desires from me some statement, or rather an exhibition to the eye, so that even slightly educated persons can grasp and comprehend that route. Although I am well aware that this can be proved from the spherical shape of the earth, nevertheless, in order to make the point clearer and to facilitate the enterprise, I have decided to exhibit that route by means of a sailing-chart. I therefore send to his Majesty a chart made by my own hands, upon which are laid down your coasts, and the islands from which you must begin to shape your course steadily westward, and the places at which you are bound to arrive, and how far from the pole or from the equator you ought to keep away, and through how much space or through how many miles you are to arrive at places most fertile in all sorts of spices and gems, and do not wonder at my

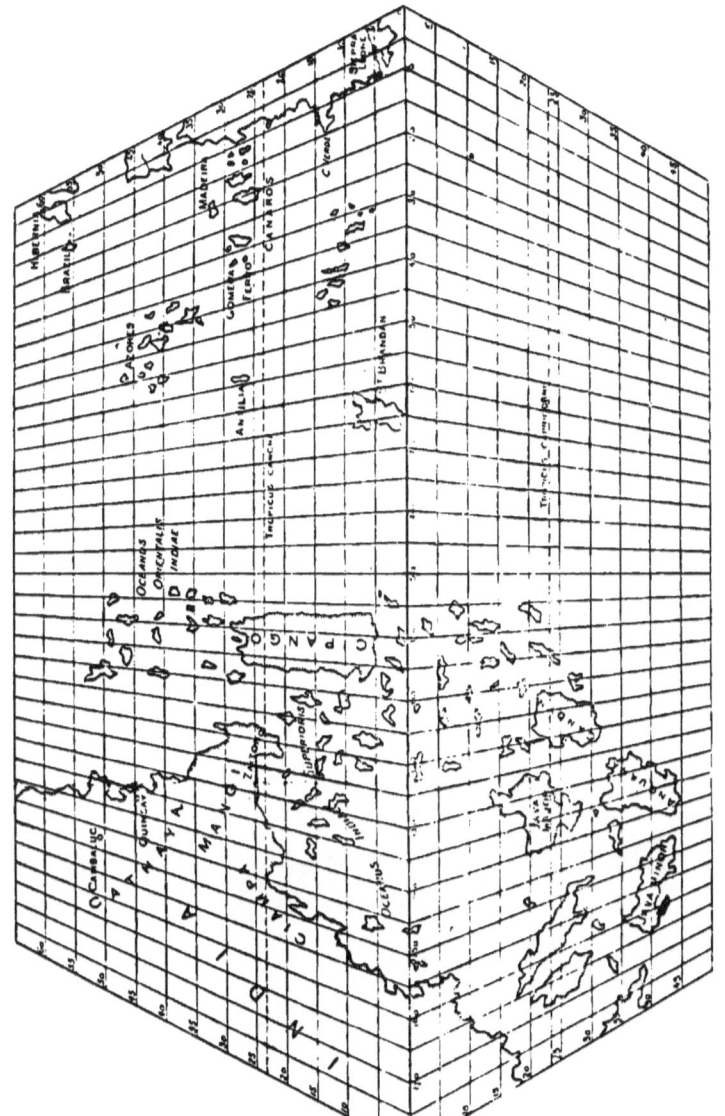

SKETCH OF TOSCANELLI'S MAP, SENT TO PORTUGAL IN 1474, AND USED BY COLUMBUS IN HIS FIRST VOYAGE ACROSS THE ATLANTIC

calling *west* the parts where the spices are, whereas they are commonly called *east*, because to persons sailing persistently westward those parts will be found by courses on the under side of the earth. For if [you go] by land and by routes on this upper side they will always be found in the east. The straight lines drawn lengthwise upon the map indicate distances from east to west, while the transverse lines show distances from south to north. I have drawn upon the map various places upon which you may come, for the better information of the navigators in case of their arriving, whether through accident of wind or what not, at some different place from what they had expected; but partly in order that they may show the inhabitants that they have some knowledge of their country, which is sure to be a pleasant thing. It is said that none but merchants dwell in the islands.[1] For so great there is the number of navigators with their merchandise that in all the rest of the world there are not so many as in one very splendid port called Zaiton.[2] For they say that a hundred great ships of pepper unload in that port every year, besides other ships bringing other spices. That country is very populous and very rich, with a multitude of provinces and kingdoms and cities without number, under one sovereign, who is called the Great Khan, which name signifies King of Kings, whose residence

---

[1] Toscanelli's theory as to the islands was founded, in part at least, upon information derived from the book of Marco Polo, which proves, if any proof were necessary, the extent of the influence of that work in connection with the various circumstances which led up to the discovery of the Western Hemisphere, the outlying portions whereof were first discovered by Columbus.

[2] Zayton, Zaitun, the great mediæval port of China. Now called Chang-chow. See *ante*, pp. 23, 24.

is for the most part in the province of Cathay. . . . This country is worth seeking by the Latins, not only because great treasures may be obtained from it—gold, silver, and all sorts of jewels and spices—but on account of its learned men, philosophers, and skilled astrologers. . . . This for some sort of answer to his request, so far as haste and my occupations have allowed, ready in future to make further response to his royal Majesty as much as he may wish. Given at Florence, 25th June 1474.'[1]

"From the city of Lisbon, due west, there are twenty-six spaces marked on the map, each of which contain two hundred and fifty miles, as far as the very great and splendid city of Quinsay.[2] For it is a hundred miles in circumference and has ten bridges, and its name means City of Heaven, and many wonderful things are told about it, and about the multitude of its arts and revenues. This space is almost a third part of the whole sphere. That city[3] is in the province of Manzi, or near the province of Cathay, in which land is the royal residence. But from the island of Antilia,[4] which you know, *to the very splendid island of Cipango*,[5] there are ten spaces. For that island abounds in gold, pearls, and precious stones, and they cover the temples and palaces with solid gold. So through the unknown parts of the route the stretches of sea to be traversed are not great. Many things might perhaps have been stated more clearly, but

---

[1] Here ends the copy letter enclosed in Toscanelli's letter to Columbus.
[2] Kinsay (Kingssé, or Capital), *i.e.* the city now called Hangchau-fu.
[3] See *ante*, p. 24. [4] See *ante*, p. 31 ; also pp. 43-53.
[5] See *ante*, p. 24.

one who duly considers what I have said will be able to work out the rest for himself. Farewell, most esteemed one."

Columbus also received another letter from Toscanelli, in which the latter says: "I have received your letters with the things which you sent me, for which I thank you very much. I regard as noble and grand your project of sailing from east to west, according to the indications furnished by the map which I sent you, and which would appear still more plainly upon a sphere. I am much pleased to see that I have been well understood, and that the voyage has become, not only possible, but certain, fraught with honour as it must be, and inestimable gain. . . . When that voyage shall be accomplished, it will be a voyage to powerful kingdoms, and to cities and provinces most wealthy and noble, abounding in all sorts of things most desired by us; I mean with all kinds of spices and jewels in great abundance." . . .

Mr. Henry Harrisse[1] says: "A letter lately brought to light shows that Toscanelli's notions were current in Italy, and that the news of the discovery achieved by Columbus was considered as a confirmation of the theories of the Florentine astronomer. It is a dispatch from Hercules d'Este, Duke of Ferrara, addressed to his ambassador at Florence, as follows: 'Messer MANFREDO: Intendendo Nuy, che il quondam Mastro Paulo dal Pozo a Thoscanella medico fece nota quando il viveva de alcune Insule trovate in Ispagna, che pare siano quelle medesime che al presente sono state ritrovate per aduisi che se hanno de quelle

[1] P. 44.

bande, siamo venuti in desiderio de vedere dicte note, se lo è possibile. Et però volemo, che troviate incontinenti vno Mastro Ludovico, Nepote de esse quondam Mastro Paulo, al quale pare rimanesseno li libri suoi in bono parte ed maxime questi et che lo pregiati strectamente per nostra parte chel voglia essere contento de darvi una nota a punctino de tuto quello chel se trova havere apresso lui de queste Insule, perché ne riceveremo piacere assai et ge ne restaremo obligati, et havuta che la haverite, ce la mandareti incontenenti. Ma vsati diligentia per havere bene ogni cosa a compimento di quello Io ha sicome desideramo. *Ferrarie*, 26 *Junis* 1494.'—' Mr. MANFREDO: As we have just heard that the late Paul dal Pozzo Toscanelli, a physician, penned in his lifetime a note concerning several islands found in Spain (*sic*), which it seems are the same which have been rediscovered (according to news received from there), we desire, if possible, to see said notes. That is the reason why we want you to find immediately one Mr. Ludovico, who is a nephew of the late Mr. Paul, and who appears to have inherited most of his books, and particularly those notes. We also wish you to request him on our part to give you an exact list of all he has with him concerning those islands; for we should be happy to obtain it, and shall be thankful for the favour. And do you, as soon as you are in possession of it, send the same at once. But do not fail to do everything in your power to get from him all that he has; for such is our desire.—*Ferrara, June* 26*th*, 1494.' "

It will thus be seen that all the circumstances warrant our recognition of Toscanelli's theory—

for, after all, it was only a theory—as one of the most potent factors associated with the events that occurred during the lifetime of Columbus. Toscanelli's support led Columbus to insist on the practicability of a voyage over the storm-tossed ocean, the paths of which were yet unknown. And, in like manner, it would be unfair entirely to ignore, in connection with the good work performed by John Cabot, the originator of the map or chart upon which were shown the oceanic paths—the parallels of latitude—which, if followed, Toscanelli asserted, would lead the explorers to the lands of the Grand Khan, " to cities and provinces most wealthy and noble, abounding . . . with all kinds of spices and jewels in great abundance," in other words, to the golden lands of their day-dreams.

Again, in connection with the developments of evolutionary fancies and beliefs, and the practical application of the ideas which preceded and led up to the Great Discovery, we should not forget the marvellous work of that intelligent pioneer of the golden age of exploration, Prince Henry of Portugal, to whom nautical science owes so much, of whom his country is so justly proud. The Rev. M. Harvey, LL.D., of St. John's, Newfoundland, in a paper on the Cabot voyages, speaks as follows of this period: " The narrow strip of earth consisting of parts of Europe, Asia, and Africa, on which history had hitherto transacted itself, was suspected not to be the whole. The Portuguese led the way in the new career of discovery. Away down the African coast their daring mariners crept, passing Cape Bojador," —the fearful outstretcher, as the name signifies,— " which had barred the way for twenty years, penetrating the dreaded torrid zone, crossing the line, losing sight of the North Polar Star, and gazing in rapture on the Southern Cross and the luminaries of another hemisphere, till at length Bartholomew Diaz discovered [1] the Cape of Good Hope in 1486, thus opening a new way to the shores of India. The earth was continually widening in man's view. What new discoveries might not the abysses of ocean yet disclose!"

But, above all, in the past history of the Italian republics, there appears an influence of paramount importance, among the many influences which directly or indirectly led to the discovery of the Western Hemisphere. This is the marvellous spread of learning which was due to the Italian renaissance.[2] The great struggle for the supremacy of the Mediterranean, which had been waged for a long period of time, had been the means of producing among the men of the maritime republics of Italy, some of the most intrepid sailors the world had ever seen. The wealth produced by the vast and increasing commerce of Venice, of Genoa, and of Florence had gradually created a taste for classical learning, for the fine arts, for architectural splendour, and for eastern luxuries. The founders of the Italian renaissance

---

[1] History somewhat repeats itself in this narration. This is really a record of a *re-discovery* of the Cape Land, now called "The Cape of Good Hope" (*ante*, pp. 3, 4). Bartholomew Columbus took part in the important and successful expedition of Diaz.

[2] The term "renaissance" or "renascence" has been used in the sense that it denotes a period of time—a state of transition—during which an intellectual wave gradually spread over Europe, the first appearance of which can be traced to the Italian republics. In its truest sense the term contains a suggestion or metaphor of re-birth, as applied to the new growth of knowledge after a long period of intellectual torpor; in other words, we may use it to describe the rejuvenation of ancient art and of ancient learning.

developed new instincts and roused men's minds from a long lethargy, which, in the end, not only led Italians of all classes towards a study of the works of ancient and contemporary writers, but also prompted them to inquire into and criticise the truths and theories contained in those works. It was a period of transition, somewhat difficult to be included between any given chronological dates. In the pagan past, Europe beheld a noble civilisation, first in republican, later in imperial, Rome, and prior to that an even nobler development when Greece was in her prime. Then came the fall of the Roman Empire, and the terrible story of Roman provinces overrun by hordes of men—Goths, Visigoths, Vandals, and Huns—who were merely in the upper status of barbarism. Ruin and desolation marked the progress of these destroyers of the grand and of the beautiful. The Roman territories were left in possession of men who were complete strangers to the arts and sciences which had been patronised by the Romans. It has been truly said that from this period Europe may be described as having commenced a second infancy, and that a long period elapsed before any substantial intellectual advance was made. The buried seed of learning remained a long time underground; the young sapling that came forth had to endure many hardships, many cold blasts, many checks to its growth; the tree of knowledge was slow in arriving at maturity. It was only natural that the revival of classical literature, in the middle of the fifteenth century, should spring up in modern Italy. The Italians of all classes had long been accustomed to view with wonder and ever-increasing interest the numerous monuments of classical antiquity which had not been swept away by the waves of barbarism. From the early part of the fifteenth century the signs of a considerable advance in learning may be clearly traced. The approach of more enlightened times was heralded in a variety of ways. One of the most important helps which culture received consisted in the recovery and preservation of many manuscript works of ancient Roman and Greek writers, some of which had been left to perish in out-of-the-way places. Among some of the works which were thus rescued was a copy of Quintilian, in most excellent preservation; the three first books, and part of the fourth, of the *Argonautics* of Valerius Flaccus; and several of the orations of Cicero. Cardinal Giordano Orsini purchased of Nicholas of Treves, a German monk, a complete copy of Plautus. Various persons volunteered to go into other countries in quest of hidden literary treasures. In the year 1423, Aurispa, who had visited Constantinople and other places, arrived in Venice with no fewer than two hundred and thirty-eight manuscripts, including all the works of Plato, of Xenophon, the histories of Dio, and of Diodorus Siculus, the poems of Pindar, of Callimachus, of Oppian, of those attributed to Orpheus, the geography of Strabo, etc. In the year 1427 a further addition was made upon the return of Filelfo to Italy. From this period we are enabled to trace the origin of some of the splendid Italian libraries with their vast stores of ancient literary works.[1]

[1] Niccolo Niccoli, a learned man of this period, succeeded in making a large collection of ancient manuscripts, which included about eight hundred volumes of Roman, Greek, and Oriental writings.

Thus was gradually produced an ambition to excel in literary pursuits. One of the results of a study of the historical past was the creation of a taste for the possession of the productions of the fine arts among the various classes. From ancient art they requisitioned the most precious remains for the purposes of ornamentation; modern art, the outcome of the new learning, yielded pictures, statues, busts, vases, and artistic productions of every kind. A renewed acquaintance with the great stores of Grecian literature was one of the most important factors which operated as an impetus to the advanced studies of the Italians, and opened the way for a variety of researches. In the year 1453, the Turks, under the command of Mahomet II., succeeded in capturing Constantinople, till then the capital of the Eastern Empire and the home of Greek civilisation. The encouragement hitherto given to Greek professors to settle in Florence now induced a large number of learned Greeks to seek Italian hospitality. A kind of rivalry, of the better kind, sprang up between the Greek[1] and Italian professors.

The facilities which the newly-discovered art of printing gave for the diffusion of knowledge, became a marvellous help to the cause of letters.

The Italian printing-presses became very active.

Niccoli died in 1436, and by his will bequeathed his library to the use of the public. One of the curators of his will, Cosmo de Medici, managed to obtain the sole direction of the manuscripts, which he deposited in the Dominican monastery of S. Marco, at Florence. This collection was the origin of the celebrated Bibliotheca Marciana in Florence.

[1] Cardinal Bassarion, a Greek by birth, was one of the disputants on behalf of the doctrines of Plato. In the year 1468, Bassarion befriended the cause of literature, by a magnificent gift of ancient Greek and Latin manuscripts, which he deposited in the church of S. Mark, in Venice, for the public use.

As against one hundred and forty-one books, the total number known to have been printed in England before the end of the fifteenth century, there had been produced in Venice alone two thousand eight hundred and thirty-five. In the course of time new ideas, founded upon reason, became current, which had the effect of destroying old limitations as to the unrevealed secrets of nature—of the physical world; and it destroyed many illusions and many superstitions, founded upon theological fictions, as to the geography of the earth. The revival of learning had an important effect on navigation; it gave an impulse to the sciences connected therewith; it corrected many errors in ancient maps; and it spread before the inquisitive and inquiring minds of that period, the outlines of a new cosmography. The practical application of the compass to the navigation of vessels, and an improvement of the astrolabe,[1] together with an increase of astronomical knowledge, had enabled nautical men to extend their voyages to distant parts of the ocean. As the art of printing made progress, books became more common throughout Europe. The grace and elegance of Greek and Latin classics slowly awakened the imaginative faculties of the better classes and of the most intelligent men of the principal European nationalities; an intellectual change of front eventually

[1] "Astrolabes, designed for the determination of time and geographical latitudes by meridian altitudes, and capable of being employed at sea, underwent gradual improvement from the time that the astrolabuim of the Majorican pilots was in use, which is described by Raymond Lully in 1295, in his *Arte de navegar*, till the invention of the instrument made by Martin Behaim in 1484, at Lisbon, and which was, perhaps, only a simplification of the meteoroscope of his friend Regiomontanus."—Humboldt, *Cosmos*, Otte's trans., vol. ii. pp. 630, 631.

became an accomplished fact. Very slowly, however, did progress extend its influences; prejudice, which is ever difficult to conquer, is both blind and deaf when any attempt is made to disturb existing and implicit ideas; the vast majority of mankind in all countries and in all ages afford no active sympathy with originality of thought, and rarely, if ever, lend a helping hand to seekers after truth. Gradually, notwithstanding all obstructions, whether natural or artificial, the imperturbable march of progress acted upon the common mind, and men were imperceptibly drawn towards fact instead of myth, one of the many results of recognising the necessity of searching for a higher knowledge. After a time sound views commenced to supplant some of the dogmatic subtleties of theology, and much of the darkness which had long enveloped men's vision began to disperse. Then England, which, owing probably to her insular position, had remained in the rear of intellectual activity, came under the influence and the awakening power of the new learning. Thus the common mind was opened and enlarged, and prepared for the investigation of new hypotheses, and for the reception of new truths; and eventually the eyes of all men were turned towards the Western Ocean with one common object in view, namely, the discovery of lands beyond the horizon. And herein, as in other matters, it was the unexpected that happened.

. . . .

Never, perhaps, in the history of the deeds most pregnant for humanity, has it happened that an achievement like Cabot's has been relegated to comparative obscurity for several centuries. When we consider the surpassing results and the wide-spreading consequences of Cabot's discovery, we cannot be surprised at the pride which every citizen of Bristol feels in the fact that Bristol sent the Genoese forth on his perilous enterprise. There cannot be a doubt that Bristol townsmen were the principals who supplied the means for the hazardous undertaking. The Bristol men who accompanied Cabot were described in a letter, written after the result of the voyage had become known, as "great mariners that now know where to go" (*infra*, p. 150); and this tells us plainly that some of them, at least, were men of great nautical intelligence. We find, moreover, that they had "placed their fortunes[1] with him" [*i.e.* with Cabot] (*infra*, p. 148). Their share in the arduous undertaking cannot be overrated, and to their courage and devotion we should render unstinted praise. It must, therefore, be a source of unalloyed satisfaction to the citizens of Bristol to know that their townsmen in the reign of Henry the Seventh were among the pioneers in the desire for discovery, which was one of the first-fruits of the Renaissance; that the enterprise of the men of the period had made their town and port a formidable rival to London; and that the adventurous spirit, which was so characteristic of the age, culminated in a suitable and appropriate triumph when land was first sighted from the deck of the little *Matthew*, and the continent of North America was first revealed to Europeans. And further, from distant climes the thoughts of men will be turned towards Bristol, in kindly sympathy with the efforts of the citizens to

[1] This might mean their chances of surviving the risks of the voyage.

suitably commemorate,[1] in June 1897, the quatercentenary of an event in which Bristol played such an important part—alike conspicuous and honourable—which has been aptly described as "Bristol's greatest achievement." And in honouring the memory of the worthy John Cabot, they will pass at the same time a well-deserved tribute of gratitude and respect to the zeal, courage, and perseverance of their own folk of the fifteenth century. At the same time, a famous exploit which forms a grand feature in one of the most important epochs of the world's history, cannot be treated as a merely local episode; it is an event of national and international importance.

[1] The commemoration will be celebrated at Bristol by the erection on the summit of *Brandon Hill* of a square tower adapted from a well-known example in the Department of the Loire in France. At the stages of the balconies there will be arched openings which will form "look-outs." The floor of the upper balcony will be 75 feet from the base, and an octagonal addition of 30 feet will make the total height about 105 feet. At the base provision will be made for the insertion of panels with bronze bas-reliefs. It is intended that suitable inscriptions will be made, one of which will be fitted in by Americans residing in England, and another by the Peace Society.

CHAPTER III

THE petition to King Henry VII. asking him to grant letters-patent unto John Cabot and his three sons "to seek out, discover, and find whatsoever islands, countries, regions, or provinces of the Heathens and Infidels, in whatsoever part of the world they be, which before this time have been unknown to all Christians," is, so far as we know up to the present time, the earliest document which in any way relates to the discovery of North America by John Cabot.

[COPY PETITION]

"To the Kyng our souvereigne lord,—

"Please it your highnes of your most noble and haboundant grace to graunt vnto John Cabotto Citizen of Venes [Venice], Lewes Sebastyan and Sancto his sonnys your gracious letters-patentes vnder your grete scale in due forme to be made according to the tenour hereafter ensuying. And they shall during their lyves pray to God for the prosperous continuance of your most noble and royall astate long to enduer."

The above very quaint petition, the original of which was written in English, has been slightly altered by the expansion of a few contracted words.

The petition bears no date, but from the following entry in the Roll of the Privy Seal for March, 2 Henry VII., it will be seen that it was delivered to the chancellor to be acted upon on the 5th of March [1496].

"M⁴ q̃d quinto die Marcii Anno r̃r Henr̃ septimi vndecimo ista billa delib̃ar̃ fuit d̃no Canc̃ Angł apud Westm̃ exequend̃."

The letters-patent granted by King Henry VII. to John Cabot and his three sons, in accordance with the prayer of the petition, were witnessed " by the King at Westminster, on the 5th day of March, in the eleventh year of his reign." Henry VII. ascended the throne "by just title of inheritance, and by the sure judgment of God, who had given him the victory over his enemy in the field" on the 22nd of August 1485; consequently the eleventh regnal year commenced on the 22nd of August 1495,[1] and ended on the 21st of August 1496. The date of the letters-patent is therefore the 5th March 1495-6.

A copy of the petition precedes the copy of the letters-patent in the Roll of the Privy Seal. The following is a copy of the king's grant of

---

[1] There is a curious historical incident in connection with this date. Immediately after the king's accession to the throne he obtained from a servile Parliament authority to attaint a number of noblemen and gentlemen for being guilty of high treason, a conviction for which involved the confiscation of their estates to the king. He wanted money: he was unscrupulous. None of the persons charged could possibly be convicted of the offence, having regard to the date of the king's accession. He therefore antedated his reign by one day, and the bills for attainder recited that "on the 21st day of August, the first year of the reign of our sovereign lord," certain persons did a certain act. The 21st of August was the eve of the battle of Bosworth, at which time the crown was on the head of Richard.

letters-patent for the discovery of hitherto unknown lands. Having regard to its great historical importance, it has been thought desirable to give it first in the exact words, and then in a translation :—

R Oīnibȝ ad quos ᵗi saltm Notum sit ᵗ manifestum q̃d dedim͛ ᵗ concessim͛ ac p p̃sentes dam͛ ᵗ concedim͛ p noḃ ᵗ heredibȝ n̄ris dilc̃is noḃ Joĥi Cabotto Cui Veneciaȥ ac Ludouico Sebestiano ᵗ Sancto filiis dc̃i Joĥis ᵗ eoȥ ac cuiustt eoȥ heredibȝ ᵗ deputatis plenam ac liḃam auctoritatem facultatem ᵗ potestatem nauigandi ad oīnes partes regiones ᵗ sinus maris Orientalis occidentalis ᵗ Septemtrionalis sub banneriis vexillis ᵗ insigniis n̄ris cum quinq̧ nauibȝ siue nauigiis cuiuscumq̧ portiture ᵗ qualitatis existant ᵗ cum tot ᵗ tantis nautis ᵗ ĥoibȝ quot ᵗ quantis in dc̃is nauibȝ secum duc̃e voluĩnt suis ᵗ eoȥ ppriis sumptibȝ ᵗ expensis ad inueniend discooperiend ᵗ inuestigand quascumq̧ Insulas p̃rias regiones siue puincias gentiliū ᵗ infideliū quoȥcumq̧ in quacumq̧ parte mundi positas que xp̃ianis oīnibȝ ante hec tempora fuerunt incognite. Concessim͛ cciam eisden ᵗ eoȥ cuitt eoȥ q̧ ᵗ cuiustt eoȥ heredibȝ ᵗ deputatis ac licenciam dedim͛ affigendi p̃dc̃as bannerias n̄ras ᵗ insignia in quacumq̧ villa oppido Castro Insula seu ᵗra firma a se nouiť inuentis et q̃d p̃nōiati Joĥes ᵗ filii eiusdem seu heredes ᵗ eoȥdem deputati quascumq̧ huiusmodi villas Castra Oppida ᵗ Insulas a se inuentas que subiugari occupari ᵗ possideri possint subiugare occupare ᵗ possidere valeant tanq^{n}m vasalli n̄ri ᵗ Guḃnatores locatenentes ᵗ deputati caȥdem d̃nium titulum ᵗ iurisdicc̃oem coȥdem villaȥ Castroȥ Oppidoȥ Insulaȥ ac ᵗre firme sic inuentoȥ noḃ acquirendo Ita tamē vt ex oīnibȝ fructibȝ pficuis

emolumentis cōmodis lucris τ obuencōibͥ ex huiusmodi nauigacōe puenientibͥ p̄fati Joħes τ filii ac
heredes τ eoʒ deputati teneant⁽ʳ⁾ τ sint obligati nob̄ p
ōmi viagio suo tociens quociens ad portum ñrm
Bristrollie applicuerint ad quem ōmino applicare
teneant⁽ʳ⁾ τ sint astricti deductis ōmibͥ sumptibͥ τ
impensis necessariis p eosdem factis quintam partem
tocius capitalis lucri sui fc̄i siue in m̄cibͥ siue in
pecuniis psolūᵉ dantes nos τ concedentes eisdem
suisqͥ heredibͥ τ deputatis vt ab ōmi solucōe
custumaʒ ōim τ singuloʒ bonoͥ ac m̄ciū quas secum
reportarint ab illis locis sic nouit⁽ᵖ⁾ inuentis libi sint τ
Immunes. Et insup dedim⁽ᵖ⁾ τ concessim⁽ᵖ⁾ eisdem ac
suis heredibͥ τ deputates q̄d tre ōmes firme Insule
ville Oppida Castra τ loca quecumq̨, a se inuenta
quotquot ab eis inuenire contigit non possint ab
aliis quibusuis ñris subditis frequentari seu visitari
absq̨ licencia p̄dc̄oʒ Joħis τ eius filioʒ suoʒ q̨,
deputatorʒ sub pena amissionis tam nauiū siue
nauigioʒ qᵘm bonoʒ ōim quoʒqumq̨, ad ea loca sic
inuenta nauigare p̄sumenciū volentes τ strictissime
mandantes ōmibͥ τ singˡlis ñris subditis tam in tra
qᵘm in mare constitutis vt p̄fato Joħi τ eius filiis ac
deputatis bonam assistenciam faciant τ tam marin-
andis nauibͥ seu nauigiis qᵘm in puisione δmetaᵗ⁽ᵖ⁾ τ
victualiū p sua pecunia emendoʒ atq̨ aliaʒ ōim reʒ
sⁱ puidend p dc̄a nauigacōe sumend suos ōmes fauores
τ auxiliᵃ imparciant⁽ʳ⁾ In cuius τc̄."

[TRANSLATION]

"The king, etc., to all to whom these presents
shall come, greeting:

"Let it be known and made manifest that we

have given and conceded, and by these presents do give and concede, for us and our heirs, to our well-beloved John Cabot, citizen of Venice, and to Lewis, Sebastian, and Sanctus, sons of the said John, and to the heirs and assigns of them, and to the heirs and assigns of each of them and their deputies, full and free authority, faculty and power of navigating to all parts, countries, and seas of the east, west, and north,[1] under our banners, flags, and ensigns, with five ships or vessels of what burden or quality soever they be, and with as many mariners or men as they will have with them in the said ships, upon their own proper costs and charges; to seek out, discover, and find whatsoever islands, countries, regions, or provinces of the heathens or infidels, in whatever part of the world they be, which before this time have been unknown to all Christians.

"We also concede to them and each of them, and to their heirs and assigns, and their deputies, and we give licence to fly the said our banners and ensigns on whatever towns, cities, camps, islands, or mainlands may be newly found by them.

"And the before-named John and his sons, their heirs and assigns, may occupy and possess whatever towns, camps, cities, or islands may be discovered by them; that they may be able to conquer, occupy, and possess, as our vassals and governors, lieutenants or deputies, acquiring for us the dominion, title, and

---

[1] It should be borne in mind, when we come to consider the northerly and westerly courses taken by Cabot, that he—and the King of England also—knew that both the Spanish and Portuguese ambassadors would be watching every detail of his voyage with the greatest interest. The southern seas, in which each of those powers had long since acquired the right to certain possessions by their occupation thereof, were, therefore, expressly excluded when this charter was drawn up.

jurisdiction over these towns, camps, islands, and mainlands so discovered.

"Providing that the said John and his sons, their heirs and assigns, and their deputies, shall be bound and under obligation to us, from all the fruits, profits, emoluments, advantages, gains, and incomes accruing from this voyage, for every their voyage, as often as they shall arrive at our port of Bristol (at the which port they shall be bound and holden to arrive), to deduct a fifth part of the whole capital, whether in goods or in money, for our use.

"We give and concede to them, their heirs and assigns and deputies, that they shall be free from all payments of customs on all and singular the goods and merchandise that they may bring from those newly-discovered places.

"And we further give and concede to them, their heirs and assigns, and their deputies, that all mainlands, islands, cities, towns, camps, and other places, whatsoever by them discovered, shall not be frequented or visited by any others of our subjects without the licence of the said John and his sons,[1] or of their heirs and assigns, on pain of for-

[1] In the papal bull dated in 1493, the pope grants to the Spanish Crown all the regions and lands "found in the West Ocean Sea by the navigation of the Spaniards," "under the pain of the sentence of excommunication . . . that they [*i.e.* other persons] in no case presume, without special licence of you, your heirs and successors, to travail for merchandise . . . to the said lands or islands." The words in the papal bull, such as, for example, "lands and islands . . . hitherto unknown, . . . with their dominions, territories, cities, castles, rivers, places, and villages," bear a suspicious resemblance to some of those used in the letters-patent. It is quite possible that the papal bull had been read by the scribe who drew up the letters-patent, or a copy of it may have been actually before him for the purpose of gaining assistance therefrom.

feiting, as well the ships or vessels as all the goods whatsoever.

"We further will and strictly command all and singular our subjects, as well by land as by sea, that they shall render good assistance to the aforesaid John, his sons, their heirs and assigns; and that they shall give them all favour and help, as well in arming their ships or vessels, as in supplying them with stores and victuals paid for by their money."

The words in the petition, which suggest that the letters-patent should "be made according to the tenour hereafter ensuing," most certainly point to the conclusion that there had been negotiations between Cabot and the king as to the terms, and that the petition was drawn up at a time when the form of the letters-patent had been definitely settled. With all the frankness of conscious merit, with all the eloquence enthusiasm could bring to his assistance would the intrepid navigator place his proposals before the king, in the full hope that the monarch would treat him fairly and grant him favourable terms. But Cabot was dealing with an unscrupulous money-grabber.[1] Henry the Seventh was a man of great ability, but so fond of money and so wholly devoted to its cares, so reserved in matters involving considerations of finance, that he never, or rarely,

---

[1] The Milanese Envoy in London, Raimondo de Soncino, in a letter dated September 4, 1497, addressed to Ludovic Sforza, Duke of Milan, refers to the accumulation of money by King Henry VII. as follows :—"I am informed that he has upwards of six millions of gold, and it is said that he puts by annually five hundred thousand ducats, which is of easy accomplishment, for his revenue is great and real; . . . nor does he spend anything."

arrived at quick decisions; hence it has been said of him, that only on very rare occasions was he able to convince his subordinates that he was acting in a straightforward manner. However, in a variety of ways he showed remarkable proofs of his ability and industry, and tenacity of purpose. On the one hand, he not only realised the importance of commerce and the necessity for keeping the navy in a sound condition, but did all in his power to obtain trading concessions from the kings and rulers of other countries, as the result of which the English merchants, particularly those of Bristol, derived great advantages. On the other hand, his avarice induced him to fleece his subjects, particularly the merchants, with the most unsparing rigour.[1] The period was one of unwonted activity and enterprise in commercial adventures. It was gradually dawning on the minds of men that there was room for improvement in the system which allowed each town or community the privilege of exclusive trading—of trading, that is, in which no "outsider"[2] might participate. It may be affirmed that in the reign of Henry the Seventh the upbreak of exclusive trading was begun,

---

[1] In 1498 Don Pedro de Ayala, the Spanish Ambassador, wrote to their Catholic Majesties, Ferdinand and Isabella, as follows:— "The custom-house revenues, as well as the land rents, diminish every day. As far as the customs are concerned, the reason of their decrease is to be sought in the decay of commerce, caused partly by the wars, but much more by the additional duties imposed by the king. There is, however, another reason for the decrease of trade, that is to say, the impoverishment of the people by the great taxes laid on them. The king himself said to me *that it is his intention to keep his subjects low*, because riches would make them haughty."

[2] By "outsider" was meant all persons not actually either (*a*) "free" by virtue of birth, marriage, servitude, or other special qualification or privilege, or (*b*) residents paying "scot or lot" of the town or community.

although not till many years later was it finally consummated. As a sequence to the gradual encroachment on the privileges of the land-owners under the feudal laws and customs, there had been an appreciable growth in previous reigns of the power of the towns, and a corresponding betterment in the position of wealthy merchants. This by slow degrees resulted in a recognition—not quite disinterested, perhaps—by royalty of the benefits which accrued to the nation, and yet might accrue, through an extension of commerce. King Edward IV. was himself a shipowner and merchant, and the mind of the prudent Henry VII. was *par excellence* that of a practical, circumspect merchant. Having regard to all the circumstances, it is not unreasonable to suppose that the king would be quick to see how desirable it was to arrange with Cabot, a man whom he might have regarded as the equal of Columbus in matters pertaining to navigation and cosmography. In all probability the merit of Cabot's plans was fully appreciated by Henry; who would remember what was brought to his notice prior to the result of Columbus's voyage being known, and would thus grasp the importance of the discoveries promised by Cabot and the danger of abandoning the advantages they might bring to the Crown.[1] It will be remembered that King Henry[1] had missed the opportunity of engaging Christopher Columbus by a mere mischance. Christopher, despairing of obtaining terms at the Court of Spain, had sent his

---

[1] "Henry VII., disappointed in his hope of forming an engagement with Columbus, gladly extended his protection to the Venetian, John Gavotta or Cabot, whose reputation as a skilful pilot was little inferior to that of the celebrated Genoese" (Lardner's Cyclopædia, *Maritime and Island Discovery*, vol. ii. p. 136).

brother, Bartholomew, to England to make an offer of his services to King Henry.

Hakluyt[1] refers to the offer by Christopher Columbus to King Henry VII. in the year 1488 the 13 of February : " With the King's acceptance of the offer, and the cause whereupon he was deprived of the same : recorded in the thirteenth chapter of the history of Don Fernando Columbus of the life and deeds of his father Christopher Columbus. Christopher Columbus, fearing lest, if the King of Castile in like manner (as the King of Portugal had done) should not condescend unto his enterprise, he should be inforced to offer the same again to some other prince ; and so much time should be spent therein, sent into England a certain brother of his which he had with him, whose name was Bartholomew Columbus, who, albeit he had not the Latin tongue, yet nevertheless was a man of experience and skilful in sea causes, and could very well make sea-cards and globes, and other instruments belonging to the profession, as he was instructed by his brother. Whereupon, after that, Bartholomew Columbus was departed for England, his luck was to fall into the hands of pirates, which spoiled him with the rest of them which were in the ship which he went in. Upon which occasion, and by reason of his poverty and sicknesse which cruelly assaulted him in a country so far distant from his friends, he deferred his ambassage for a long while, until such time as he had gotten somewhat handsome about him with making of sea-cards. At length he began to deale with King Henry VII. unto whom he presented a mappe of the worlde, wherein these verses were

[1] Vol. iii., edition of 1600.

written, which I found among his papers, and I will here set them downe, rather for their antiquity than for their gooduesse—

> 'Thou which desirest easily the coast of land to know,
> This comely mappe right learnedly the same to thee will shew:
> Which Strabo,[1] Plinie, Ptolomey and Isodore maintaine:
> Yet for all that they do not all in one accord remaine.
> Here also is set downe the late discovered burning zone
> By Portingals, unto the world which whilom was unknown,
> Whereof the knowledge now at length thorow all the world is blown.'"

In a recent English publication[2] appear the following references to Columbus's offer to King Henry the Seventh :—"On his way to England[3] he [Bartholomew Columbus] was taken by pirates and made by them to labour as a slave, and when he escaped and reached London, he was first so ill and then so poor as to be unable to press his brother's designs upon the King until 1488. In the interval he supported himself by making charts and globes, and, on being at length introduced to King Henry,

---

[1] Here we have evidence that the views of the ancient writers had been closely studied.

[2] Traill's *Social England*, vol. ii. p. 495.

[3] It appears that Bartholomew Columbus, who, having regard to his great nautical experience, is considered by many to have been in no way inferior to his brother, sailed with the intention of landing in Bristol, on his way to London to interview King Henry VII. "It was natural enough that Bartholomew should first set out for Bristol, where old shipmates and acquaintances were sure to be found. . . . On the way he was captured by pirates (Fiske, vol. i. p. 404). Some writers have come to the conclusion that it is extremely likely that some of the Bristol men of the period had some personal knowledge of Christopher himself, an idea which appears to have originated from a belief that in his voyage to Iceland, he (Christopher) either called at or started from Bristol, or returned thither at the conclusion of his voyage. Sir Clements Markham says: "Canynge [a Bristol merchant] lost a vessel of 160 tons on the Iceland coast, and in 1477 Columbus himself learnt from English sailors of Bristol the management of an ocean voyage, when he visited Ultima Thule."

he presented his majesty with a map of the world.[1] The King listened to Columbus's plans, and readily promised to assist in carrying them out; but delays supervened, and ere Bartholomew was in a position to carry a definite commission to his brother Christopher, the latter had not only obtained the cooperation of Spain, but had actually accomplished his first voyage and made his great discovery. The news of this naturally created great stir in all the seaports of Europe, and induced Giovanni Caboto [John Cabot], . . . *who had long been settled at Bristol*[2] and who was already favourably known to Henry, to make application to the King for encouragement to attempt further discoveries to the westward, and especially to look for *a north-west passage to India.*"[3]

With regard to the statement that John Cabot "had long been settled at Bristol and who was already known to Henry," the following extract from *A History of Newfoundland*, by L. A. Anspach, p. 25, seems to show that it is not entirely without confirmation:—" The Venetians had factories in the different towns and cities of the northern kingdom, and agents wherever they deemed it advantageous to preserve an intercourse. John Gabota or Cabot, . . . was employed in that

[1] This would probably be a map which included information founded on the theory of Toscanelli (*ante*, p. 80). King Henry would, therefore, have been in possession of some knowledge of the subject prior to Cabot's application for the grant of the letters-patent.

[2] This statement must be accepted with caution and reserve. It may or may not be correct. In the absence of any written contemporary record, it is impossible to fix a precise date, either for his arrival in England or for his first arrival in Bristol.

[3] The popular and generally accepted idea that John Cabot sailed from Bristol for the purpose of finding "a north-west passage to India" rests on no foundation whatever.

capacity at Bristol; he had long resided in England, and a successful negociation in which he had been employed in the year 1495, with the Court of Denmark, respecting some interruptions which the merchants of Bristol had suffered in their trade to Scotland, had been the means of introducing him to Henry VII."

Mr. Henry Harrisse, in his splendid work on the Cabots (London, 1896), says: "Englishmen having killed the Governor of Iceland in a riot, King Christian I. embargoed four British vessels laden with valuable merchandise. As Edward IV. made no reply to the complaints of the Danish monarch, the latter allowed the cargoes to be sold. This brought about an open war between the two nations. . . . It is possible, therefore, that John Cabot may have been engaged by Bristol shipowners to prosecute their claims in 1495." Of course this is a mere matter of detail which may not be capable of strict proof; but it is beyond doubt that immense wealth was accumulated by the merchants of Bristol in connection with the trade carried on between that port and Iceland and the Northern Seas.

"In 1450, we find by a treaty with Christian, King of Denmark (Rymer, tom ii. p. 264), three places prohibited us [English] from trading to, namely, Iceland, 'Halgeoland,' and Finmark"; this treaty, however, was "dispensed with in favour of Canynges (Fœdera, tom xi. p. 277), the Danish King allowing Canynges in consideration of the great debt due to him [Canynges] from his [the king's] subjects of Iceland and Finmark, to lade certain English ships with merchandize for those prohibited places, and there to lade fish and other

ST. MARY REDCLIFF CHURCH, BRISTOL (NORTH VIEW)
[This Illustration is taken from a Block kindly lent by Messrs. MACK & Co., of Bristol.]

goods in return : wherefore during his mayoralty of Bristol, because Canynges had done good service unto the King; he allowed the same to be done for two years to come in two ships " (Price's *Canynges Family*, pp. 100, 101). Although the evidence is not conclusive, there is yet a probability that the British merchants, in the reign of Henry VII., may have selected John Cabot for employment as their agent or factor abroad to look after their interests. It appears to be true that not only the Venetians, but the English also had recognised agents or factors abroad, for we find that King Henry VI. sent letters of commendation to the magistrates of Dantzic praying them to favour his factors established within their jurisdiction, and to advance the interests of " his beloved eminent merchant of Bristol " [William Canynges].[1]

[1] William Canynges, a Bristol merchant, one of the richest English merchants in the reigns of Henry VI. and Edward IV. During the reign of Edward IV., William Canynges was *compelled*, as one of the richest merchants, to *lend* the king 3000 marks. According to Wyrcestre, p. 99, "Canynge employed 800 men for eight years ; and his ships included *Le Marie Canyng*, 400 tons ; *Le Marie Redclive*, 500 ; *
Le Marie and Johan, 900,† which had cost him 4000 marks ; *Le Gallyote*, 50 ; *Le Katerine*, 140 ; *Le Marie Batt*, 220 ; *Le Margaret of Tylnay*, 200 ; *besides a ship lost in Iceland of 160 tons burthen*."
Barrett ‡ says : " On the floor of the chancel [of St. Mary Redcliff]

* Named after the beautiful Church of St. Mary Redcliff, in Bristol. Canynge devoted a large portion of his wealth to the completion of the Church of St. Mary Redcliff, of which noble edifice the architectural details were designed upon a style of cathedral magnitude. The church is rich in fifteenth century associations, and among its monuments will be found one erected to the memory of John Jay, whose family name is associated with the first recorded voyage in quest of the island of Brasil. *Ante*, p. 58.
† There is reason to believe that the actual burthen is not here represented. It has been suggested that the measurements show the actual carrying capacity as represented by "tuns" of Spanish wine. It is impossible, however, to come to any certain conclusion.
‡ *History of Bristol*, p. 586.

The inevitable "fish story" having cropped up in connection with the Cabot history, it may be as well to give it a little passing attention. In the church of St. Mary Redcliff, according to Britton, the historian, there "is an object of popular curiosity, traditionally called a rib of the noted Dun-Cow, slain by Guy, Earl of Warwick; but it is more likely to be the rib of a whale, or of some other monstrous fish!" (*sic*). A variant of the story, told by many of the "old parishioners," described the "curiosity" as a rib of the "Dun-Cow"—it is desirable to be very precise in giving the details when matters of importance are involved—which supplied milk to the men who built the church. Another

is a large black marble stone with brass curiously laid in, and engraved with the figures of a man and woman, with six sons underneath the man and eight daughters under the woman, with the following inscription:—'Hic jacet Johannes Jay quondam vicecomes istius villæ, et Joanna uxor ejus; qui quidem Johannes, obiit die 15 mensis Maii, A.D. 1480, quorum animabus propitietur Deus, Amen.' This John Jay was a merchant of great eminence, as appears by William of Wyrcester, p. 267, and Joanna was sister to William of Wyrcester." In the year 1456-57, William Canynge was mayor, William Daine was sheriff, and Henry Chester and John Jay, senior, were bailiffs. In the year 1458-59 John Jay, junior, was one of the bailiffs of Bristol. In the year 1472-73, John Jay was sheriff.

The Jay family appear to have been connected with the parish of St. Mary Redcliff.* John Jay, whose will, dated 13th April 1468, was

---

* This church is one of the favourite visiting places for American and Canadian visitors to England. It contains a memorial of Sir William Penn, knight, the father of William Penn, the founder of Pennsylvania. Dr. Justin Winsor, the American historian, who visited the church many years since, made the following entry about the Penns in the visitors' book :—"When Admiral Penn died, the English Government voted him a large sum for his service; and when this was paid to his heirs, and a grant of land was made to his son, the Quaker William Penn, the latter, in settling in the country, named it, as he himself says, in memory of his father, Pennsylvania.—Justin Winsor, librarian of Harvard University." The admiral's armour and the tattered remains of some Dutch flags taken by him in a naval engage-

THE JAY BRASSES IN ST. MARY REDCLIFF CHURCH

variant, which a former sexton implicitly believed in
and invariably repeated to the visitors to the church,
associated the "curiosity" with a cow which, in ancient
times, supplied the whole of the parish with milk.
But in late years it has been seriously related to
visitors to the church that the "curiosity" is a relic
of a Cabot voyage. In a recent issue of a Bristol
newspaper it was stated that the tradition as to the
rib of the Dun-Cow slain by Guy, Earl of Warwick,
"has long been exploded," and that a belief was
now current that this "bone" belonged to "a big
fish! brought across the seas at the exact time of
the discovery of the American continent."

proved at Bristol "before Robert Jakys, mayor, and John Hoper, sheriff, on Wednesday in the feast of St. Margaret Virgin, 8 Edward IV.—that is, the 13th July 1468—desired to be buried in the choir of the parish church of St. Mary Redcliff, to which church, for his burial, he gave xx^s., and to the vicar for tithes, vi^s. viii^d." Among the bequests, his sons John and Henry to have his share of the ship called "*Trinite.*" * Testator appointed his son John to be the executor, and one of the overseers of the will was testator's brother John. It is exceedingly difficult to trace the pedigree of the Jay family, in consequence of the name of John having been given to several members of the same family. In the "good old times," when, in consequence of the absence of proper sanitary arrangements, and the almost entire ignorance of medical science, life was a glorious uncertainty, it was a matter of frequent occurrence for persons who wished to perpetuate a particular name, to give it to more than one child in the same family.

---

ment may yet be seen in the church. The church is associated with the unfortunate Thomas Chatterton, whose father was the sexton. The boy had access to the muniment room, and a study of the writing in the ancient deeds enabled him to concoct the Rowley forgeries. Rowley, described as a monk who, Chatterton alleged, was the intimate friend of Canynge, was altogether an imaginary person. There are seven old chests yet remaining in the muniment room, but the MSS. have disappeared. The chests show traces of great antiquity, and are now in a state of decay. Chatterton described the church as "the pride of Brystowe and the westerne lande."

* "Item volot lego duobus filiis meis Johanni t Henrico partem meam de naui que vocatur *Trinite*" (Jay's will). This may have been the ship which made the attempt, in 1480, to find the mythical island of Brasil.

In the *Dictionary of Bristol*, p. 100, we find the following : " Dun-Cow, the rib in St. Mary Redcliff Church, on the left hand of the western entrance. It is a rib of the cow-whale, which was placed in the church in 1497, and is *supposed* to have been presented by Sebastian Cabot to the corporation as a trophy of his enterprise in discovering Newfoundland.'

The association of the whale's rib with the Cabot voyage is due to the appearance, in the *Bristol Observer*, February 8th, 1868, of an entry—which purported to have been taken from an old book—as follows :—" 1497. Pd for settynge upp ye bone of ye bigge fyshe and [writing illegible] hys worke brote over seas, vid. For two rings of iron, iiijd."[1] Search has been made for the purpose of verifying the statement, but the original entry has not as yet been discovered.

. . . . .

It appears that on the 21st January 1496, forty days before the date of the grant of the letters-patent, the Spanish Ambassador in London made a communication as to John Cabot to their Catholic Majesties, Ferdinand and Isabella of Spain. Searches have been made for this letter, but as yet no trace of it has been discovered. The following reply of their Catholic Majesties to their Ambassador, Ruy Gonzales de Puebla, dated 28th of March 1496,[2] has been copied from the *Jean et Sébastian Cabot* of H. Harrisse, p. 315.

" Quanto a lo que desis que alla es yda uno como colon para poner al Rey de ynglaterra en otro

---

[1] St. Mary Redcliff Church is not mentioned in the entry.
[2] This letter was apparently received about twenty-three days after the grant of the letters-patent.

THE PENN MEMORIAL IN ST. MARY REDCLIFF CHURCH

negocio como el de las yndias syn perjuysio de
españa ni di portogal sy asy le acude a el como a
nosotros lo de las yndias bien librado estara crehemos
que esto sera echadiso del Rey de françia por poner
en esto al Rey de ynglaterra para le apartar de otros
negocios mirad que procureis que en esto ny enlo
semejante no Resciba engaño el Rey de ynglaterra
que por quantas partes pudieren trabajaran los
franceses de gelo hazer y estos cosas semejantes son
cosas muy ynçiertas y tales que para agora no
conviene entender en ellas y tanbien mirad que
aquellas[1] . . . no se puede entender en esto syn
perguisio nuestro o del Rey de portogal.
"*Tortosa, à 28 de Marzo de* 1496."

[TRANSLATION]

"You write that a person like Columbus has come to England for the purpose of persuading the king to enter into an undertaking similar to that of the Indies, without prejudice to Spain and Portugal. He is quite at liberty. But we believe that this undertaking was thrown in the way of the King of England by the King of France, with the premeditated intention of distracting him from his other business. Take care that the King of England be not deceived in this or in any other matter. The French[2] will

---

[1] Simancas, Estado ; *Capitulaciones con Inglaterra*, Leg. 2°, fol. 16².
[2] In all probability the King of France had intimated his intention not to be bound by the papal bull. There is evidence that his successor, Francis I., asked by what right the kings of Spain and of Portugal undertook to monopolise the earth? "Had our first father Adam made them his sole heirs?" And he naïvely suggested that it would be necessary to produce a copy of Adam's will! Pending the production of this interesting document, "he should feel at liberty to seize upon all he could get."

try as hard as they can to lead him into such undertakings, but they are very unpleasant enterprises, and must not be gone into at present. Besides, they cannot be executed without prejudice to us and to the King of Portugal.[1]

"*Tortosa, 28th of March* 1496."

. . . .

Ruy Gonzales de Puebla was a doctor of laws, whom Ferdinand and Isabella sent to Henry VII., in 1488, to negotiate the marriage of Catherine of Aragon with Arthur, Prince of Wales. He came to England a second time about 1494, as Spanish Ambassador, and represented not only Castile and Aragon, but also the pope and the emperor until 1509, when he died.[2] Puebla was well known to the Genoese residents in London, and it is recorded that he accepted bribes from some Genoese merchants for using his influence with Henry VII. in order to obtain a remission of certain fines that had been imposed.[3] Puebla's knowledge of the Genoese resident in London should be borne in mind in giving consideration to the facts which go to prove

---

[1] This is, of course, a reference to the claims of Portugal and Spain by virtue of the papal bulls, etc.

[2] Harrisse, p. 14.

[3] It may be worth while to mention here that, in cases of piracy by persons belonging to any of the Southern nations, which involved loss to English merchants or shipowners, the merchants of the particular nationality by whose men the wrong had been inflicted, who happened to be residing in London, were mulcted in penalties with a view to stop the practice of piracy. Thus, for example, the Genoese merchants of London were fined and committed to prison in consequence of the spoliation by Genoese of a large vessel belonging to Robert Sturmye, a merchant of Bristol (Fabyan's Chronicle). The Robert Sturmye who is referred to in the Chronicle is probably the merchant of that name who was shipwrecked at Modon, on the Greek coast, in a ship of Bristol called the *Cog-Anne*, after a voyage with 160 pilgrims for Jerusalem (Wyrcestre's MS. Itin.).

that John Cabot was a Genoese by birth. In a subsequent despatch from Puebla to their Catholic Majesties,[1] he described Cabot as "another Genoese like Columbus." It should be remembered also that Puebla was a Spaniard, and that his letter was written to the Spanish sovereigns. It is a fair inference that Puebla believed that John Cabot was a Genoese by birth, and it is not at all improbable that he derived his belief either from the king or his officials, or from Cabot himself, or, what is very likely, from the gossip of the Genoese colony. John Cabot's proceedings would naturally have become a topic of conversation both at Court and among the Italians resident in London. We have evidence as to Puebla's intercourse with the Genoese merchants; it is also a well-established fact that he attended the Court of King Henry VII. in his official capacity of Ambassador to their Catholic Majesties of Spain, and that he sometimes dined with the king. It is clear that he frequently availed himself of his official position to join the king's table. On one occasion King Henry "asked his courtiers if they knew the reason why De Puebla was coming. They answered, 'To eat,'[2] and the king laughed."[3]

Although the letters-patent of King Henry VII. bear date the 5th March 1495-96, for some inexplicable reason the expedition was not embarked upon until the following year. Whether the delay arose in consequence of any diplomatic difficulty connected with the rights which, legally or illegally, were

[1] *Infra*, p. 159.
[2] He was regarded at Court as a man who was of a very parsimonious disposition, so far as money was concerned.
[3] *Report of Londoño*, Nos. 204, 207.

claimed by the sovereigns of Spain and Portugal under the papal bull;[1] or whether it was caused by unforeseen difficulties of a financial or other kind; or whether it was merely that there was not sufficient time to make preparations for a voyage in 1495-96, —will in all probability ever remain unexplained. It should be borne in mind that an important factor in the calculation of those connected with the arduous undertaking would be the value and the possible loss of the ship or ships in which the intrepid explorers were to navigate the "Sea of Darkness." Leaving these conjectural matters, we now come to the important reality, namely, that John Cabot set sail in the *Matthew* (or *Mathew*), of

---

[1] King Henry VII. was descended from a son of John of Gaunt and Catherine Swynford. At a very early age he was initiated into the mysteries of theology, and he soon realised the advantages which the spiritual teaching would afford him. He thus fully comprehended the effect which a papal dispensation would have upon the popular mind. He made a pretence that he had conscientious scruples as to the lawfulness of his marriage with the Princess Elizabeth, eldest daughter of Edward IV., the authority for which had been given by the Bishop of Imola, papal legate, and asked the pope himself to personally confirm the dispensation. This the pope assented to, and, what is more, he, at the request of the king, confirmed the Act of Settlement passed by Parliament, and put an interpretation on that Act. According to the papal definition, the Act should read that if Queen Elizabeth should die without issue before the king, or if the issue should not outlive the king, then in that case the Crown should pass to Henry's children (if any) of a subsequent marriage. Sentence of excommunication was to be given against any person who should dare to question the pope's interpretation. And the same sentence was thundered forth against all who should disobey the papal bull which divided all the newly-found lands, etc., between Spain and Portugal. But the wily Henry was not in fear of the supposed damnation which, in the popular mind, would be the fate of a person who disobeyed a papal bull. Accordingly, inasmuch as there was a chance of getting money out of Cabot's proposal, he very soon saw his way to ignore the papal bull, under which any person was to be excommunicated who interfered with the pope's division of the newly-found lands.

Bristol, in the early part of the month of May 1497. "In the drama of maritime discovery, as glimpses of new worlds were beginning to reward the enterprising Crowns of Spain and Portugal, for a moment there came from the north a few brief notes fraught with ominous portent. The power for whom destiny had reserved the world empire, of which these Southern nations . . . were dreaming, stretched forth her hand, in quiet disregard of papal bulls, and laid it upon the western shore of the ocean. It was only for a moment, and long years were to pass before the consequences were developed. But in truth the first fateful note that heralded the coming English supremacy was sounded when John Cabot's tiny craft sailed out from the Bristol Channel on a bright May morning of 1497" (*The Discovery of America*, by John Fiske, vol. ii. pp. 1, 2). "Cabot's voyage of 1497 takes precedence of every recorded voyage between the two continents in the Northern hemisphere, and . . . the frail craft, *The Matthew*, with a crew of eighteen Bristol sailors, may be viewed as the forerunner, the primitive embryo, of the magnificent fleets of ships that now traverse the ocean with so much regularity between the Old and New Worlds" (*Canada and Ocean Highways*, by Sandford Fleming, C.M.G., Journal of the Royal Colonial Institute, London: Session 1895-96, p. 584).

In Barrett's *History of Bristol*, p. 172, the following bald entry as to the Cabot voyage appears:— "In the year 1497, the 24th of June, on St. John's Day, was Newfoundland, found by Bristol men in a ship called the *Mathew*."[1] According to an entry which was copied many years ago from a MS.

[1] Barrett adds: "As it is in a manuscript in my possession."

chronicle, formerly in the possession of the Fust family of Hill Court, Gloucestershire, the *Mathew* sailed from the port of Bristol on the 2nd day of May [1497].

[COPY ENTRY]

" 1496. John Drewes [Mayor].   Thomas Vaughan
         Hugh Johnes [Sheriff].   John Elyott
                                                [Bailiffs].

" This year, on St. John the Baptist's Day,[1] the land of America was found by the Merchants of Bristow in a shippe of Bristowe, called the *Mathew*; the which said ship departed from the port of Bristowe, the second day of May, and came home again the 6th of August next following.

" 1497. Henry Dale [Mayor].   John Spencer
         Richard Vaughan [Sheriff].   William Lane
                                                [Bailiffs]."

NOTE.—The old-time civic entries of years date from the 29th of September and end on the 28th of September, consequently the above record, according to the present style of reckoning, refers to an event of the year 1497.

Inasmuch as the original MS. Chronicle, which purported to contain entries relating to the history of Bristol down to the year 1565, was destroyed by fire in the year 1860, it is absolutely necessary that the facts relating to the history of the Chronicle should be given in detail.

Richard Fust,[2] the first of his family who settled at Hill Court, Gloucestershire, died in 1614.

Samuel Fust, of Bristol, merchant, born in 1570,

---

[1] The 24th of June.

[2] I am indebted to Mr. H. Jenner Fust, a son of Sir H. Jenner Fust, Bart., for information as to the Fust family; also to Mr. F. A. Hyett, J.P., of Painswick House, near Stroud, who, in addition, has forwarded a number of notes as to the Cabots.

was the third son of Edward Fust, of London, merchant, and uncle to Sir Edward Fust, Baronet.

Sir Edward Fust, the first baronet, possessed property in Bristol.

Sir Francis Fust, the fifth baronet, married Fanny, daughter of Nicholas Tooker,[1] a Bristol merchant. Sir Francis, who died in 1769, was a book collector; he had several book plates, one a very remarkable one showing the arms of various families with whom the Fusts had intermarried. One or more of these he was in the habit of inserting in all the books, journals, magazines, etc., in his library. He was succeeded by Sir John Fust, the sixth baronet, the last male of his line, who d.s.p. 1779.

Now, we may fairly assume, as we are asked to do, that some members, at least, of his family would feel an interest in Bristol history.

Sir John Fust entailed his property upon his widow, and successively upon his nieces Fanny Fust (who died unmarried) and Flora Langley, who took the name of Fust, and with whom the entail of the personalty ceased. Miss Langley died unmarried in 1841, and left the great part of the personalty, including the contents of Hill Court, to her step-nephew, Sir John Dutton Colt, Bart., the entailed estates passing to Sir Herbert Jenner, who assumed the name and arms of Fust in accordance with Sir John Fust's will. Sir John Dutton Colt remained as tenant of Hill Court until his death in 1845, and after his death the MS. Chronicle hereafter referred to, in which the dates of the sailing and of the return

[1] In the Bristol Poll Books for 1734 and 1739 he is described as follows :—" Nicholas Tooker, Gent., St. James's Parish."

of the *Matthew* were given, passed to the Rev. Sir E. H. Vaughan Colt, Bart., vicar of Hill from 1839 to 1882, as executor of his uncle, Sir John Dutton Colt. Sir E. H. Vaughan Colt sold the MS. Chronicle to Mr. William Strong, bookseller, 30 College Green, Bristol.

Prior to the publication of Barrett's *History of Bristol* (1789) the various events relating to the town were found in MS. Chronicles alone, and in casual entries inserted either in books of national history, or works relating to particular branches of historical inquiry. Following Barrett's publication came several histories in the form of guides; but it may be accepted as a fact that no historical publication containing much original information was published until the Rev. Samuel Seyer, M.A., an eminent Bristol man, issued his *Memoirs of Bristol*, in two volumes, 1821. Now Mr. Strong, after purchasing the MS. Chronicle, requested his assistant, Mr. William Pickering Talboys, to collate the entries therein with Barrett's and Seyer's Histories, with a view to the extraction from the Chronicle of all the entries which were yet unpublished, or which contained information supplemental to any matter or event already published in either of those histories. Mr. Strong subsequently sold the MS. Chronicle, together with the excerpta, which was made up into a MS. volume, to Mr. John Hugh Smyth-Pigott, of Brockley Hall, Somersetshire.

Mr. Smyth-Pigott, who was a natural and recognised son of the late Sir Hugh Smyth, Bart., of Ashton Court, North Bristol, adopted the name of Pigott many years after his marriage with Miss Ann Provis, the heiress of the Pigott estates, in accordance with a wish expressed in the will of Wadham Pigott, of Brockley and Weston-super-Mare, the uncle of Ann Smyth neé Provis, that her husband, Mr. John Hugh Smyth, should adopt the name and arms of Pigott.

Mr. Smyth-Pigott, who was a man of superior education, was a keen collector of curios and rarities. He took an intelligent interest in the history of the City of Bristol, and in its welfare, and he became possessed of a large number of manuscripts, printed books, and pamphlets, relating to Bristol, with which the family of Smyth, of Ashton, had been connected for a long period. The founder of the Smyth family was a Bristol merchant, and there have been connecting links, from the reign of Henry VIII. to the present time, between the Ashton Court family and the City of Bristol.

In the year 1849 a sale was held of the effects of Mr. J. H. Smyth-Pigott of Brockley Hall, Somerset. To give an idea of its magnitude, it should be mentioned that it occupied twenty-three days. From a printed "Catalogue of the costly and highly interesting effects of John Hugh Smyth-Pigott, Esq., which will be sold by auction by Messrs. English & Son, on Monday, October 8 [1849], and following weeks," we learn that the Fust manuscript was included in the sale. The description is as follows:—"Lot 1554, 'A Brief Chronicle, conteyninge the accompte of the Reignes of all the Kings in the Realme of Englande, from the entering of Brutus untill this present yeere, with all the notable acts done by the dyvers of them, and wherein is also conteyned the names of all the Mayors, Stewardes, Bayliffes, and Sheriffes, of the laudable town of Bristowe, now at this time called ye Worshippfull City of Bristowe, with all the notable acts done in those days, from the first yeere of Bristowe, with all the notable acts done in those days, from the first yeere of King Henry ye 3rd, A.D. 1217, untill the present yeere, 1565'; a very curious MS., containing many facts not recorded by the historians of Bristol, from Sir Francis Fust's library, folio."

This sale took place in the lifetime of Mr. J. H. Smyth-Pigott,[1] and the MS. Chronicle appears to have been bought in. Mr. Smyth-Pigott died in the year 1853, and the MS. Chronicle (with the excerpta) was taken to London and sold by auction at the well-known saleroom of Messrs. Sotheby & Wilkinson (now Sotheby, Wilkinson, & Hodge). In the "Catalogue of the remaining portion of The Valuable Library of the late John Hugh Smyth-Pigott, Esq., of Brockley Hall, Somerset, . . . which will be sold by Messrs. S. Leigh Sotheby & John Wilkinson, on Monday, December 19th, 1853, and five following days, at one o'clock precisely," there appears the following description of the "Chronicle" and the Excerpta:—"Lot 2040. A briefe Chronycle conteyning the accompte of the Reynes of all the Kynges in this realme of England, from the entering of Brutus until this present yeere (1595),[2] with the names of all the Mayors, Stewardes, Bayliffes, and Sheriffes of Bristow (by Maurice Toby).

"Autograph Manuscript, from the library of Sir Francis Fust, folio.

---

[1] "Literature, and all the liberal arts, had in Mr. Pigott a munificent patron. No one paid with more prompt liberality every variety of talent. He delighted to patronize painters, sculptors, engravers, and many other branches of art."—*Bath and Cheltenham Gazette.*

[2] A printer's error for 1565.

⁎ "This most valuable chronicle will enable any future Historian of Bristol to correct the errors of his predecessors. The Preface commences, 'Maurice Toby, Gent., the Author of this Chronicle, to the Reader.' A modern Collation of its statement of Facts, with the Histories of Barrett and Seyer, will be sold with this Volume." Mr. Thomas Kerslake, a well-known Bristol bookseller and antiquarian, became the purchaser of this lot. A copy of the catalogue of the sale is in the possession of Mr. Ernest E. Baker, F.S.A., of Weston-super-Mare, and against lot 2040, there is written in the margin in pencil (in the handwriting of the late Mr. Henry Bush of Bristol), "Kerslake, £11, 5s. 0d."; also the words "ends with Queen Mary, 1565."

Upon application being made to Messrs. Sotheby, Wilkinson, & Hodge, for corroboration of the annotation in Mr. Baker's catalogue as to the name of the purchaser of lot 2040, the following reply came:—

"13 WELLINGTON STREET, STRAND,
LONDON, W.C., *Sep.* 28, 1896.

"DEAR SIR,—All our catalogues containing the record of our sales (except those of the last 10 years) are now at the British Museum: we regret, therefore, that we are unable to give you the information you require. Our Catalogue can be seen there, or probably one of the Officials in the Library department would give you the amount the lot realised,—Yours faithfully,
"SOTHEBY, WILKINSON, & HODGE."

In response to an application, Dr. R. Garnett, C.B., of the British Museum, has kindly sent the following information :—"The price and purchaser of the MS. Chronicle, according to the annotated copy of Messrs. Sotheby's catalogue in the Museum, are the same as those stated in Mr. Baker's copy of the catalogue—Kerslake, £11, 5s."

The "Chronicle" was burnt in the disastrous fire which occured at Mr. Kerslake's shop in Park Street, Bristol, February 14, 1860, when many rare and unique volumes and manuscripts then perished, but the excerpta or "collations" happily escaped. The following extracts have been taken from an account in the *Bristol Times and Felix Farley's Journal*, of Saturday, February 18, 1860, under the heading, "Destructive Fire in Park Street."

"Mr. Kerslake's stock of books, MSS., etc., is known to everyone almost as one of the most valuable and extensive in the country, out of London. . . . The door of the private room in which were the accumulated treasures of Mr. Kerslake's life had been broken open and a few of the treasures removed, but the devouring element soon seized upon the rest, and they became a heap of ashes."

About ten years after the fire, the volume of the excerpta or collations was purchased of Mr. Kerslake by Mr. William George, of Bristol, and is still in his possession.

CHAPTER IV

"Thus it came to pass that early in May 1497, a little vessel called the *Matthew*, of the caravel class, most likely, sailed out of the port of Bristol and turned her prow towards the West. . . . Never was a voyage of discovery, the consequences of which were so far-reaching, entered upon with less pomp and circumstance. Without flourish of trumpets or any outward demonstrations, Cabot and his English sailors sailed away into the unknown waste of waters. What dangers they encountered; through what storms they passed; what fears and alarms they conquered; what feelings gladdened their hearts at the close—of all these we know nothing. No diary of the voyage has been preserved." These words have been taken from Rev. M. Harvey's paper on the Cabot voyages, because they truly represent the scarcity of material which the historian has to guide him in dealing with this memorable adventure.[1] Referring to the two chronicles, the one known to Barrett, and the Fust MS., Mr. Harvey remarks as follows:—"Both of these ancient records agree as to the date of the discovery of the land, and the name of the ship, and both ignore the discoverer whose genius and courage pointed the way which so many thousands have since followed. Such, too often, is fame among contemporaries. After generations recognise the merits of great men, but too frequently the prophets are stoned or treated with bitter contempt in their own day."

In the MS. Fust or Toby Chronicle it is stated that the *Matthew* "came home again the 6th of August" [1497]. This date may be fairly received as the correct one, in the absence of any contradictory evidence to merit our attention. It receives some confirmation from an entry, dated 10th August [1497], in the Remembrancer's office, in connection with the privy purse expenses of the king, in which it is recorded that the king on that day gave £10 "To hym that founde the New Isle" (British Museum, additional MSS., No. 7099, 12 Hen. VII. fol. 41).

It may be assumed that after his arrival in Bristol, Cabot lost no time in making his way to the king's Court[1] with a view to acquaint the king with the result of his voyage, and therefore we naturally find him at Court four days after his return from his voyage. It appears from contemporary evidence[2] that the king was greatly pleased with John Cabot's report of his discovery, and that negotiations were at once commenced for another expedition, to start early in the following year.

John Cabot's arrival must have caused much pleasurable excitement, not only at the king's Court, but in all grades and classes of society—from the highest to the lowest. To the king it would point to accessions, both of power and wealth

---

[1] The king, on August 10, appears to have been at Westminster. —E. Chishom Butler, in *Proceedings of Som^t Arch^l Society*, xxv. p. ii. p. 61.
[2] *Infra*, p. 140.

in the near future, for it was popularly believed that His Majesty had "gained a part of Asia without a stroke of the sword";[1] by merchants and traders the adventure would be regarded as a harbinger of voyages to the promised lands, where gold and gems and aromatic spices would be found, with an early prospect of making "London a greater place for spices than Alexandria";[2] to others, again, of his Majesty's subjects, it might seem that their day-dreams of those pleasant islands in the Western Ocean would soon be realised. Ambassadors and others became interested in the reports of the voyage. Raimondo de Soncino wrote to the Duke of Milan, with a long account of what he had been told by John Cabot, who is described in the despatch as "a popular Venetian";[3] and Lorenzo Pasqualigo, a native of Venice, in a letter to his brothers, informed them that great honour was paid to Cabot, who "is called the great admiral; ... he dresses in silk, and these English run after him like insane people."[4]

Tarducci, writing with reference to Cabot after his arrival in England from his successful venture, says: "John Cabot's return seems to have wonderfully stirred and warmed up the cold nature of the English. He returned with the announcement that he had landed in the Grand Khan's empire, and was naturally believed by everybody. This announcement meant that he had opened the treasures of all wealth to their ships and commerce. ... They called him 'High Admiral,' the king promised him a fleet for a new expedition in the fine season, and the principal merchants of Bristol vied to take part in it.

[1] *Infra*, p. 148. [2] *Infra*, p. 150.
[3] *Infra*, p. 148. [4] *Infra*, p. 140.

These honours seem to have gone a little to his head, for he put on showy garments of silk; and in his confidence that he had discovered extensive regions, he invited his companions and friends to share in his fortune, bestowing islands and lands on some. Those selected for his generosity rejoiced in the greatness of their future honour, and he in their midst esteemed himself a prince. Still, in this cheap vanity there is a good and beautiful side; it is to see that his heart was not shut up with pride in the sentiment of his grandeur, but gladly opened to share his happiness with others."

From a perusal of the contemporary letters it may be thought by some that the king may have made Cabot small presents, in addition to the recorded gift of £10.[1] In all probability some negotiation took place between the king and the successful voyageur, for a settlement of any claim to which the latter might reasonably believe he was entitled under the letters-patent. From a perusal of contemporary documents, it seems almost certain that no claim could arise in respect of any "goods and merchandise that they [the adventurers] may bring from those newly-discovered places";[2] and Cabot derived no benefit in this way, either directly or indirectly, because we find that he merely brought back with him "certain snares which had been set to catch game, and a needle for making nets." Nor gold, nor precious stones, nor merchandise of any kind came home with the adventurers—there was nothing of any value to be dealt with. We are, therefore, left to consider any claim that might arise under the clause of the letters-patent, which seems

[1] This sum represents in present value about £120.   [2] *Ante*, p. 99.

to point out that no English subject would be allowed to visit the lands that might be discovered without the licence of the discoverers.[1]

Considering the hazy notions that existed as to what Cabot had discovered—beyond a belief that it was a part of Asia—or as to what its value really was; considering, too, the vagueness of the language that describes the concession granted by the letters-patent, a lawyer of that or of any other period would sorely have been puzzled to state what the legal claim of Cabot actually was. Ultimately the king agreed to grant an annuity to John Cabot of £20 per annum, payable half-yearly out of the customs and subsidies due to the king from goods and merchandises brought into the port of Bristol. The question arises, Why did the king "for certain considerations, us [the king] specially moving," arrange to pay Cabot an annual sum, which represents about £240 per year in present value? Bearing in mind the fact that the arrangements for the payment of the annuity were followed by the grant of new letters-patent in the name of John Cabot only, it may fairly be assumed that a final settlement had been come to between the king and Cabot, as to the claims of the latter under the first letters-patent, which, presuming they did not expire on the ending of the voyage, were completely put an end to by the grant of the annuity or pension. And, in passing, we might ask, Does not the absence of the names of John Cabot's sons, whether in connection with the gift of £10 or in the grant of the annuity, justify us in regarding this as an additional argument, perhaps of a negative character,

[1] *Ante*, p. 99.

against the probability of the presence of any of these sons in the memorable voyage of the *Matthew*?

The following is a copy of the document, dated December 13, 1497, by which John Cabot became entitled to an annuity of £20 per annum.

"Henry, by the grace of God king of England and of France, and lord of Ireland—To the most reverend fadre in God, John Cardinal archiebisshop of Cantrebury prymate of all England and of the apostolique see legate our chauncellor greting.—We late you wite that We for certaine consideracions us specially moevyng have geven and granted unto Welbilouved John Calbot [*sic*] of the parties of Venice an annuitie or anuel rent of twenty pounds sterling. To be had and yerely perceyved from the feast of thanunciacion of or lady last passed [the Feast of the Annunciation of our Lady last past, *i.e.* the 25th of March 1497] during our pleasur of our custumes and subsidies comying and growing in our Poort of Bristowe by thands of our custums ther for the tyme beyng at Michelmas and Estre [Easter] by even porcions. Wherfor we wol [will] and charge you that vnder [under] our grete seal ye do make heruppon our lettres-patent in god and effectuall forme.—Yeuen vndre [Given under] our Pryue Seal at o^r paloys [palace] of Westminster the xiijth day of Decembre, the xiijth yere of our Reigne.

"HORWOOD."

(Public Record Office, Privy Seal, Dec. 13, Henry VII., No. 40.)

It appears from a perusal of the following document that Cabot experienced some difficulty in obtaining payment of his annuity.

COPY WARRANT from Henry VII., dated 22nd February 1498, for the payment of John Cabot's pension.

"Henry, by the grace of God, king of England and of France and lord of Ireland.—To the Tresourer and Chaubrelaines of oure Eschequier greting.— Whereas we by oure warrant under oure signet for certain consideracions have geven and graunted unto John Caboote xx li. [£20] yerely during oure pleasure to be had and prayved by the hands of our custumers in our poorte of Bristowe, and as we be enformed the said John Caboote is delaied of his payement because the said custumers have no sufficient matier of discharge for their indempnitie to be yolden at their accompt before the Barons of our Eschequier. Wherefore we wol [will] and charge you that ye our said Tresourer and Chaubrelaines that now be and hereafter shal be that ye unto suche tymes as ye shall have from us otherwise in comandement do to be levied in due fourme II. several tailles every of them conteignyng x li. [£10] upon the customers of the revenues in oure said poorte of Bristowe at two usual termes of the yere whereof oon taill to be levied at this time conteignyng x li. of the revenues of oure said poort upon Richard Meryk[1] and Arthure

[1] Richard Meryk or Merryk, otherwise A' Meryk or A' Merryeke, was elected Sheriff of Bristol in 1503. He died during his year of office, and Robert Thorne succeeded him. He [Merrick] was a very wealthy man and bought several estates in Somerset, amongst others, the manor of Ashton Philips, near Bristol. His daughter and heiress, Johanna or Joan, married John Brooke, of Bristol, sergeant-at-arms, who resided in Redcliff Street, and was buried in St. Mary Redcliff Church, where there are brasses to the memory of himself and his wife. David Brooke, recorder of Bristol (1541), was his son. Meryk was a very common name in Bristol at that period. In a Cause Book

Kemys[1] late custumers of the same. And the same taill or tailles in due and sufficient fourme levied ye delyver unto the said John Caboote to be had of our gift by way of rewarde without prest or any other charge to be sette upon hym or any of them for the same. And thes our lettres shal be youre sufficient warrant in that behalf.—Geven undre oure prive seal at oure Manor of Shene the xxii. day of ffebruary the xiii. yere of oure reign.

"BOLMAN."

(Warrants for Issues of the 13th of Henry VII.)

An important entry, recently discovered in the account of the collectors of the customs and subsidies due to the king at the port of Bristol, has been transcribed, and the following copy thereof *is now published for the first time.*

of the ancient Tolzey Court of Bristol (now in the possession of Alderman F. F. Fox, of Bristol), which contains a large number of contemporary names, "Richard Meryk" appears twice. He is once styled a merchant; and "Richard ap Meryk," with no trade, occurs thrice.

[1] By an indenture of covenant, dated 26 Hen. VI., that is, 1449-50, between John Kemys and William Arthur, arrangements were made for a marriage between Roger, the son of the said John, and Alice, daughter of the said William. Arthur Kemys "of Bedminster," son of Rodger Kemys, by his wife Alice, daughter and heire of William Arthur, of Bedminster, Bristol, appears in a list of names referred to in the Visitation of Somerset, 1591 (Harleian MS., No. 1559, in British Museum). Arthur Kemys (great-grandson of the Arthur of Bedminster) appears to have been living at the date of visitation (1591). There is a Kemys aisle in St. Philip's Church in which "oon John Kemys, Esquier," founded a chantry, but the date is not recorded. The name of John Kemys, son and heir of John Kemys, deceased, appears in a grant of wardship, dated 10th March 1486, in respect of land which John Kemys, deceased, held of the king *in capite*. In the will of Joan Forde, the widow of John Forde, deceased, which was proved in the parish church of St. Mary Redcliff, Nov. 16, 1464, "a legacy was bequeathed to Isabel, wife of William Kemys, mercer."—*Bristol Wills,* No. 250.

It is a very interesting entry, and it seems to prove conclusively that he received a proportion of his annuity of £20 up to and inclusive of the 25th of March 1498; consequently it was at some time after that date that he started upon his new expedition.

Bristoll.

"Visus compĩ Arthuri Kemys ⁷t Riči A' Meryk Collčoʒ Custumaʒ ⁷t Subs̃ d̃ni Regis in port ville Bristolt ⁷t in sing̃lis portub; ⁷t locis eid̃m portui adjacentibus vidett de h̃uj cust̃ ⁷t subs̃ d̃ni Regis ib̃m a ffesto sc̃i Michis Archi Anno xiij° d̃ni Regis nunc Henrici septimi vsque ffestum Pasche accideñ xv^mo die Aprilis tunc prox̃ sequeñ scitt p medietatem vnius Anni ⁷t xvj dies ut supra.

. . . .

"Sm^u Re^t—Dliiij^li xviij^s v^d ob D quib; Resp^r eisd̃m Collčorib;—lxxij^s iiij^d q̃ feodo suo. . . . Et eisd̃m—x ti p ip̃os solut̃ Joh̃i Calboto veniciano nup de villa Bristoll p̃dict̃ p Annuitate sua ad xx ti p Annũ sibi p d̃cm d̃ñm Regem nunc p tras suas pateñ concess̃ pcipient ad duas Anni Terminos de Cust̃ ⁷t Subs̃ in d̃co portu ville Bristolt pveñ ⁷t cresceñ vidett p Termino Annunc̃ b̃te Marie virginis infra tempus huj visus accideñ p vnam Acquietanc̃ ip̃ius Johis inde sup hunc visum ostens̃ ⁷t penes d̃cos Collčores remañ."

(Exchequer Q. R. Custom ⅌⅋. Public Record Office, London.)

[TRANSLATION]

"View of the account of Arthur Kemys and Richard A' Meryk, collectors of the customs and subsidies of the lord the king, in the port of the town of Bristol and in all parts and places to the same port adjacent, to wit, of such customs and subsidies of the lord the king there from the feast of St. Michael the Archangel in the 13th year of the lord the King Henry VIIth that now is up to the feast of Easter happening on the 15th day of April then next following, to wit, for the moiety of one year and 17 days as above.

"Sum of the receipts, £554, 18s. 5½d., whereof there is answered to the said collectors for their fees 72s. 4d. . . . And to the same—£10 paid by them to John Calbot [sic], a Venetian, late of the said town of Bristol for his annuity of £20 a year, granted to him by the said lord the king, by his letters-patent, to be taken at two terms of the year out of the customs and subsidies forthcoming and growing in the said port of the town of Bristol, to wit, for the term of the annunciation of the Blessed Virgin Mary happening within the time of this view, by an acquittance of the said John to be shown thereof upon this view, and remaining in the possession of the said collectors. . . ."

[NOTE.—A full translation of the account in which the entry as to the payment to Cabot appears will be found in Appendix C. The account for the half-year immediately preceding this account, in which the payment of the first moiety of the annuity would probably be found, cannot be discovered. Diligent search has been made for the subsequent accounts, but, so far, without success. The next entry of the account of the Bristol customs is for the 19 Hen. VII., that is, A.D. 1504.]

The following account will show who Kemys and

OLD BRISTOL BRIDGE

[Showing the Chapel of the Assumption of the B.V. Mary built across the Bridge, and "St. Nicholas's Gate," one of the City Gates, with the Chancel of the Church of St. Nicholas over the Gateway.]

A' Meryk were, and how it was they served "the lord, the king, in the port of the town of Bristol." It was customary in Bristol, at that period, for the collectors of the king's customs[1] and subsidies to take the same, either at the quay on the waters of the Frome, "or in a certain place called *the Backe*, between Baldwin Street and *the bridge*" (Bristol Bridge).[2] The king directed his collectors of customs "to overlook the lading of all merchandise and

[1] A very curious entry in the Rolls, under date 13th July 1489, contains a special pardon for John Rowley and William Rowley, merchants of Bristol, for entering the name of John Rowley only in the books of the collectors of customs at Bristol, the goods being the joint property of John and William, contrary to the provisions of an Act of Parliament. It was from the name of a member of this family that Chatterton borrowed his "monk Rowleie."

[2] This arrangement was made in pursuance of an order of King Henry VI., which recites that "very many persons, residents of the town aforesaid, have put divers customable goods and merchandizes in ships and boats, by night and by day, upon the water of Avon, running through the middle of the town, and do carry the same to foreign parts, we being subtilely defrauded of the customs thereof to us belonging." Not only were the places for ships to take goods in defined, but it was ordered that all customable goods, on pain of forfeiture, were to be carried out of the town "in the daytime, *between the rising and the setting of the sun*,* and not in the nighttime, nor at any time in a secret way, . . . and shall be put into ships paying the customs thereof, due at the said key, or at the said place called the Backe" . . . It was also ordered to be publicly proclaimed in the town, "That no one shall presume to load their ships with wool, or other customable merchandises, but at the place aforesaid, *between the rising and setting of the sun*, as is aforesaid, under forfeiture of the same wools and merchandise."

---

* By letters-patent of Queen Elizabeth, after reciting an enactment as to the time for loading and unloading, it is stated that the queen, having been informed that the port of Bristol (except at spring tides) was very dangerous, and deficient in depth of water, and that no great ship or vessel, being laden with wares and merchandise, was able to approach *within four miles*; that the sea there quickly ebbed and flowed, and that each flowing did not continue above five or six hours, and not more than six in days of spring tide, authority was granted for loading and unloading "at any time between the hours of four in the morning and eight in the evening."

other goods, laden in the town aforesaid, and to take into your hands, as forfeited to us, all customable goods and merchandises which shall happen to be loaded into ships elsewhere than at the said key, or the said place called *the Backe,* or at any other time than between the rising and setting of the sun, contrary to the form of the ordinance aforesaid, and to keep in safe custody the same for our use, so that to us, for the forfeitures aforesaid, you may answer at our exchequer" (Rol. Pat. 16 Hen. VII. part i. m. 9).

The kings of England were entitled to certain customs and subsidies in respect of certain towns, of which Bristol was one, which were royal demesnes.[1] King Edward I., much against his will, being compelled to bend before the storm, confirmed the celebrated charters, together with the statute, "De Tallagio non concedendo," and from that period it was illegal for the king to make a seizure of wools,

---

[1] The town of Bristol, together with the castle, the walls, cottages, stalls, tofts, mills, rents, landgable tolls, pleas of court, fairs, and markets, were frequently leased by the king, for the time being, to the mayor and commonalty of Bristol. As an example, King Henry VI. "committed to our well-beloved Hugh Wythyford, Mayor of our town of Bristol, and to the commonalty of the same town, and their successors, the same town, with the suburbs of the same, etc. etc., . . . to have and to hold the same, to him and his successors, from the feast of St. Michael the Archangel, next happening, unto the end of twenty years next following. . . . And that the same mayor and commonalty, and their successors, during the term aforesaid, shall have the same privileges, profits, etc., . . . as fully and entirely as we should have had them, if we had retained the said town in our hands." The mayor and commonalty bound themselves to pay the following yearly sums during the continuation of the lease : To the king, £102, 15s. 6d. ; to the Abbot of Tewkesbury, in Gloucestershire, £14, 10s., for tithes of the town ; to the Prior of St. James's, of Bristol, for the annual rent of the town mill, £3 ; to the Constable of Bristol and his officers . . . and to the Forester of Kingswood, £39, 14s. The king also granted certain customs of Bristol for goods coming by land or water, except *wool, leather and woolfells.*

skins, etc., or to take toll upon them without the assent of parliament. But, notwithstanding the charters, etc., the parliaments were unable to restrain the royal authority, and, at times, the kings resorted to various devices for the purpose of obtaining money. Henry V. obtained a grant from the commons of the tonnage and poundage for life. After the battle of Bosworth, the parliament, which was composed of servile tools of Henry VII., settled the tonnage and poundage on the king for life, adding a request or condition that he should remedy his assumption of the crown by contracting a marriage with Elizabeth, the representative of the York family. King Henry VII., during the whole of his reign, was practically independent of parliamentary control, inasmuch as there never existed any real restraint upon his conduct. Notwithstanding the existence of the limitations imposed by the charters, etc., the exercise of the royal authority in matters of taxation was not properly safeguarded. The customs, or portions thereof, taken by the king at the port of Bristol, were claimed to be a part of the inheritance of the crown, and consequently were probably regarded as outside the sphere of parliamentary influence. In the fourth year of his reign the king appointed Adam Oxenbridge to collect customs on wool and skins in the port of Bristol, and in the same year a similar appointment was made in favour of Richard ap Myryk. A commission was also granted him for the collection of the customs of worsted cloth in the port of the town of Bristol; a similar commission was also granted him in respect of the customs for woollen cloth, skins, and furs (Fine Roll, 4 Hen. VII.).

It was, apparently, usual for the king to have two collectors. By reason of the vacation of office by the then joint-holder with Myryk, the king, in the ninth year of his reign, appointed Arthur Kemmeys[1] as one of his collectors. Extract from the Fine Roll.—" The King, to his beloved Arthur Kemmeys. Know thou that we in full confidence of thy fidelity and circumspection appoint thee to raise and collect our customs on wools and skins, in the port of the town of Bristol, and in ports and places lying near the said port, and to receive the same to our use, to keep our seal called Coket, in the ports and places aforesaid, to pay the money accruing therefrom into our exchequer. In witness whereof, etc., the King, at Westminster, 1st October" (Fine Roll, 9 Henry VII.). By a commission of same date, Arthur Kemmeys was appointed collector of customs on coloured cloth in the port of the town of Bristol, etc. By another commission of same date, Arthur Kemmeys was appointed collector of customs on tonnage and poundage in the port of the town of Bristol, etc.

. . . .

Within a comparatively recent period the archives of foreign countries have been found to contain some exceedingly important evidence relating to the voyages of 1497 and 1498. The documents have altered the whole complexion of affairs, in so far as they throw light upon the services of John and Sebastian Cabot in connection with the two voyages, and assist us to form an opinion as to the compara-

---

[1] Under date 7th Jan. 1488, there is an entry of the grant of a reward of 100 marks to Arthur Kemys, "in recompense for his losses in the King's victorious battles."—Pat. p. 1, m. 16 (11).

tive agency of the father and the son. Here and there among these writings we may detect a verbiage that makes it doubtful whether John Cabot's own words are exactly given by the authors; we may detect language which merely expresses some opinion or some passing thought of the writer; yet, again, some of the details may have been derived from rumour or from gossip; but, on the whole, having regard to the certainty that they are original and authentic documents, beyond the suspicion of forgery of any kind whatsoever, the contents must be accepted as absolutely first-class evidence of the events and circumstances to which they severally refer. Besides, the style of the narrations of these contemporary writers is of a character so unique, and the narrations shed a light so clear on details of importance which were formerly in a state of great obscurity, that we ought to be exceedingly grateful to the gentlemen whose exertions have brought the documents to light. The effect of the publication of these documents, coupled with the production of additional information lately exhumed from original records contained in the various rolls kept at the Public Record Office in London, is that at the present time no history of the voyages of 1497 and 1498, or of either of them, which was published prior to the date of the discovery of the documents now about to be transcribed, can be accepted as a trustworthy guide to seekers after the truth. The following relate to the voyages of 1497; subsequently, copies of certain documents which relate only to the voyage of 1498 will appear.

It is proposed to give copies of all the documents in the language in which they were originally written, each copy to be followed by a translation.

COPY LETTER written by Lorenzo Pasqualigo in London, on the 23rd August 1497, to his brothers residing in Venice.

"Copia de uno capitolo scrive in una lettera q. Lorenzo Pasqualigo fo di q. Filippo da Londra adi 23 Avosto. A q. Alvise e Francesco Pasqualigo suo fradeli. In *Veniexia recevuta adi* 23 septembrio 1497.

"L'e venudo sto nostro Veneziano, che andò con uno navilio de Bristo (Bristol) a trovar Isole nove, e dice haver trovato lige 700 lontano de qui terra ferma, chè el paese del Gran Cam, ed è andato per la costa lige 300 ed è desmontato, e non ha visto persona alguna, ma ha portato qui al Re certi lazi che era tezi per prender salvadexine, e uno ago da far rede, e à trovato certi albori tajati, sichè per questo judicha che sce persone. Vene in nave per dubito et è stato mexi tre sul viazo, e questo è certo, e al tornar al dreto a visto do Isole, ma non ha voluto desender, per non perder tempo, chè la vituaria li manchava, sto Re nè habuto grande apiacer; e dize che le acque è stanche, e non hano corso come qui. El Re li ha promesso a tempo novo, navilii 10 armati, come lui vorà, e dali dato tutti i presonieri, da traditori in fuora, che vadano con lui, come lui à richiesto; e ali dato danari, fazi bona ziera, fino a quel tempo, ed è con so mojer veniziana, e con so fioli a Bristo, el qual se chiama Zuam Calbot, e chiamasi el gran Armirante, e vienli fato grande honor; era vestido de seda, e sti Inglexi li vano driedi a modo pazi; e pur ne volese tanti quanti n'avrebbe con lui, et etiam molti de nostri furfanti. Sto inventor de queste cose à impiantato suli tereni, à trovato uno gran croxe con una bandiera de Ingilterra e una di San Marco per esser lui Veneziano, sichè el nostro Confalone se stese molto in quà."

. . . .

[*Diarii di Marin Sanuto*, tom. i. fol. 374. MS. in Marciana Library, Venice; Calendar of State Papers and Manuscripts relating to English Affairs in the Archives of Venice and other Libraries of Northern Italy. Edited by Rawdon Brown, vol. ii. p. 262.]

[TRANSLATION]

"The Venetian, our countryman, who went with a ship from Bristol to search for new islands, is returned, and says that seven hundred leagues from here he discovered main land (*terra firma*), *the territory of the Grand Khan*.[1] He coasted for three hundred leagues and landed; saw no human beings, but he has brought here to the king certain snares which had been set to catch game, and a needle for making nets; he also found some felled trees, by which he judged there were inhabitants, and returned to his ship in alarm. He was three months on the voyage,[2] and on his return saw

[1] It seems tolerably clear that they believed they had found a part of the mainland of Asia.
[2] This is consistent with the entries in the Fust MS. Chronicle.

two islands to starboard, but would not land, time being precious, as he was short of provisions. He (Cabota) says that the tides are slack there, and do not flow as they do here.[1] This has greatly pleased the King of England. The king has promised him in the spring ten ships, armed to his order, and at his request has conceded him all the prisoners, except those confined for high treason, to man his fleet. The king has also given him money with which he may amuse himself until that time, and he is now at Bristol with his wife, who is also a Venetian, and with his sons. His name is John Calbot (*sic*), and he is called the great admiral. Great honour is paid him; he dresses in silk, and these English run after him like insane people, so that he can enlist as many of them as he pleases, and a number of our own rogues[2] besides. The discoverer of these places planted on this newly-found land a large cross, with one flag of England and another of St. Mark[3] on account of his being a Venetian, so that our banner has floated very far afield."

This despatch contains a decisive record which will dispel all doubt—if, indeed, any doubt yet exists—as to John Cabot's belief with regard to

---

[1] The rise of the tide in those regions, which rarely exceeds three or four feet, would have been a surprise for the Bristol men on board the *Matthew*. In Bristol the tide varies from 20 feet (neap) to 36 feet (spring).

[2] Italians.

[3] St. Mark had long been regarded as the patron Saint of Venice. In the ninth century the celebrated Church of St. Mark was commenced. Some historians say that this church was built on the site of the temple of St. Theodorus. From this time "St. Mark became, instead of St. Theodorus, the patron of Venice."

the land he had met with. He describes it as "the territory of the Grand Khan," thus proving his acquaintance with the ideas of Toscanelli, which had been for a long period prevalent, not only in his native Republic of Genoa, but generally accepted by most educated Italians. And for all we know to the contrary, Cabot may have been personally acquainted with Toscanelli, may have gained from him the belief or inspiration he held as to the actual existence of land in the far Western waters.

Lorenzo Pasqualigo's letter tells his brothers in Venice that the land found by Cabot was situated "seven hundred leagues from here," [1] whereas Don Pedro de Ayala, in a letter to Ferdinand and Isabella of Spain, expresses a belief it "was not further distant than four hundred leagues." [2] Don Pedro had actually seen Cabot and entered into a discussion with him; and, further, he had in his possession a map given him by Cabot, which, we have good reasons for believing, he subsequently forwarded to Spain. The best opinions seem to favour the suggestion that this map must have been the foundation for the references to the English discoveries which appear upon the celebrated La Cosa Map.[3]

With regard to the "two islands to starboard," inasmuch as no authentic record of Cabot's landfall exists, it is impossible to identify them: various writers have endeavoured to locate them, but any attempt to do so must of necessity end in conjecture. There can be very little doubt that Cabot saw two islands, because the Milanese envoy,

[1] England is perhaps meant, but the writer would have had the port of Bristol in his mind's eye.
[2] *Infra*, p 162.   [3] *Infra*, pp. 292, 293.

Raimondo de Soncino, in writing to the Duke of Milan on the subject of Cabot's discovery, playfully observes that these two islands had already been disposed of,—one to a Burgundian, "a companion of Messer Joanne," and the other to Cabot's barber,[1] whom Raimondo describes as being a Genoese!"

"On landing on the new shore," says Tarducci, "after planting there the cross, after the custom of all discoverers, as a sign that they had taken possession in the name of Christ for the spreading of His faith and His law, he planted by its side the banner of England, to mark the new country as the property of the English Crown. And then, drawn by that mysterious bond which at every distance of time and place brings us to the image of those dear to us, especially in the most solemn and consoling moments of life, he crossed in thought through the ocean, passed over England, traversed Europe, and sought on the shore of the Adriatic the glorious Queen of the Lagoons [Venice]. Twenty years had passed since he left her, but neither length of time nor distance of place could weaken his tender affection. And in the new land he had discovered, by the side of Christ's Cross with the banner of England he planted the flag of Venice."

. . . .

EXTRACT from a DESPATCH, in August 1497, from Raimondo de Soncino to the Duke of Milan.

"Oltre a ciò alcuni mesi dopo S. Maestà mandò un Veneziano che è un distinto marinajo, e che aveva molta capacità nelle scoperte di nuove isole, ed è ritornato salvo, ed ha scoperto due isole fertili molto

---

[1] Probably a barber-surgeon.

grandi, avendo del pari scoperto le setta città quattrocento leghe dall' Inghilterra dalla parte verso occidente. Questi tosto esternò a S. M. l'intenzione di mandarlo con quindici o venti bastimenti. . . . Londra, 24 Agosto 1497." (*Archives des Sforza*, Milan.[1])

[L'original, paraît-il, n'a pu être retrouvé dans les archives milanaises. Nous croyons donc utile de reproduire la copie que M. Kingston a eu l'obligeance de prendre sur le texte envoyé par M. Rawdon Brown au Public Record Office.]

"Item la Majesta de Re sono mesi passate havia mandato uno Veneciano el quel e molto bono marinare et a bona scientia de trovare insule nove, e ritornato a salvamento et a ritrovato due insule nove grandissime et fructiffere et etiam trovato le septe citade lontane da l'insula de Ingliterra lege 400 per lo camino de ponentela Maesta de Re questo primo bono tempo gli vole mandare xv. in xx. navili" (*Jean et Sébastian Cabot*, by H. Harrisse, p. 323.)

[TRANSLATIONS]

"News received this morning from England by letters dated the 24th of August.[2]

"Also, some months ago, his Majesty sent out a Venetian, who is a very good mariner,[3] and has good

[1] Rawdon Brown's *Calendar*, t. iii. p. 260, No. 750.

[2] In the original there is no address to this document, but from Sanuto's diaries the notices it contains were evidently written to the Duke of Milan, in August 1497, by his envoy, Raimondo de Soncino, accredited to Henry VII. The name Soncino is given by Sanuto in his diaries, date 21 August 1497. The letters of this envoy, in the Sforza Archives, merely bear the name "Raimundus."—(Rawdon Brown's *Calendar*, p. 260, No. 750.)   [3] John Cabot.

skill in discovering new islands, and he has returned safe, and has found two very large and fertile new islands; having likewise discovered the seven cities, 400 leagues from England,[1] on the western passage. This next spring his Majesty means to send him with fifteen or twenty ships."

In this despatch we have confirmatory evidence as to the "two islands." It seems pretty clear, too, that at this period a much larger expedition than that which subsequently was fitted out was talked about. Pasqualigo, in his letter, refers to a contemplated expedition of ten ships "armed to his [Cabot's] order"; in all probability, however, the second account, which states that the king "means to send him with fifteen or twenty ships," was the result of the exaggerated additions to an original story which we may naturally expect to find in a case of the kind. We will now proceed to look at a subsequent despatch of Raimondo de Soncino, in order to ascertain to what extent it throws light upon our subject.

. . . . . .

Copy of the SECOND DESPATCH of Raimondo de Soncino, dated the 18th of December 1497, to the Duke of Milan.

[*Archivio di Stato in Milano*; Potenze Estere, Inghilterra, 1497, dicembre.]

"Illustrissimo et excellentissimo signor mio Forsi che tra tante occupatione de V. Ex. non li

[1] In the former letter it is stated that "seven hundred leagues from here he discovered firm land."

sarà molesto intendere come questa Maestà ha guadagnato una parte de Asia senza colpo de spada. In questo regno è uno populare Venetiano chiamato Messer Zoanne Caboto de gentile ingenio, peritissimo dela navigatione, el quale visto che li serenissimi Re prima de Portugallo poi de Spagna hanno occupato isole incognite, deliberò fare uno simile acquisto per dicta Maestà. Ed impetrato privilegi regie, che lutile dominio de quanto el trovasse fossi suo, purchè lo diretto se reserva alla Corona, cum uno piccolo naviglio e XVIII. persone se pose ala fortuna, et partitosi da Bristo porto occidentale de questo regno et passato Ibernia più occidentale, e poi alzatosi verso el septentrione, comenciò ad navigare ale parte orientale, lassandosi (fra qualche giorni) la tramontana ad mano drita, et Navendo assai errato, infine capitoe in terra ferma dove posto la bandera regia, et totto la possessione per questa Alteza, et preso certi segnali, se ne retornato. Al ditto Messer Zoanne, como alienigena et povero, non aria creduto, se li compagni chi sono quasi tutti inglesi, et da Bristo non testificassero ciò che lui dice essero vero. Esso Messer Zoanne ha la descriptione del mondo in una carta, et anche in una sphera solida che lui ha fatto et demostra dove è capitato, et andando verso el levante ha passato assai el paese del Tanais. Et dicono che la è terra optima et temperata, et estimanno che vi nasca el brasilio et le sete, et affermanno che quello mare è coperto de pessi li quali se prendenno non solo cum la rete, ma cum le ciste, essendoli alligato uno saxo ad ciò che la cista se impozi in laqua, et questo io lho oldito narrare ad dicto Messer Zoanne.

"Et ditti Inglesi suoi compagni dicono che portaranno tanti pessi che questo regno non havera più bisogno de Islanda, del quale paese vene una grandissima mercantia de pessi che si chiamanno stochfissi. Ma Messer Zoanne ha posto l'animo ad magior cosa perche pensa, de quello loco occupato andarsene sempre a Riva *Riva* [*sic*] più verso el Levante, tanto chel sia al opposito de una Isola da lui chiamata Cipango, posta in la regione equinoctiale, dove crede che nascano tutte le speciarie del mundo et anche le gioie, et dice che altre volte esso è stato alla Meccha, dove per caravane de luntani paesi sono portate le speciarie, et domandati quelli che le portanno, dove nascono ditte speciarie, respondenno che non sanno, ma che venghono cum questa mercantia da luntani paesi ad casa sua altre caravane, le quale ancora dicono che ad loro sono portate da altre remote regioni. Et fa questo argumento che se li orientali affermanno ali meridionali che queste cose venghono lontano da loro, et cosi da mano in mano, presupposta la rotundità della terra, è necessario che li ultimi le tolliano al septentrione verso l'occidente. Et dicello per modo che non me costando più como costa, ancora io lo credo. Et che è maggior cosa, questa maestà che è savia et non prodiga, ancora lei li presta qualche fede, perchè do poi chel è tornato, li dà asai bona provisione come esso Messer Zoanne me dice. Et a tempo novo se dice che la Maestà prefata armarà alcuni navilii, et ultra li darà tutti li malfatori et andarano in quello paese ad fare una colonia, mediante la quale sperano de fare in Londres magior fondaco de speciarie che sia in Alexandria. Et li principali dell' impresa sono di Bristo, grandi marinari li quali hora che sanno dove andare, dicono che là non è navigatione de più che xv. giorni, ne hanno mai fortuna come abbandonano Ibernia. Ho ancora parlato cum uno Borgognone compagno di Mess. Zoanne chi affermatutto, et vole tornarci perche lo armirante (che già Messer Zoanne cosi se intitula) li ha donato una Isola; et ne ha donato una altra ad un suo barbero da castione Genovese, et intrambi se reputanno Conti, ne Monsignor Larmirante se estima manco de principe. Credo ancora andarano cum questo passaggio alcun poveri frati Italiani li quali tutti hanno promissione de Vescovati. Et per essere io fatto amico di Larmirante, quando volessi andarvi, haverei uno Archivescovato, ma ho pensato chel sia più secura cosa li beneficii quali V. Ex. me ha reservati, et perhò' supplico che quando vacassero in mia absentia la me faccia dare la possessione, ordenando fra questo megio dove bisogna, che non me siano tolti da altri, li quali per essere presenti possono essere più diligenti di me, el quale sono redutto in questo paese ad mangiare ogni pasto de x. o xii. vivande, et stare tre hore ad tavola per volta ogni giorno due volte per amore de' Vostra Excellentia. A la quale humilmente me recomando. *Londoniae xviii. Decem.* 1497.

"Eccelentiae Vestrae,
"Humilissimus Servus,
"Raimundus."

[Dall' *Annuario Scientifico* . . . del 1865, Milano, 1866, p. 700; ma collazionato coll' originale per cura cortese di quella Sovrantendenza.]

[Translation of the Foregoing Letter]

"Perhaps your Excellency, in the press of so much business, will not be disturbed to learn that his

Majesty (Henry VII.) has gained a part of Asia without a stroke of the sword. In this Kingdom is a popular Venetian called Messer Joanne Caboto, a man of considerable ability, most skilful in navigation, who having seen the most serene Kings, first him of Portugal, then him of Spain, that they had occupied unknown islands, thought to make a similar acquisition for his Majesty [Henry VII.]. And having obtained the royal privileges which gave him the use of the land found by him, provided the right of possession was reserved to the Crown, he departed in a little ship from the port of Bristol, in the western part of this kingdom, with eighteen persons, who placed their fortunes with him. Passing Ireland more to the west, and then ascending towards the north, he began to navigate the eastern part of the ocean. Leaving, for some days, the north to the right hand, and having wandered enough, he came at last to main land, where he planted the royal banner, took possession for his Highness [Henry VII.], made certain marks and returned. The said Messer Joanne, as he is a foreigner and poor, would not be believed, if his partners,[1] who are all Englishmen, and from Bristol, did not testify to the truth of what he tells. This Messer Joanne has the representation of the world on a map (in una carta),[2] and also on a globe (in una sphera solida), which he has made, and he shows by them where he arrived, and going towards the East, has passed much *of the country of Tanais.*[3]

---

[1] This may be translated "companions." In all probability they were co-adventurers with Cabot.

[2] This is a very important statement, *infra,* pp. 162, 163.

[3] Dr. Dawson says: "No certain meaning can be given for the word

And they say that the land is fertile and temperate, and think that the red wood (el brasilio) grows there, and the silks, and they affirm that there the sea is full of fish that can be taken not only with nets, but with fishing baskets, a stone being placed in the basket to sink it in the water, and this, as I have said, is told by the said Messer Joanne.

"And the said Englishman, his partners, say that they can bring so many fish that this kingdom will have no more business with Islanda (Iceland), and that from that country there will be a very great trade in the fish which they call stock-fish (stoch-fissi). But Messer Joanne has his thoughts directed to a greater undertaking, for he thinks of going, after this place is occupied, along the coast farther toward the east until he is opposite the island called Cipango, situate in the equinoctial region, where he believes all the spices of the world grow, and where there are also gems. And he says that he was once at Mecca, where from remote countries spices are carried by caravan, and that those carrying them, being asked where those spices grew, said they did not know, but that they came with other merchandise from remote countries to their home by other caravans, and that the same information was repeated by those who brought the spices in turn to them. And he argues that if the oriental people tell to those of the south that these things are brought from places remote from them, and thus

Tanais, but inasmuch as in those days the Tanais was held to separate Europe from Asia, it may be taken as a vague term for Asiatic lands. That the land discovered was supposed to be a part of Asia appears very clearly." "Tanais" is regarded to be synonymous with the river Don. In ancient times it was believed that the "Tanais" was the chief boundary of Asia.—*Geog. of Strabo* (Bohn's edition), vol. ii. p. 224.

from hand to hand, presupposing the rotundity of the earth, it follows that the last carry to the northern, toward the west. And he tells this in a way that makes it quite plain to me, and I believe it. ⁾ And what is a greater thing, his Majesty, who is learned and not prodigal, places confidence in what he says, and since his return, provides well for him, as this Messer Joanne tells me.

"And in the spring he says that his Majesty will arm some ships, and will give him all the criminals, so that he may go to this country and plant a colony there.

"And in this way he hopes to make London a greater place for spices than Alexandria. And the principals of the business are citizens of Bristol, great mariners that now know where to go. They say that the voyage will not take more than fifteen days, if fortune favours them after leaving Ireland. I have talked with a Burgundian,[1] a companion of Messer Joanne, who affirms the same, and who is willing to go, since the Admiral, as Messer Joanne is already styled, has given him an island, and has also given another to his barber, a Genoese, and they regard the two as counts, and my lord, the admiral, the chief. And I believe that some poor Italian friars will go on the voyage, who have the promise of being bishops. And I, being a friend of the admiral, if I wished to go, could have an archbishoprick. . . . ."

[1] Some writers argue that the statement as to the Burgundian and the Genoese indicate that among the eighteen persons on board two were foreigners. This is one of the moot points in connection with the Cabot controversies. It seems to be a matter of no very great importance. The Genoese was probably a barber-surgeon.

It has been assumed from the words, "who having seen the most serene kings, first him of Portugal, then him of Spain, that they had occupied unknown islands, thought to make a similar acquisition for his Majesty," coupled with an extract from a despatch by Don Pedro de Ayala, written in the following year, in which reference is made to visits of John Cabot to Seville and Lisbon, that Cabot proffered his services, first to Spain and next to Portugal without success, and as a last resort came to England. It is quite clear, however, that the words first quoted merely mean that John Cabot knew of the maritime successes achieved by the Portuguese, and that he knew of the Columbus' discovery. It does not follow that Cabot used the exact words, and, in all probability, it was a statement of the writer, which was used for the purpose of leading up to the announcement of Cabot's discovery. Be that as it may, it is certain that the words used by Don Pedro de Ayala, in a communication made to Ferdinand and Isabella, at a time when the second voyage of John Cabot had actually commenced,[1] refer to actual visits made by him to Spain and Portugal. "I have," says Ayala, "seen the map which the discoverer has made, who is another Genoese, like Columbus, and who has been in Seville and in Lisbon, asking assistance for his discoveries." It is not unreasonable to conclude that at some time between the date of his arrival in Bristol in August 1497, after his return from his first voyage, and the date of his departure for his second voyage, Cabot had deemed it expedient to visit both Seville and Lisbon for the purpose of

[1] The despatch was forwarded to Spain in July 1498, *infra*, p. 162.

obtaining the assistance of skilful pilots—men whose scientific knowledge had been supplemented by actual experience.

Dr. Samuel Edward Dawson in his monograph on the Cabot voyages (pp. 59, 60), says: "There resided in London at that time a most intelligent Italian, Raimondo di Soncino, envoy of the Duke of Milan, Ludovico Sforza, one of those despots of the Renaissance who almost atoned for their treachery and cruelty by their thirst for knowledge and love of arts. Him Soncino kept informed of all matters going on at London, and specially concerning matters of cosmography, to which the duke was much devoted. From his letters we are enabled to retrace the momentous voyage of the little *Matthew of Bristol* across the western ocean—not the sunny region of steady trade-winds, by whose favouring influence Columbus was wafted to his destination, but the boisterous reaches of the northern Atlantic —over that "still vexed sea" which shares with one or two others the reputation of being the most storm-tossed region in the world of ocean. Passing Ireland, he first shaped his course north, then, turning westwards and having the pole star on his right hand, he wandered for a long time, and at length he hit upon land. The letter indicates that, after he changed his course, his wandering was continuously westwards, in the same general direction, as far as the regions of the Tanais. . . . The land was good and the climate temperate, and Cabot intended on his next voyage, after occupying that place, to proceed further westwards until he should arrive at the longitude of Japan, which island he thought to be south of his landfall and near the Equator. It should be carefully noted that in all the circumstances on record, which are indisputably referable to this first voyage, nothing has been said of ice,[1] or of any notable extension of daylight. . . . If anything unusual had existed in the length of the day it would have been at its maximum on midsummer day, June 24, the day he (Cabot) made land."

NOTE.—Dr. Dawson's remarks have been specially selected for insertion here, because they lead up to what is probably the most important point in the history of the Cabot voyages of 1497 and 1498. Dr. Dawson's reference to the existence of ice, the length of the day, etc., refer to what purports to be an account of the first voyage of John Cabot, that is, the voyage referred to in the letter of Raimondo di Soncino, dated December 18th, 1497, as it is described in a book, *De Orbe Nova Decades,* Decade iii. Cap. vi., by Pietro Martire (Peter Martyr) of Anghiera, written in 1515.[2]

It is now proposed to set out certain entries and documents which relate exclusively to the second voyage of John Cabot, that is, an expedition con-

[1] He (Sebastian Cabot) "directed his course so far toward the North Pole, that even in the month of *July* he found monstrous heaps of ice swimming on the sea" (Peter Martyr's account, published in 1515, *infra,* p. 172). He (Sebastian Cabot) "set sail in the spring of the year, and they sailed westward till they came in sight of land, in 45 degrees of latitude towards the north, and then went straight northwards until they came into 60 degrees of latitude, where the day is eighteen hours long, and the night is very clear and bright. There they found the air cold, and great islands of ice" (Galvao's account, published in 1550, *infra,* p. 191). " He (Sebastian Cabot) relates how that, in the month of July, it was so cold, and there were such great pieces of ice, that he could get no farther" (Gomara's account, published in 1552, *infra,* pp. 193, 194).
[2] *Infra,* p. 167.

sisting of five vessels which left Bristol in 1498. As to the exact date of the departure of the expedition, the only definite information we have is that it must have been at some time after March 1498, because we find that Cabot was in Bristol for the purpose of receiving the half-yearly payment of his annuity up to the Feast of the Annunciation of the Blessed Virgin (25th March).

⸢The voyage of 1497 was apparently carried out without the slightest assistance in the way of financial aid from the king. It appears, however, that the second expedition was aided by the king to the extent of making certain gifts or loans towards the expenditure.⸥ The following entries relate to payments made under the head of the king's private expenses

"13 Hen. 7. March 22.   £ s. d.
Itm to Lanslot Thirkill of Lond apon a
  Prest for his Shipp going towards
  the new Ilande   .   .   . 20 0 0

Itm delivd to Launcelot Thirkill going
  towards the new Ile in Prest   . 20 0 0

Apr. 1.
Itm to Thomes Bradley and Launcelot
  Thirkill going to the new Ile   . 30 0 0

Apr. 1.
To Jn Carter going to the Newe Ile in
   rew^d . . . . . 0 40 0"
(British Museum Add. MS. No. 7099, fo. 45.)[1]

It does not follow from the above entries that all or any of the persons named went with the expedition.

From a perusal of the following copy of the letters-patent it will be seen that John Cabot only is named therein; having regard to what has been already said as to the legal effect of the clauses in the letters-patent previously granted to John Cabot and his three sons, it may be safely assumed that all rights thereunder were at an end when the letters-patent, which are hereafter transcribed, were granted.

So far as we have proceeded with the narrative, the name of Sebastian Cabot appears only in the first grant of letters-patent, in common with those of his two brothers; it may perhaps be desirable to repeat here that if we are to assume that Sebastian sailed with his father in 1497, simply because his name appears in the letters-patent, then we must assume that the three sons were with their father in the voyage made by him in the *Matthew*. And if the presence of their names in the letters-patent is to be accepted as evidence of their presence in the first voyage, then, by parity of reasoning, the absence of the names in the second letters-patent must equally be conclusive of their absence in the second expedition. But surely, so far as the evidence goes, the presence or the absence of any of the sons

---

[1] These amounts represent a present value of (at a low calculation) two sums of £240 paid to Thirkill, £360 to Bradley and Thirkill, and £24 to Carter. The amounts paid to Thirkill were probably for the compulsory purchase, in other words, for the *impressment*, of his vessel or vessels ("Prest money").

must be treated as pure conjecture.[1] Hereafter, we shall come to a consideration of statements in which the name of Sebastian appears, either with or without his father, in such a way that it is suggested that he (Sebastian) did take an active part in the enterprise of 1497.

COPY of the PETITION of John Cabot for the grant of Letters-Patent for his Second Voyage.

"To the Kinge,—

"Pleas it your highnesse of yor moste noble and habundant g^{a}ce to graunte to John Kabbatto Veneciam y^r g^{a}cious tres patente in due fourme to be made Accordyng to the tenor hereafter ensuying. And he shall contynually praye to god for the ∽ p̃seruacion of your moste noble and Roiall astate longe to endure."

In the Roll of the Privy Seals for February 13. Henry VII., the following entry appears:—

"M^d q̃d tcio die ffebruarii Anno r̃r Henr̃ septimi xiij° ista billa delib̃ata fuit d̃no Canc̃ Angł apud Westm̃ exequend̃."

In this roll the entry of the petition is followed by the following entry (in English) of the grant of the letters-patent to John Cabot on the 3rd of February 1498:—

"Rex to all men to whom thies p̃sentis shall come send gretyng knowe ye that we of o^r g^{a}ce esp̃all and for dyuers causis vs movyng we have geven and graunten and by thies p̃sentes geve and graunte

---

[1] This is the view taken by the best authorities on the history of the Cabotian voyages, namely, Mr. H. Harrisse, Dr. Dawson, and Sir Clements Markham.

to oʳ welbeloved John Kabote Venician sufficiente auctorite and power that he by hymn his Deputie or Deputies sufficient may take at his pleasure vj englisshe Shippes in any Porte or Portę or other place within this our Realme of England or Obeisaunce so that and if the shippes be of the bourdeyn of cc tonnes or vnder wᵗ their apparaill requisite and necessarie for the saueconduct of the said Shippę And theym conuey and lede to the londe and Iles of late founde by the seid John in oure name and by oʳ ~ cōmaundmente Paying for theym and eũy of theym as and if we shuld in or for oʳ owen cause paye and noon otherwise And that the seid John by hym his Deputie or Deputies sufficiente maye take and Receyve into the seid shippes and eũy of theym all suche Maisters Maryners pages and oʲ Subiecte as of their owen free wille woll goo and passe with hym in the same Shippes to the seid londe or Iles wᵗoute any impedymente lett or pturbaunce of any of oʳ Officers or Ministers or Subiectę whatsoeuir they be by theym to the seid John his Deputie or Deputies and all other our seid Subiectę or any of them passing wᵗ the seid John in the seid Shippes to the seid londe or Iles to be doon or suffer to be doon or attempted. Yeving in cōmaundement to all and eũy our Officers Ministers and Subiectę seying or heryng thies our łres patentę withoute any ferther cōmaundement by vs to theym or any of theym to be geven to pfourme and socour the seid John his Deputie and all our seid Subiectę so passyng with hym According to the tenur of thies oʳ łres patentę Any statute Acte or ordenᵃnce to the contᵃrye made or to be made in any wise notwithstanding" (Privy Seals, February 13, Henry VII.).

(An entry of the letters-patent, in Latin, appears in another Roll.)

Copy.

D licencia Caboto.

"R̈ Omibz ad quos t̃c sałtm. Sciatis q̃d nos de g̃ra ñra sp̃ali ac c̃tis consideracõibȝ nos sp̃alĩ mouentibȝ dedim̂ t concessim̃ ac p p̃sentes dam̃ t concedim̂ dilc̃o nob̃ Joh̃i Caboto Veniciario sufficientem potestatem t auctoritatem q̃d ip̃e p se deputatum seu deputatos suos sufficientes sex naues huius regni Augł in quocumq, portu seu portub̃ȝ siue aliis locis infra idem regnũ ñrm aut obedientian̂ ñram sic q̃d dc̃c naues sint portajii ducentoȝ dolioȝ vel infra cum apparatibȝ suis p saluo conducti caȝdem nauiũ ad libitum suũ capiendi t p̂uidendi neausq, illas ad t̂ram t Insulas p ip̃m Joh̃em nupim̃c inuentas conducendi soluendo p eisdem nauibȝ t eaȝ quałt tantum quantum nos solũcm᷎ t non vlt si p ñro negocio t causa capte fuissent t p̂uise. Et q̃d idem Joh̃es p se aut deputatum siue deputatos suos sufficientes om̃es t singulos marinarios Mag̃ros pagettos ac subditos ñros quoscũq, qui ex coȝ lib̃a voluntate secum in dc̃is nauibȝ v̂sus t vsq, t̂ram t Insulas p̃dc̃as tⁿnsire t tⁿnsmeare volũint in naues huiusmodi t eaȝ quamłt cape t recipe possit t valeat absq, impedimento impeticõc seu pturbacõc aliquoȝ Officiarioȝ Ministroȝ seu subditoȝ ñroz quoȝcumq, p ip̃os seu eoȝ aliquem p̃fato Joh̃i deputato siue deputatis suis aut aliis subditis ñris p̃dc̃is seu coȝ alicui in comitiua eiusdem Joh̃is in nauibȝ p̃dc̃is ad t̂ram t Insulas p̃dc̃as tⁿnseuntibȝ inferend̂ aut attemptari p̃mittend̂ Dam᷎ vniũsis t singulis offici-

ariis Ministris ᵗ subditis ñris p̃sentes fras ñras
visuris ᵗ audituris absq̃ vlͭiori mandato p nos eisdem
siue eoᷤ alicui faciend̃ tenore p̃sentiū firmiͭ in
mandatis q̃d eidem Joħi ac deputatis suis p̃dc̃is
aliisq̃ ñris subditis secum vt p̃mittitʳ tⁱnseuntibᷣ in
p̃missis faciend̃ ᵗ exequend̃ fauentes sint consulentes
ᵗ auxiliantes in om̄ibz diligenͭ. In cuius ĩc̃. T̃
R̃ apud Westm̃ ͭcio die ffebruarii.
                            p ip̃m Regem ᵗ de dat ᵗc."
(Fr. Roll. 13 Hen. VII. No. 439, memb. (1) 6.)

EXTRACT from a DESPATCH from Dr. Puebla, the
    Senior Spanish Ambassador to England, to their
    Catholic Majesties, Ferdinand and Isabella of
    Spain, written on or about the 25th of July
    1498.

" El Rey de Inglaterra embio cinco naos armadas
con otro genoves como colono a buscar la Isla de
Brasil y las vicinidades,[1] fueron proveydos por un
año. Dicen que seran venidos para al el Septiembre.
Vista la derrota que llevan allo que lo que buscan
es lo que Vuestras Altozas poseen. El rey me ha
fablado alcunas veces subrello espera haver muy gran
interesse. Creo que no hay de aqui alla cccc leguas."
(Jean et Sebastian Cabot, par Henry Harrise, p.
328.)

[TRANSLATION]

"The King of England sent five armed ships
with another Genoese like Columbus to search for

[1] Desimoni thinks that "vicinidades" should read "septecitades,"
that is, the seven cities (*Intorno a Giovanni Caboto*, Pref. p. 15). Desimoni's opinion is endorsed by Tarducci.

the island of Brasil, and others near it. They were victualled for a year. They say that they will be back in September. By the direction they take, the land they seek must be the possession of your highnesses.[1] The king has sometimes spoken to me about it, and seems to take a very great interest in it. I believe that the distance from here is not four hundred leagues."

There is yet another document which has reached us from the Spanish archives.

COPY DESPATCH from Pedro de Ayala to their Catholick Majesties, dated 25th July 1498.

"Bien creo, Vuestras Altezas an vido, como el rey de Ynglaterra ha fecho armada para descubrir ciertas islas y tierra firme que le han certificado hallaron ciertos que de Bristol armaron año passado para lo mismo. Yo he visto la carta que ha fecho el inventador que es otro genoves como Colon que ha estado en Sevilla y en Lisbona procurando haver quien le ayudasse a esta invencion. Los de Bristol, ha siete años que cada año an armado dos, tres cuatro caravelas para ir a buscar la isla del Brasil y las siete ciudades con la fantasia deste Ginoves. El rey determino de enbiar porque el año passado le truxo certenidad que havian hallado tierra. Del armada que hizo que fueron cinco naos fueron avitallados por un año. Ha venido nueva, la una en

---

[1] It is important that this view of the Spanish ambassador as to the ownership of the land, more especially when we consider the words used by their Catholic Majesties (*ante*, p. 112), should not be lost sight of in considering the probabilities as to the fate of John Cabot's expedition.

que iva un otro Fai (*sic pro* Fray?) Buil aporto en Irlanda con gran tormento rotto el navio.

"El ginoves tiro su camino. Yo, vista la derrota que llevan y la cantitad del camino hallo que es lo que han hallado o buscan lo que Vuestras Altezas poseen, porque es al cabo, que a Vuestras Altezas capo por la convencion con Portugal Sperase seran venidos para el Setiembre. Hago lo saber a Vuestras Altezas. El Rey de Ynglaterra me ha fablado algunas vezes sobre ello. Spero aver muy gran interesse. Creo no ay quatro cientos leguas. Lo le dixe, creya eran las halladas por Vuestras Altezas, y aun le did la una razon, no lo querria. Porque creo, Vuestras Altezas ya tendran aviso de todo lo y asymismo al carta o mapa mundi que este ha fecho, yo no la enbio agora, que aqui la ay, y a mi ver bien falsa por dar a entender, no son de las islas dichas."

(Simancas, Estado, Tratado con Inglaterra. Legaio 2.)

[TRANSLATION]

. . . . . .

"I think your Majesties have already heard that the King of England has equipped a fleet in order to discover certain islands and continents which he was informed some people from Bristol, who manned a few ships[1] for the same purpose last year, had

---

[1] As to this statement, we can come to no other conclusion than that the writer had been misinformed. Lorenzo Pasqualigo says: "The Venetian, our countryman, who went with a ship from Bristol, is returned" (*ante*, p. 139). Raimondo di Soncino says: "He (Cabot) departed in a little ship from the port of Bristol" (*ante*, p. 148).

found. I have seen the map which the discoverer
has made, who is another Genoese, like Columbus,
and who has been in Seville and in Lisbon, asking
assistance for his discoveries. The people of Bristol
have, for the last seven years, sent out every year
two, three, or four light ships (caravelas), in search
of the island of Brazil and the seven cities, according
to the fancy of this Genoese. The king determined
to send out (ships), because, the year before, they
brought certain news that they had found land. His
fleet consisted of five vessels, which carried provisions
for one year. It is said that one of them, in which
one Friar Buil[1] went, has returned to Ireland in great
distress, the ship being much damaged. The Genoese
has continued his voyage. I have seen, on a chart,
the direction which they took, and the distance they
sailed; and I think that what they have found, or
what they are in search of, is what your Highnesses
already possess. It is expected that they will be
back in the month of September. I write this because the King of England has often spoken to me
on this subject, and he thinks your Highnesses will
take great interest in it. I think it is not further
distant than four hundred leagues. I told him that,
in my opinion, the land was already in the possession
of your Majesties; but, though I gave him my reasons,
he did not like them. I believe that your Highnesses
are already informed of this matter, and I do not now
send the chart or *map mundi* which that man has

[1] Harrisse asks, with regard to the suggestion that this person is
the same Friar Buil who went with Columbus to evangelise the natives,
"Might he not be the same?" It is possible that he was brought from
Spain by Cabot. Tarducci refers to "his (Friar Buil's) infamous con-
duct towards Christopher Columbus."—Tarducci's *Life of Christopher
Columbus*, bk. i. ch. xxxi.

made, and which, according to my opinion, is false, since it makes it appear as if the land in question was not the said islands.[1]

(Calendar of State Papers, England and Spain. By G. A. Bergenroth, vol. i., 1485–1509. No. 210, pp. 168-179.)
London, 25th July.
Indorsed: " To their Highnesses, 1498. From Don Pedro Ayala, 25 July '98."
The greater portion of this letter is in cipher, which is deciphered by Almazan, First Secretary of State—Spanish.

By the letters-patent, John Cabot was authorised to take at his pleasure six English ships. The words in the document seem to imply that Cabot was given power to take ships, not exceeding six, from any port in the kingdom, paying to the owners about the same amount that would be paid for them to the owners by the king had they been requisitioned directly by the king for his own use. It was clearly provided that the men who were to join him in the expedition were to act of "their own free will," which is an enactment directed against an exercise of a power of compulsorily manning the ships. But this clause would at that period be practically inoperative, *so far as it was thought necessary to have recourse to the prisons for many of the sailors.* We have seen that "in the spring. . . . his Majesty will arm some ships, and will give him all the criminals, so that he may

[1] This paragraph is so much curtailed in the deciphering made by Almazan, that it was necessary to decipher it again from the original despatch in cipher.

go to this country and plant a colony there,[1] and also that "the king. . . at his (Cabot's) request, has conceded him all the prisoners, except those confined for high treason, to man his fleet."[2] It was probably thought undesirable to make the service compulsory, having regard to the fact that it was an expedition which was setting out, not for the arduous task of finding new lands, but with the peaceful object of founding a colony. They were going "to the londe and Iles of late founde by the seid John."[3]

Therefore, if recourse were had to the prisons it would have been very unwise to make men cross the stormy ocean against their will; motives of prudence would dictate a free pardon, with a view to a willing acquiescence in a scheme of colonisation. Be this as it may, we know for certain that John Cabot sailed for the purpose of taking possession of the land he had previously discovered and taken over on behalf of the English Crown.

EXTRACT from an Anonymous Chronicle, part of Robert Cotton's Collection in the British Museum :—

"In anno 13 Henr. VII. This yere the kyng, at the besy request and supplication of a straunger venisian, wich by a Cocart made hymself expert in knowying of the world, caused the kyng to manne a ship wt vytaill and other necessairies for to seeke an iland wheryn the said straunger surmysed to be grete commodities; w^t which ship, by the kynges grace, so rygged, went 3 or 4 moo owte of Bristowe,

[1] *Ante*, p. 150. [2] *Ante*, p. 140. [3] *Ante*, p. 157.

the said straunger beyng conditor of the said flete, whereyn diuers merchantes as well of London as Bristow adventured goodes and sleight merchandises,[1] which departed from the west cuntrey in the begynning of somer, but to this present moneth came nevir knowledge of their exploit."—MS. Cott. Vitellius, A xiv., f. 173.

'From the date of the sailing of the expedition down to the present time the fate of John Cabot and of his co-adventurers has been enshrouded in mystery. Even his name does not appear as the discoverer of North America until quite a late period. It is true that his name is found associated with that of his son, Sebastian, in connection with the discovery, but the accounts in the various historical works have merely served the purpose of glorifying the memory of the son. To quote Dr. Dawson's expression : "John Cabot had a narrow escape from complete suppression. It was the fortunate preservation of the Spanish, Milanese, and Venetian correspondence which has given a firm basis to his reputation." Tarducci says as follows : " The American, Richard Biddle,[2] the first to give to history a profoundly thought-out book on Sebastian Cabot, wished to blot out completely the rest of that

---

[1] In another MS. chronicle the following words are used :— "Fraught with sleight and grosse merchandises, as coarse cloth, caps, laces, prints, and other trifles." In the Corte Real voyages some evidences of the presence of John Cabot's expedition were met with. " A piece of a broken sword, gilded," and "a native boy had two silver rings in his ear, which, without doubt, seem to have been manufactured in Venice."

[2] In justice to Biddle, it should be stated that he wrote in 1831, long before the documents which prove the position of John Cabot were known to be in existence.

figure which appeared in the background of the picture, and concentrates the spectator's whole attention on the figure of Sebastian, sparkling in the richness of the colouring and drawing. But his efforts were idle, for the more he laboured to persuade the beholder that the figure of Sebastian rose all alone by itself, and had no support from another figure, no relation with it, the more the eye felt drawn to the mysterious figure there in the background of the picture, and to the ear came more sensibly distinct his question, 'And I then?'"

"In these last years the truth has finally triumphed, and the documents discovered, though few in number, yet sufficient for the purpose, have restored to John the light that was due to him, and drawn his figure out of the shade and placed it in full view. If the love of my subject does not veil my judgment, it seems to me that one of the very first places in the history of discoveries belongs to John Cabot. For without any impulse or guidance from others, by the mere force of his will and strength of his enthusiasm, he raised himself above the common herd of navigators for commerce and wealth."

CHAPTER V

In passing from the contemporary records, consisting of letters-patent, ambassadors' despatches, etc., in which it is clearly set forth that John Cabot was the moving spirit, the organiser, and equipper in connection with the two "Cabot voyages" of 1497 and 1498—in passing from these to entries made by foreign, that is, Spanish, Portuguese, and Italian historians and chroniclers, we must state here that nothing of importance is known about Sebastian Cabot, from the date of the entry of his name in the letters-patent of 1496 until the year 1512, beyond the fact that he was a maker of maps and charts. In the year 1512 we find that he made a map of Gascony and Guyenne for the English Government, for which he was paid twenty shillings. We shall presently see that in the same year (1512) Sebastian Cabot went to Spain, and subsequently settled at Seville, and accepted employment under the Spanish Government.

There are several accounts which ascribe the discovery of America to Sebastian Cabot. Harrisse says: "The first is Peter Martyr's, written in 1515, in Spain, which, from his frequent intercourse and personal intimacy with Sebastian Cabot, we must believe to have been derived from the latter's own lips."[1] This appears to be the reasonable and almost the only conclusion we can arrive at; it should be borne in mind, however, that this view of the matter is not absolutely free from doubt, and therefore we should pause before arriving at an opinion hostile to Sebastian until we have had an opportunity of reviewing the whole of the evidence. Pietro Martire d'Anghiera, generally called Peter Martyr, who was born in 1455, belonged to a distinguished family in Milan. He went to Rome in 1477, and we find that while he remained in that city he was much esteemed as a literary student by some of the most distinguished men of that period. He went to Spain in 1487, as a member of the suite of the Spanish Ambassador, and subsequently obtained the situation of instructor of the royal pages, which, while giving him a competence, also enabled him to apply himself to literary pursuits. He was afterwards called to more active duties, being sent on missions to Venice and Egypt. On his return he was elected prior of the Cathedral Church of Granada, which, with other posts, he held until his death, which took place in 1526. He was the author of several important works (*Biographie Universalle, Ancienne et Moderne*, etc., tome deuxieme).

[1] "Furthermore, it was published at Alecala, whilst Cabot was frequenting the Court." Martyr speaks of Sebastian as his "Concurialis," the correct interpretation of which, according to d'Avezac, is that Cabot "is here with me at Court" (*Revue Critique d'Histoire et de Litterature, Premier Semestre*, p. 265). Eden, in his translations, interpreted the word to mean that Sebastian Cabot was associated with Martyr as a member of the "Supreme Council of the Indies." Herrera has given a complete list of the members of the Council, but the name of Cabot is not found therein.

ACCOUNT given by Pietro Martire (Peter Martyr) of Anghiera.

"Scrutatus est eas glaciales oras Sebastianus quidam Cabotus genere Venetus, sed a parentibus in Britanniam insulam tendentibus (uti moris est Venetorum, qui commercii causa terrarum omnium sunt hospites) transportatus pene infans. Duo is sibi navigia propria pecunia in Britannia ipsa instruxit, et primo tendens cum hominibus tercentum ad septentrionem, donec etiam Julio mense vastas repererit glaciales moles pelago natantes, et lucem fere perpetuam, tellure tamen libera gelu liquefacto. Quare coactus fuit, uti ait, vela vertere et Occidentem sequi: tetenditque tamen ad meridiem, littore sese incurvante, ut Herculei freti latitudinis fere gradus equarit: ad Occidentemque profectus tantum est, ut Cubam insulam a leva, longitudine graduum pene parem, habuerit. Is ea littora percurrens, quæ Bacallaos appelavit, eosdem se reperisse aquarum, sed lenes, delapsus ad Occidentem, ait, quos Castellani, meridionales suas regiones ad navigantes, inveniunt, ergo non modo verisimilius, sed necessario concludendu est, vastos inter vtranque ignotam hactenus tellurem iacere hiatus, qui viam prœbeant aquis ab Oriente cadentibus in Occidentem. Quas arbitror impulsu cœlorum circulariter agi in gyrum circa terræ globum; non autem Demogorgone anhelante vomi, absorberiq, vt nonnulle senserunt: quod influxu & refluxu forsan assentire daretur. Bacallaos Cabottus ipse terras illas appellavit, eo quod in eorum pelago tantam repererit magnorum quorumdam piscium, tinnos æmulantium, sic vocatorum ab indignenis, multitudinem, ut etiam illi navigia interdum detardarent. Earum regionum homines pellibus tantum coopertos reperiebat, rationis haudquaquaq expertes. Ursorum in esse regionibus copiam ingentem refert, qui et ipsi piscibus vescantur. Inter densa nanque piscium illorum agmina sese immergunt ursi, et singulos singuli complexos, unquibusque inter squamas immissis in terram raptant et comedunt. Propterea minime noxios hominibus ursos esse ait. Orichalcum in plærisque locis se vidisse apud incolas prædicant. Familiarem habeo domi Cabotum ipsum et contubernalem interdum" (Petri Martyris ab Angleria, *De Rebus Oceanicis et Orbe novo*, dec. iii. lib. vi.).

Peter Martyr's work was translated into English by Richard Eden, and, inasmuch as this translation has been dealt with in various ways by various subsequent writers, it is desirable to give a few particulars as to Eden and his works.

Richard Eden, translator, was born in Herefordshire about 1521, and studied at Queen's College, Cambridge, 1535–44, under Sir Thomas Smith;[1] held a position in the treasury 1544–46, and married in the following year. He was private secretary to Sir W. Cecil, 1552. He published, in 1553, a translation of Münster's *Cosmography*. Next year he obtained a place in the English treasury of the Prince of Spain, and in 1555 published his great work, *The Decades of the Newe Worlde, or West India*, a collection of travels of great interest, translated from many sources, part of which, *The Travels*

---

[1] Eden says, "that the ryght worshypfull and of singular learnynge in all sciences, Syr Thomas Smyth, in my tyme the floure of the University of Cambridge, and some tyme my tutor."

of *Lewes Vertomannus*, 1503, is reprinted in Hakluyt's *Voyages* (iv. 547, ed. 1811). Thereupon he was cited by Thomas Watson, Bishop of Lincoln, before Bishop Gardiner, for heresy, but escaped with the loss of his office. Eden died in 1576, having achieved great reputation as a scholar and man of science.[1]

The following translation of that portion of Peter Martyr's work, which purposes to relate to the Cabot voyage, is taken from—

The Decades of the newe worlde of West India, conteynyng the nauigations and conquestes of the Spanyardes, with the particular description of the moste ryche and large landes and Ilandes lately founde in the West Ocean perteynyng to the inheritaunce of the Kinges of Spayne. In the which the diligent reader may not only consyder what commoditie may hereby chaunce to the hole Christian world in tyme to come, but also learne many secreates touchynge the lande, the sea, and the starres, very necessary to be knowe to al such as shal attempte any navigation, or otherwise have delite to beholde the strange and woonderfull woorkes of God and nature. Written in the Latine tounge by Peter Martyr of Angleria, and translated into Englysshe by Richard Eden. Londini, In ædibus Guilhelmi Powell, Anno 1555. "These northe seas haue byn searched by one Sebastian Cabot, a Venetian borne,[2] whom beinge yet but in maner an

[1] *Dict. of Nat. Biog.*, vol. xvi. pp. 359, 360.
[2] This statement must not be hastily accepted as one which is entirely free from doubt. See *infra*, pp. 177–181.

infante, his parentes caryed with them into Englande, hauyng occasion to resorte thether for trade of marchandies, as is the maner of the Venetians too leaue no parte of the worlde unsearched to obteyne richesse. He therfore furnisshed two shippes in England at his owne charges: And fyrst with three hundreth men, directed his course so farre toward the north pole, that euen in the mooneth of July he founde monstrous heapes of Ise swimming on the sea, and in maner continuall day lyght. Yet sawe he the lande in that tracte, free from Ise, whiche had byn molten by heate of the sunne. Thus seyng suche heapes of Ise before hym he was enforced to tourne his sayles and folowe the weste, so coastynge styll by the shore, that he was thereby brought so farre into the southe by reason of the lande bendynge so muche southward that it was there almoste equall in latitude with the sea cauled Fretum Herculeum[1] hauynge the north pole eleuate in maner in the same degree. He sayled lykewise in this tracte so farre towarde the weste, that he had the Ilande of Cuba [on] his lefte hande in maner in the same degree of longitude. As he traueyled by the coastes of this greate lande (which he named Baccallaos) he sayth that he found the like course of the waters toward the west, but the same to runne more softely and gentelly than the swifte waters whiche the Spanyardes found in their nauigations southeward. Wherefore, it is not onely more lyke to bee trewe, but ought also of necessitie to been concluded, that betwene both the landes hetherto vnknowen, there shulde bee certeyne great open places whereby the waters shulde thus continually passe from the Easte

[1] The Straits of Gibraltar.

into the weste: which waters I suppose to bee
dryuen about the globe of the earthe by the vn-
cessaunt mouynge and impulsion of the heauens:
and not to bee swalowed vp and cast owt agayne by
the breathynge of Demogorgon [1] as sume haue imagined bycause they see the seas by increase and
decrease, to flowe and reflowe. Sebastian Cabot him
selfe, named those landes Baccalaos, bycause that in
the seas therabout he founde so great multitudes of
certeyne bigge fysshes much lyke vnto tunies (which
the inhabitantes caule Baccalaos) that they sumtymes
stayed his shippes. He found also the people of
those regions couered with beastes skynnes: Yet
not without thi use of reason. He saythe also that
there is greate plentie of beares in those regions,
which vse to eate fysshe. For plungeinge theym
seluces into the water where they perceu a multitude
of these fysshes to lye, they fasten theyr clawes in
theyr scales, and so drawe them to lande and eate
them. So that (as he saith) the beares beinge thus
satissfied with fysshe, are not noysom to men. He
declareth further, that in many places of these
regions, he sawe great plentie of laton amonge the
inhabitantes. Cabot is my very frende, whom I vse
famylierly, and delyte to haue hym sumtymes keepe
mee company in myne owne house."

In Peter Martyr's account of the alleged voyage
of Sebastian Cabot, we have a part of the foundation
for the statement made by successive historians, that
he (Sebastian) was the discoverer of America, thus
ignoring the name of John Cabot altogether. And
it may be safely asserted that this belief would never
have been dispelled had the archives of foreign

[1] The spirit or ruler of the waters.

countries never have yielded up evidence sufficient to disprove it. Let us review Martyr's statement from a rational point of view. What materials were at the historian's disposal? He and Sebastian Cabot were on very familiar terms, and, according to Martyr's own statement, Cabot was a frequent visitor. It may be fairly assumed that they also met elsewhere and had many opportunities for conversation. And it should be remembered, that exactly at this period Martyr was engaged in writing and publishing the work in which the reference to the friendship which subsisted between himself and Sebastian is given. Tarducci aptly remarks that Martyr, "in his account, joins the information concerning Cabot with the fact that he has Cabot a guest in his house. Thus [says Tarducci] it is clear, natural, undoubtable, that he had his information from Sebastian's own mouth, for it cannot be supposed that with such opportunity as he had of learning the truth from the very lips of one who was at his side, at his table, at his conversation, he, an historian, would fail to question him *and learn the truth from him.*"

The italics have been added to draw the reader's attention to the exact words that are used. It is not at all certain, supposing Sebastian did tell Martyr exactly what the former relates, that the statement recorded by Martyr is "the truth"! It is now a matter placed beyond conjecture—that John Cabot was the discoverer of North America. Martyr and his friends apparently knew nothing of John. We now know that there were two early voyages in which John acted the parts of organiser, equipper, and leader; Martyr knew of only one voyage:

and it seems also certain that the facts related by him apply to neither of the two voyages of John Cabot, that is, of 1497 and of 1498. At anyrate, it requires a great deal of "faith" to enable us to accept Martyr's description as being a true account of either voyage. Sebastian Cabot, either by actual statements of what purported to be fact or by *suppressio veri*, had led the Spaniards to regard him as the discoverer of the territory now known as the continent of North America. And further, we are justified in concluding that he took no steps to enlighten them as to the part his father took in the enterprise. As a *soi-disant* successful *voyageur*, he would be *persona grata* to a man who was gathering information about the discovery of land in the Atlantic Ocean with a view to insert it in a book. And he who was regarded, rightly or wrongly, as the discoverer of an immense territory, would be received as a man of light and learning, a great navigator, an important personage. The popular mind would accept as positive evidence of the truth of his position as a discoverer, the fact—and a fact it undoubtedly was—that he was a highly-skilled constructor of charts and of maps. In all probability he was unusually clever in this particular direction. This is a circumstance which should be borne in mind by those who wish to form an accurate judgment in matters relating to the history of John and Sebastian Cabot. It was due to his knowledge of map-making—or at least that was probably the reason—that he was selected to join the army which King Henry VIII. sent to Spain, and which landed at Passages, near San Sebastian, in June 1512. It is said that Henry VIII. was anxious to obtain the title of "Most Christian King" from the pope, which title had been annexed to the Crown of France, and that King Ferdinand of Spain, being in possession of the knowledge that Henry coveted the title, induced him to join in a league against the King of France. Be that as it may, it is clear that the fitting out of the English expedition had the effect of taking Sebastian Cabot to Spain in the year 1511, and that he thereupon made up his mind to settle in that country. In 1515 he was appointed a pilot to the King of Spain, under his Majesty's pilot-major. All these circumstances tend to show that Sebastian would have been received everywhere with the greatest favour, and there existed no reason why anyone should have expressed the slightest distrust of the current story that he, and he alone, was the discoverer of a vast country. Peter Martyr knew of the fish which abounded in the seas adjacent to the territory of Baccalaos. Consequently we may readily conclude that he would have accepted all Sebastian Cabot's statements without the slightest idea that there was any necessity for further inquiry; in all probability every hint from Sebastian was swallowed with avidity. No man at that time was better able to supply Peter Martyr's demand for materials for his proposed publication. If either a man or a book may be drawn upon in support of the subject a man is engaged upon, the tendency is to accept what is said without inquiring into the truth, and this applies more particularly when the information adds either details or confirmation to some theory or preconceived idea of the author. History, in reality, frequently records the thought tendencies of the writer rather than the facts of the case; once an idea obtains a firm impression on the mind, it is difficult to dislodge it,—in many cases it is useless to make the attempt. Peter Martyr, in good faith, would probably have recorded, without the·slightest hesitation, whatever the supposed discoverer of America had vouchsafed to tell him. In 1515 Peter Martyr says : " Cabot is here with us, looking daily for ships to be furnished for him to discover this hid secret of nature," which evidently refers to an idea Sebastian had formed that there was a north-west passage, of which some account will be given later in the narrative. The historian must have implicitly believed that " this hid secret of nature" was something more than a conjecture, and, as a true son of mother church, he sent a communication on the subject to Rome. No blame is to be imputed to the historian; he, in common with others, never grasped the idea that it is absolutely necessary for a recorder of events which are not either before his actual view, or brought within his own actual knowledge, to inquire carefully into the matter in all its bearings before placing it on record *as a fact.*

We will now proceed to consider some of the statements contained in Peter Martyr's work. He speaks of Sebastian Cabot as " a Venetian borne, whom being yet but in maner an infante, his parentes caryed with them into Englande, hauyng occasion to resorte thether for trade of merchandies," etc.[1] All the probabilities seem to point out that he was born in Venice, but there is no certainty that he was born there ; on the other hand, Richard Eden, in his translation of Ramusio's work, opposite the words " a Venetian borne," has a marginal note as follows :—" Sebastian Cabote tould me that

[1] Richard Eden's translation.

he was borne in Brystowe, and that at iiii. yeare ould he was carried with his father to Venice, and so returned agayne into England with his father after certayne years, whereby he was thought to have been born in Venice." This statement is the sole authority for the allegation that Sebastian Cabot was born in Bristol. Other statements have been made to the effect that he was an Englishman, and these have been accepted as corroborating the communication which Eden says Sebastian made to him with regard to his birthplace. Tarducci supposes that Eden had the information from Cabot, "but from lack of attention or other cause he misunderstood his words, and gave them a meaning quite opposite to the true." "Let us [says Tarducc] compare the words of Eden with those of Peter Martyr, and we shall see that this supposition is well founded." And he goes on to suggest that if, in Eden's statement, "Venice" and "Bristol" are transposed, the two accounts agree. D'Avezac, a writer who has devoted much time to the subject, is not satisfied with Eden's statement, nay, he seems to hint that he has been guilty of intentional misrepresentation. He says: "Nous croyons raisonnable de soupçonner un qui pro quo dans l'esprit aventureux du compilateur, à qui probablement Cabot avait dit en réalité, comme à tous les autres, qu'il était né à Venise, et avait été, dés son jeune âge (quattre ans expressément cette fois), amené a Bristol par son père,"—and he afterwards suggests that Eden wrote in bad faith, "Il n'y aura qu'une falsification fantaisiste de plus à porter au compte de Richard Eden." Dr. Justin Winsor, referring to the question as to where Sebastian was born, says: "There is a dispute over his birthplace more perplexing than that which concerns his father's nativity. Sebastian told Eden that he was born in Bristol, England, whither his father had come not long before. On the other hand, he assured Contarini[1] that he was a native of Venice, —a statement now accepted by Deane, Tarducci, and most of the other authorities." Having regard to all the circumstances, it is a better and a safer course not to raise the question as to the exact words he may have used in speaking to persons of his birthplace; let us loyally accept the statements,—whether they name either Venice or Bristol, —and, without any attempt to bespatter those who have left us written records of what purports to be Sebastian's statements, let us apply to each the question : "*Is this capable of proof?*"

It is as strange as it is true, that not one man in a thousand understands that it is necessary to be guided in historical matters by rules of evidence which are as clearly defined as are those of the courts of law. In this case it is certain that Eden knew Sebastian Cabot. And it is equally clear that Peter Martyr knew him, because he says: "Cabot is my very friend," and he also says that he "sometimes keeps me company in mine own house." Here we are brought face to face with the testimonies of two friends of the man whose birthplace is the subject of dispute, and each tells a different story.[2] Now it must be remembered

[1] *Infra*, p. 220.
[2] Gaspar Contarini, in the course of a conversation with Sebastian, was told by the latter with regard to his birthplace as follows :—" I was born in Venice, but was brought up in England."

that in those days there were no convenient registers to apply to for information in cases of necessity. We must conclude, then, that unless some evidence of an affirmative character can be found in confirmation of either of the two statements, we must reject both as matters which, at least for the present, are not capable of proof. These contradictory statements have produced a rather anomalous state of things. Two cities contend for the honour of Sebastian Cabot's birth. It is solemnly recorded in Bristol that he was born in the city, and it is likewise recorded in Venice that he was born there. Neither record is of more than recent date, neither purports to be based upon any evidence other than that which was derived from Sebastian's uncorroborated statement. To the gentlemen of Bristol who have quite recently placed a tablet in a public position in that city, stating as *a fact*, not as a conjecture, that Sebastian was born in Bristol, it is desirable to point out that, until positive evidence is forthcoming to prove where Sebastian was born, the matter must be relegated to the realm of conjecture. If we are to accept Sebastian's own statement that he was born in Bristol, then it follows that we must accept his several statements that he was born in Venice. This is the *reductio ad absurdum* of the position taken up by those who are anxious to argue that we ought to accept the statement made by Sebastian to Eden. Sir Clements R. Markham, K.C.B., the President of the Royal Geographical Society, writing with reference to this disputed point, says: "His (Sebastian Cabot's), own words can count for nothing under the circumstances."

What is the value of a man's own unsupported evidence as to his birthplace? The prudent man will say that it is not justifiable to state *as a fact* that a man was born in a certain place, when the proof rests solely on an unsupported statement of his own, it being well known that he has stated on other occasions, when it suited his purpose, that he was born elsewhere.

What are the deductions to be drawn from Peter Martyr's statement that Sebastian Cabot "furnished *two* ships in England at his own charges, and sailed with 300 men," etc.? We have abundant testimony to prove that in the first expedition of John Cabot, in 1497, he had one ship only, namely, the *Matthew*, of Bristol, and that the second expedition, in 1498, of which John Cabot was the organiser and leader, consisted of five vessels.

Now, it should be remembered that it is *possible* that Sebastian Cabot may never have made the statements in the exact form in which they appear in Peter Martyr's book; but, on the other hand, we shall subsequently meet with what appears to be a strong corroboration that Cabot did say that he was the leader of an expedition consisting of two ships. "When my father died in that time when news was brought that Don Christopher Columbus, Genoese, had discovered the coasts of India, whereof was great talk in the Court of King Henry VII., who then reigned. . . . I thereupon caused the King to be advertised of my device, who immediately commanded two caravels to be furnished with all things," . . . etc. (Ramusio's *Mantuan Gentleman*, *infra* p. 202). Ramusio, who says that he was in correspondence with Sebastian Cabot, states elsewhere as follows :—

"Fu [Caboto] menato da suo padre in Inghilterra, da poi la morte del quale trouandosi ricchissimo, et di grande animo, deliberò si come hauea fatto Cristoforo Colombo, voler anchor lui scoprire qualche nuoua parte del mondo, et à sue spese armò duoi nauili." "He was taken by his father to England, where, after the latter's death, finding himself extremely rich, and being high-spirited, he determined, as Christopher Columbus had done, to discover some new part of the world, and at his own cost he equipped two ships" (Ramusio, *Raccolta*, 1565, vol. iii. p. 35).

What deduction is to be drawn if we believe that Sebastian said that *after his father had died* the news came of the discovery by Columbus, and that he (Sebastian) approached the king (Henry VII.) with a view to the fitting out of an expedition? Looking at all the circumstances, it is impossible to come to any other conclusion than this, that he deliberately told a lie. From this position escape is almost impossible. In order to ascertain whether Sebastian was a man who would be guilty of duplicity, it will be necessary to inquire into the truth of certain other matters—more particularly as to his intrigues with the Council of Ten of Venice[1]—with a view to guide us to a just decision as to the possibility of his having wilfully misled both Peter Martyr and Ramusio.

It may be as well to insert here the words used by Marc-Antonio Contarini, in a statement read before the Senate in Venice in 1536. "Sebastian Cabot, the son of a Venetian, who repaired to

[1] *Infra*, p. 214.

England on galleys from Venice with the notion of going in search of countries, . . . obtained two ships from Henry, King of England, the father of the present Henry, who has become a Lutheran, and even worse, navigated with 300 men, until he found the sea frozen. . . . He was obliged, therefore, to turn back without having accomplished his object, with the intention, however, of renewing the attempt when the sea was not frozen. But upon his return he found the king dead, and his son[1] caring little for such an enterprise" (*Raccolta Colombiana*, pt. iii. vol. i. p. 137).

This statement is useful in so far as it proves that the popular and unquestioned idea at that period was, that Sebastian Cabot, a Venetian,[2] discovered the continent of North America, in an expedition of discovery in which two ships only were engaged. This helps us to form a conclusion that, whatever else in the way of voyages it may possibly relate to, it certainly applies neither to the voyage in 1497, nor to the expedition of 1498.

With regard to the course which it is alleged Sebastian covered during the voyage, the following reference by Stevens, in his *Historical and Geographical Notes* (p. 35), is well worth considering. Steven's says : "The remark of Peter Martyr, in

[1] Henry VIII. So far as this statement may be considered to relate to the voyages of John Cabot in 1497 and 1498, or to either, it is meaningless.

[2] There are reasons for believing that on his first arrival in Spain, in other words, at the period when he left the expedition which he had accompanied from England for the purpose of taking employment under the Spanish Crown, he was regarded as an Englishman, which, in the truest sense, and putting aside the question of his birthplace, he really was. It seems almost certain that his appearance, his language, his surroundings, would combine to stamp him as an Englishman.

1515, about Cabot's reaching on the American coast the latitude of Gibraltar, and finding himself then on a meridian of longitude far enough to leave Cuba on his west, is simply absurd, dilemmatise it as you will. Such a voyage *would have landed him near Cincinnatti.*"

Two accounts are given by Ramusio; in the one (see preface to vol. iii.) he says that Cabot navigated the north coast, from Baccalaos to the latitude of 67°, and in the other 67½°. Inasmuch as he gives the last-named latitude on what purports to be Sebastian's own communication to him, it is desirable to give the quotation as follows :—" And he told me that having sailed a long time west and by North beyond these islands unto the latitude of 67½° under the North Pole, and, on the 11th of June, finding the sea yet open without any kind of impediment, he thought surely by that way to have passed on towards the Eastern Cathay, *and would have done so if the malice of the master and insurgent mariners had not forced him to turn back.*"[1]

[1] Ramusio, vol. iii. Harrisse (pp. 144, 145) says: "Henry VII., on March 19th, 1501, issued new letters-patent, embracing the privileges heretofore conceded to the Cabots, but this time the grantees were Richard Warde, Thomas Ashehurst, and John Thomas, of Bristol, and João Fernandez, Francisco Fernandez, and João Gonzales, of the Azores. On December 9th, 1502, letters-patent were again granted to several of these parties, with whom was associated in the privilege [*i.e.* the monopoly of trade, first for ten, then for forty years] and expedition, *Hugh Elliot, of Bristol.*"

At the time the letters-patent of the year 1502 were granted there resided in Bristol a merchant and adventurer named Nicholas Thorne. Robert Thorne, a son of Nicholas Thorne, who was residing in Seville in the year 1527, made a communication to Henry VIII. in which the following words occur :—" I reason, that as some sicknesses are hereditarous, and come from the father to the sonne, so this inclination or desire of this discoverie I inherited of my father, which with another merchant of Bristowe, named Hugh Elliot, were the discoverers of *newe found lands*, of the which there is no doubt, as now

Ramusio also narrates what the "Mantuan gentleman" told him as to Sebastian's description of his navigation, as follows :—" I began to navigate towards the west, expecting not to find land until I came to Cathay, whence I could go on to the Indies. But at the end of some days I discovered that the land tended northwards, to my great disappointment; so I sailed along the coast to see if I could find some gulf where the land turned, until I reached the height of 56° under our pole, but finding that the land turned eastward, I despaired of finding an opening. I turned to the right to examine again to the southward, always with the object of finding a passage to the Indies, and I came to that which is

plainly appeareth, *if the marriners would then have been ruled and folowed their pilot's mind*, the lands of the West Indies, from whence all the gold commeth, had beene ours."

Thorne communicated with King Henry VIII. for the purpose of advising the monarch to take steps to find a north-west passage to the Indies. Is the statement by Ramusio, that Sebastian Cabot was "forced" to turn back from some enterprise by insurgent mariners, and that made by Thorne as to what might have happened if the mariners had followed the wishes of the pilot, merely a coincidence? Of course, there may have been two voyages in which the pilot's wishes were set at nought by unruly mariners. On the other hand, is it not quite possible that Sebastian Cabot was the pilot of an expedition made in pursuance of either the letters-patent of 1501, or those of 1502? Thorne says that his father and Hugh Elliot were the "discoverers" of newe found lands; in the circumstances, is it not possible that they were on board a vessel of which Sebastian Cabot was the pilot, and that they actually succeeded in discovering "newe found lands," which was a general description used by successive explorators when they either sighted or took possession of land hitherto unknown. If this theory is worthy of consideration, then we may not unfairly suggest that what purport to be Sebastian Cabot's statements to the historians must be considered to apply to a voyage of discovery actually undertaken by him, as pilot, at some time after the grant of letters-patent of 1501. There seems to be no other mode of making anything of his statements; if, however, this theory is held to be unreasonable, we are then driven to say that Sebastian evolved the story from his fertile imagination.

now called Florida. Being in want of victuals, I was obliged to return thence to England."[1]

There is yet an extraordinary statement to be considered, namely, that Sebastian Cabot invented a name for a portion of the region which he alleged he had discovered. " Sebastian Cabot himself named those lands Baccalaos, because that in the seas thereabout he found so great multitudes of certain big fishes much like unto tunies (which the inhabitants call Baccalaos), that they sometimes stayed his ships." As to the origin of the word, Mr Harrisse says : " Baccalarius, baccallao, backljaw, Kabbljaw," in the *Bibliographia critica portugueza*, Porto, 1873–75, vol. i. pp. 373, 374. In Littré's opinion (voc. Cabilland), " Kabeljaauw " is a derivative " par renversement " of " bacailhaba," which is the Basque word for codfish, " whence the Spanish ' bacalao,' and the Flemish 'bakkeljaid.'" King Ferdinand of Aragon, at that time regent of Castile, wrote to Sebastian Cabot on the 12th September 1512, and in his letter he uses the word "Bacallos." The paragraph in which the word occurs reads as follows: " Sabeis que en Burgos os hablaron de mi parte Conchillos i el Obp. de Palencia sobre la navegacion á los *Bacallos* e ofrecistes servirnos." Dr. S. E. Dawson says : "The same writer [Pietro Martire d'Anghièra] states that [Sebastian] Cabot himself named a portion of the great land he coasted Baccalaos, because of the quantity of fish, which was so great that they hindered the sailing of his ships, and that these fishes were called baccalaos by the natives. This statement has given rise to much dispute. . . . A very exhaustive note on the word will be found at

[1] Ramusio, vol i. p. 414 ; *infra*, p. 203.

page 131 of Dr. Bourinot's *Cape Breton*. He gives the Micmac name as 'pegoo,' on the authority of Dr. Rand. Richard Brown gives it as 'pakshoo' in his *History of Cape Breton*. Lescarbot gave it in his time as 'apegé.' Kohl derives the word, by a parallel evolution, from the Dutch word 'Kabeljaaw,' but, as pointed out by Dr. Bourinot, the word is Basque. It may be called Iberian, for the Basque 'bacailaba' became in Spanish 'baccalao' and in Portuguese 'bacalhas,' and this last name is found on Pedro Reinel's map of 1505.[1] It is not likely that Cabot, in an English ship with an English crew, would have given the country an Iberian name. The probability is that the Portuguese, who flocked upon the coast after the Corte Reals, first gave the name 'Codfish land' to the country; and Cabot's claim to the name is no more true than his claim to having fitted out the expedition at his own expense. I have read somewhere in the books that Sebastian Cabot was a great sailor and also a great liar, but I think Richard Eden's naïve account of his last illness is the best explanation of his very comprehensive claims." The same author, in an appendix to the *Monograph*, from which the above quotation was taken, says: "*Diez-Dictionary of the Romance Languages* gives a clue to Kohl's etymology. He cites the word under the old French form 'cabeliau' from Dutch 'Kabeljaauw,' 'whence, too' (he adds), 'perhaps with a reference to 'baculus,' the Spanish 'bacalao,' Basque 'bacailaba,' Venetian, Piedmontese 'bacala.' When an etymology seems so simple as that of bacalao

---

[1] This is an extremely important item of evidence, and one which must not be overlooked, when Sebastian's statement is placed before us for an impartial and unbiassed criticism.

(stock-fish), from the Latin 'baculus,' a stick, it is unnecessary to go so far afield as to import such a word as 'Kabeljaauw' into the question. There is a precise parallel in the Spanish *caballo*, from the low Latin 'cabullus,' and the Basques no doubt borrowed the Spanish word and spelled it in their own way. It is a common saying concerning the Basques, that they write Solomon and pronounce Nebuchadnezzar! so difficult is their language."

Inasmuch as there is no evidence of any sort or kind at present forthcoming to prove that Baccalaos is an Indian word, it seems only a reasonable conclusion that Peter Martyr's statement is incapable of proof. Further, it is so very improbable that either John Cabot, an Italian who probably understood and spoke English, or Sebastian, his son (assuming for the convenience of argument that he was with his father in 1497), who may have had a knowledge of both English and Italian, would apply such a name to the districts from whence the Basques and the Portuguese obtained their supplies of fishes. Dr. Justin Winsor[1] says: "In Peter Martyr's account of the early voyages, it is said that Cabot found the word Baccalaos used in this coast, or, at least, that is one interpretation of his Latin. As this term was one common on the Biscayan shores for stock-fish or cod, it might be deemed conclusive evidence of a previous acquaintance by the Basques with this coast, if Martyr's language would bear such an interpretation in the opinion of all scholars, but it will not. . . ."

With our present knowledge of John Cabot's

[1] *The Cabot Controversies and the Right of England to North America.* Cambridge [America], 1896.

voyage of 1497, it is difficult to reconcile Sebastian's statements in any way whatsoever. If, as has been suggested, the attempt to find the "open places" refers to the theory as to the existence of a north-west passage to India, it proves conclusively that the account of the voyage given by Peter Martyr does not refer to the voyage of 1497. That Sebastian Cabot, at a much later period, believed that there existed a "north-west passage" cannot be doubted. But it is equally certain that John Cabot could not have entertained such an idea, because he sailed to find a part of Asia; and it is obviously apparent that he fully expected not to find any land—other than the Mythical Islands—between Europe and what he believed to be the land of the "Grand Khan," in other words, the *Asiatic territory*. Sebastian Cabot's idea as to the "open places" was probably founded upon a theory which, in the year 1515, the date of Martyr's publication, and prior thereto, was held by many to the effect that there was a south-westerly route to India by way of the Strait, now called after Magellan. It was in or about the year 1514 that Magellan began to think that the circumnavigation of the globe was a feasible undertaking. Schöner's globe, of the year 1515, shows an opening or strait, which indicates a connection between the Southern Atlantic and an expanse of water beyond the land already discovered. Its appearance on this globe might readily lead persons to believe that the strait used by Magellan in his voyage of circumnavigation had already been navigated. There seems, however, so far as one can ascertain, no proof of any navigation, other than that of Magellan. On looking back and reviewing all the circumstances connected with the Cabot voyage, it seems necessary to repeat that Peter Martyr knew of only one voyage, and that the unsatisfactory and apparently unreliable evidence which appears in Martyr's book—so far as it purports to make Sebastian the discoverer of North America — must disappear in the light which is afforded us by the contemporary writers who obtained their information from, or in connection with, the undoubted discoverer, namely, the never-to-be-forgotten John Cabot.

. . . .

The next entry of importance—treating them in order of date—is found in the Tratado of Antonio Galvão, first published in 1550.

"No anno de 1496 achandose hum Venezeano por nome Sebastiano Gaboto[1] em Inglaterra, et ouvindo nova de tam novo descubrimento como este era : et vendo em huma poma como estas jlhas acima ditas estano quasi em hum parallelo et altura et muyto mais perto de sua terra huma a outra que de Portugal nem Castolla, o amostrou a el Rey dom Annrique o septimo de que elle ficou tam satisfeito que mandou logo armar dous navios, partio na primavera com trezentos companheiros, fez seu caminho a Loeste a vista do terra, et quarenta et cinco graos d'altura da parte donorte, forano por ella

---

[1] The English translations give the name of John Cabot. Sir Clements Markham says : "'John Cabota' is the name in the English translation of Antonio Galvão; but in the Portuguese text the name so translated is 'Sebastião Gabota.' The translator probably intended to correct the mistake. In Gomara and Ramusio it is also 'Sebastian,' who evidently gave out that he was the discoverer, ignoring his father." The name Sebastian has therefore been restored in the translation.

ate sessenta onde os diam sam de dezoyto horas, et as noytes muy claras et serenas. Avia aqui muyta frialdade et ilhas de nove que nao achavam grandes regelos, do que tambem se arreceavam. É como daqui por dianta tornasse a costa ao levante, fizeramose na outra volta ao longo descobrindo toda a baya, rio, enseada, p'ra ver se passava da outra banda, et foram assi diminuindo n' altura ate trinta et oyto graos, donde se tornaram a Inglaterra. Outros querem dized que chegasse a ponta da Florida que esta em vinte cinco graos" (Edition of 1563).

[TRANSLATION]

"In the yeere 1496 there was a Venetian in England called Sebastian Cabot, who, having knowledge of such a new discoverie as this was, and perceiving by the globe that the islands before spoken of stood about in the same latitude with his country, and much nearer to England than to Portugal or to the Castile, he acquainted King Henry the Seventh, then King of England, with the same, wherewith the said king was greatly pleased, and furnished him out with two ships and three hundred men, which departed and set sail in the spring of the year, and they sailed westward till they came in sight of land, in forty-five degrees of latitude towards the north, and then went straight northwards till they came into sixty degrees of latitude, where the day is eighteen hours long, and the night is very clear and bright. There they found the air cold, and great islands of ice, but no ground in seventy, eighty, or a hundred fathoms sounding, but found much ice, which alarmed them: and so from thence, putting about, finding the land to turn eastwards, they trended along by it, discovering all the bay and river named Deseado, to see if it passed on the other side; then they sailed back again till they came to 38 degrees towards the equinoctial line, and from thence returned into England. There be others which say that he went as far as the Cape of Florida, which standeth in 25 degrees."

[From the translation published by the Hakluyt Society.]

The writer may or may not have known Sebastian Cabot, and the information he gives may have been derived either from Sebastian personally or from Martyr's work. We have no reliable evidence to guide us. If the information was obtained from Peter Martyr, very little importance can be attached to it. Sir Clements Markham says: "Antonio Galvão was a native of Lisbon, born 1503, who went to India in 1527, and became governor of the Moluccas. He was a man of great talent and learning, an able and exceptionally humane administrator. After his return to Portugal he devoted himself to the preparation of an account of all known voyages of discovery, *Descobrimentos em diversos annos e tempos, quà formam os primeros que navegarem*. It is still a valuable compilation. He died at Lisbon in 1557." In the *Biographical Dictionary*, p. 667: "Galvam (or Galvao) Antonio (died 1557), surnamed 'the Apostle of the Moluccas,' a Portuguese, who was in 1538 appointed governor of those islands. He maintained, by his military skill, the colonists against the Malays, whom he first subdued and afterwards conciliated. Refusing the sovereignty, he returned to Portugal in 1545, and notwithstanding his services, was left to die in poverty in an hospital."

. . . .

Francisco Lopez de Gomara, in his *Historia General de las Indias*, part i., cap. "De los Bacallaos," published in 1552, says—

"Qui en mas noticia traxo desta tierra fue Sebastian Gaboto, Veneciano. El qual armo dos navios en Inglaterra do tratava desde pequeno, a costa del Rey Enrique Septimo, que desseava contratar en la especiera como hazia el rey de Portugal. Otros disen que a su costa, y' que prometio al rey Enrique de ir por el norte al Catayo y traer de alla especias en menos tiempo que Portugueses por el sur. Y va tambien por saber que tierra eran las Indias para poblar. Llevo trecientos hombres y camino la buelta de Islandia sobre cabo del Labrador, hasta se poner en cinquenta y ocho grados. Aunque el dize mucho mas contando como avia por el mes de Julio tanto frio y pedaços de yelo que no oso passar mas adelante, y que los dios eran grandissimos y quasi sin noche y las noches muy claras. Es cierte que a sesenta grados son los dias de diez y ocho horas, Diendo pues Gabota la frialdad y estraneza de la tierra, dio la buelta hazia poniente y rehaziendose en los Baccalaos corrio la costa hasta treynta y ochos grados y tornose de alli a Inglaterra."

[TRANSLATION]

"He who obtained the most news of this land was Sebastian Gabot, a Venetian. He armed two vessels in England (where he had been brought up from a child), at the cost of King Henry VII., who desired to trade with the spice country like the King of Portugal. Others say that it was at his own cost, and that he promised the King of England to go by the north to Cathay, and to bring spices thence in a shorter time than the Portuguese brought them from the south. He also went to ascertain what land of the Indies could be settled.[1] He took three hundred men, and went in the direction of Iceland to the Cape of Labrador, reaching 58°, although he says much more. He relates how that, in the month of July, it was so cold, and there were such great pieces of ice, that he could get no further, that the days were very long and almost without night, and that the nights were very clear. It is certain that in 60° the days have eighteen hours. Considering the cold and the forbidding nature of the country, he turned to the south, and, passing the Baccalaos, he proceeded as far as 38°, returning thence to England" (*The Journal of Christopher Columbus*, etc., by Sir Clements R. Markham, K.C.B., President of the Hakluyt Society, p. 215).

It is highly probable that Gomara was personally acquainted with Sebastian Cabot, because, as Secretary[2] to Fernando Cortès, he was in the habit of visiting the Court of Charles I. of Spain. The words, "although he says much more," may or may not indicate that the writer had been in personal communication with Cabot. They clearly indicate that Gomara was struck with Sebastian's statement.

[1] This cannot possibly relate to the voyage in 1497.
[2] "Siendo su capellan y criada [de Cortès] despues de Marqués Cuando volvió la postrera vez á España."—Las Casas, *Historia de las Indias*, book iii. chap. cxiv. vol. iv. p. 448.

It appears that the printing of the first edition of Gomara's work was finished at Saragossa in December 1552, and that a second edition was printed in August 1553.

In Eden's translations (Arber's edition, p. 345), the following notes as to "Baccalaos" appear: "The coaste of the land of Baccalaos is a great track, and the greatest altitude thereof is 48 degrees and a half."

. . . .

Another historical record which contains a reference to the proceedings of Sebastian Cabot is the *Raccolta di Navigationi e Viaggi*,[1] a collection of voyages and travels written by Giovanni Battista Ramusio. This work was published in three volumes, of which the first was published in 1554. The author died in 1557. He was born at Tevisa in 1485. He entered the Venetian Secretaryship in the year 1505. In the year 1515 he was made Secretary of the Senate, an office which he occupied up to the 7th July 1533, when he was promoted to the high and responsible office of Secretary of the Council of Ten of Venice.

In the third volume of his collection of voyages, which was written at Venice in 1553, but not printed until 1556, Ramusio, in the preliminary discourse to his work, says: "As many years past it was *written* unto me by Signor Sebastian Gabotto, our Venetian [2] [countryman], a man of great experience,

---

[1] This work was regarded as one of the most copious and learned works on the history of navigations ever before published.

[2] There exists no reason for believing that Ramusio ever personally met with Sebastian Cabot. But Ramusio would have known of Peter Martyr's description of him, and in all probability, as Secretary to the Council of Ten of Venice, he knew of Cabot's declaration of his nationality to Contarini.

and very rare in the art of navigation and the knowledge of cosmography, who sailed along and beyond the land of New France, at the charges of King Henry VII. of England. And he advertised me, that having sailed a long time west by north, beyond those islands unto the latitude of 67 degrees and a half, under the North Pole, and at the 11 day of June, finding still the open without any manner of impediment, he thought verily by that way to have passed on still the way to Cathay, which is the east, and would have done it, if the mutiny of the Ship-markers and Mariners had not hindered him and made him to return homewards from that place."

A literary warfare has been carried on with reference to Ramusio's statement, which some contend is utterly devoid of meaning so far as it relates to any voyage ever undertaken by Sebastian Cabot; on the other hand, Mr. Harrisse, in reviewing all the facts and possibilities, cannot even come to the conclusion that it relates—as has been suggested—to a voyage in or about the year 1517.

But the most important account given by Ramusio purports to have been made by a person whose name is not disclosed. Tarducci says: "Ramusio relates that going with a friend to visit the celebrated Fracastoro at his villa of Caphi, he found him in the company of 'a gentleman who was a great philosopher and mathematician, whose name *out of respect is not given.*' This philosopher, as the conversation turned upon the 'plan of going to find the Indies by way of the north-west wind,' made on this subject 'a long and admirable discourse, and amongst other things related a visit of his to Sebastian Cabot in Spain, and the accounts the latter had given him of his voyages and discoveries. Ramusio, who was then composing his great collection of voyages and navigations, inserted in it this discourse of the gentleman, putting it in the person of Cabot himself, as the Anonymous had done. We are not told in what year Anonymous met Sebastian. D'Avezac supposes it was in 1544 or 1545; but as it is necessary to put Ramusio's visit to the villa of Caphi in 1547 or 1548 (as D'Avezac admits), it does not seem to me that, at the distance of only three or four years, Anonymous could have said, 'finding myself many years ago in the city of Seville.' I therefore think the conversation with Sebastian must have occurred some years earlier."

It is exceedingly difficult to ascertain whether we ought to attach any, and if so, what, importance to this statement. No date is given as to when the alleged conversation with Cabot took place, but inasmuch as in one part of it Cabot, so it is alleged, refers to the Rio de la Plata, it is only reasonable to infer that the conversation must have taken place just before Cabot's final departure from Spain to England in or about the year 1548.

Ramusio's account of the conversation with the Anonymous (generally designated the "Mantuan[1] gentleman")—

[1] Tomaso Guinti, who republished Ramusio's work in 1613, places "Mantuan" after the name of the anonymous gentleman. Marco Foscarini believed that the Mantuan gentleman was Giangiacomo Bartolo. There seems to be no real evidence to guide us. As an example of the value of conjecture in matters of this kind, Richard Eden thought this was a good opportunity of disclosing the name to the world. Eden gave his readers the name of a Bolognese, Galleazzo Bottrigari, the pope's nuncio in Spain. Unfortunately for Eden's reputation for accuracy, it subsequently turned out that Bottrigari died in 1518, and was buried in the Church of St. Francesco, in Bologna.

"Mi par convenevole di non lassare per modo alcuno, che io non racconti un grāde, et ammirabile ragionamento, che io udì questi mesi passati insieme coll' eccellente Architetto M. Michele da S. Michele, nell' ameno et dilettevole luogo dell' eccellente Messer Hieronimo Fracastora detto Caphi, posto nel Veronese.... Il qual ragionamento non mi basta l'animo di poter scrivere così particolarmente com' io udì, perchè vi saria di bisogno altro ingegno, et altra memoria che non è la mia, pur mi sforzerò sommariamente, et come per capi di recitar quel che mi potro ricordare. In questo luogo di Caphi adunque essendo andati a visitar detto eccellente messer Hieronimo, lo trovammo accompagnato con un gentil' huomo, grandissimo philosopho et mathematico, che allhora gli mostrava uno instrumento fatto sopra un moto de cieli, trovato di nuovo, il nome del quale per suoi rispetti non si dice, et avendo tra loro disputato lungamente sopra questo stesso nuovo moto, per ricrearsi alquāto l'animo fecero portare una balla grande molto particolare di tutto il mondo, sopra la quale questo gentil' huomo cominciò a parlare dicendo.... Non sapete a questo proposito d'andare a trovar l'Indie pel vento di maestro, quel che fece già un vostro cittadino Venetiano, ch'è cosi valente et practico delle cose pertinenti alla navigazione et alla cosmographia, ch'in Spagna al presente non v'è un suo pari, et la sua virtù l'ha fatto preporre a tutti li piloti che navigano alle Indie occidentali, che senza sua licentia non possono far quell' essercitio, et per questo lo chiamano Pilotto maggiore, et rispondendo noi, che non lo sapevamo, continuò, dicendo, che ritrovandosi già alcuni anni nella città di Sivilia, et desiderando di saper qlle navigationi de Castigliani, gli fut detto, che v'era un grã valent' huomo Venetiano che havea 'l carico di quelle, nominato 'l Signor Sebastiano Caboto, il qual sapeva far carte marine di sua mano, et intendeva l'arte del navigare più ch' alcun altro. Subito volsi essere col detto, et lo trovai una gentilissima persona et cortese, chi mi fece gran carezee, et mostrommi molte cose, et fra l'altre un Mapamondo grande colle navigationi, particolari si di Portoghesi, come di Castigliani, et mi disse che sendosi partito suo padre da Venetia già molti anni, et andato a stare i Inghilterra a far mercantie lo menò seco nella città di Londra, ch' egli era assai giovane, non già però che non avesse imparato et lettere d'humanità et la sphera. Morì il padre in quel tempo che venne nova che 'l signor Don Christoforo Colombo Genovese havea scoperta la costa dell' Indie, e se ne parlava grandemente per tutta la corte del Re Henrico VII., che allhora regnava, dicendosi che era stata cosa piuttosto divina che humana l'haver trovata quella via mai più saputa d'andare in Oriente, dove nascono le Spetie. Per il che mi nacque un desiderio grande, anzi un ardor nel core di voler fare anchora io qualche cosa segnalata, et sapendo per ragion della sphera, che s'io navigassi per via del vento di maestro, haverei minor cammino a trovar l'Indie, subito feci intendere questo mio pensiero alla Maestà del Re, il quale fu molto contento, et mi armò due caravelle di tutto ciò che era di bisogno, *et fu del* 1496 nel principio della State, et cominciai a navigare verso maestro, pensando di non trovar terra se non quella dov'è il Cataio, et di la poi voltare verso le Indie; ma in capo di alquanti giorni la discopersi che correva verso tramontana, che mi fu d'infinito dispiacere, e pur andando dietro la costa per vedere se io poteva trovare qualche golfo che voltasse, non vi fu mai ordine, che andato sino a gradi cinquantasei sotto il nostro polo, vedendo che quivi la costa voltava verso levante, disperato di trovarlo, me ne tornai a dietro a riconoscere ancora la detta costa dalla parte verso l'equinoziale sempre con intenzione di trovar passaggio alle Indie, e venni sino a quella che chiamano al presente la Florida, et mancandomi gia la vettovaglia, presi partito di ritornarmene in Inghilterra, dove giunto trovai grandissimi tumulti di popoli sollevati et della guerra in Scotia : nè più era in consideratione alcuna il navigare in questi parti, per il che me ne venni in Spagna al Re Catholic, et alla Regima Isabella" (Ramusio, *Delle Navigazioni et Viaggi*, Primo volume, Ediz. seconda, Giunta, 1554 ; pp. 414, 415).

[TRANSLATION]

"It would be inexcusable in me if I did not relate a high and admirable discourse which, some few months ago, it was my good fortune to hear in company with the excellent architect, Michael de S. Michael, in the sweet and romantic country seat of Hieronimo Fracastoro, named Caphi, situated near Verona, whilst we sat on the top of a hill commanding a view of the whole of the Lago di Garda.

"We found him, on our arrival, sitting in company with a certain gentleman, whose name, from motives of delicacy and respect, I conceal. He was, however, a profound philosopher and mathematician.

"At this point, after the stranger had made a pause of a few minutes, he turned to us and said :

"'Do you not know, regarding this project of going to India by the north-west, what was formerly achieved by your fellow-citizen, a Venetian, a most extraordinary man, and so deeply conversant in everything connected with navigation and the science of cosmography, that in those days he hath not his equal in Spain; insomuch that for his ability he is preferred above all pilots that sail to the West Indies, who may not pass thither without his licence, on which account he is denominated Piloto-mayor, or Grand-Pilot?'

"When to this question we replied that we knew him not, the stranger proceeded to tell us that, being some years ago in the city of Seville, he was desirous to gain an acquaintance with the navigation of the Spaniards, when he learned that there was in the city a valiant man, *a Venetian born*, named Sebastian Cabot, who had the charge of those things, being an expert man in the science of navigation, and one who could make charts for the sea with his own hand.

"'Upon this report of him,' continued he, 'I sought his acquaintance and found him a pleasant and courteous person, who loaded me with kindness and showed me many things; among the rest a large map of the world, with the navigation of the Portuguese and Spaniards minutely laid down upon it; and in exhibiting this to me he informed me that his father, many years ago, having left Venice to dwell in England, to follow the trade of merchandises, had taken him to London, while he was yet very young, yet having, nevertheless, some knowledge of letters of humanity, and of the sphere. "And when my father died," said he, "in the time when news was brought that Don Christopher Colonus, Genoese, had discovered the coasts of Indies, whereof was great talk in all the Court of King Henry VII., who then reigned, insomuch that all men, with great admiration, affirmed it to be a thing more divine than human, to sail by the West into the East, where spices grow, by a way that was never known before; by this fame and report there increased in my heart a great flame of desire to attempt some notable thing; and understanding by the sphere that, if I should sail by way of the northwest, I should, by a shorter track, come into India. I imparted my ideas to the king, who immediately commanded two caravels to be furnished with all things necessary for the voyage, being much pleased therewith. This happened in 1496, in the early part of summer, and I began to sail towards the north-west,[1] with the idea that the first land I should make would be Cathay, from which I intended afterwards to direct my course to the Indies; but, after the lapse of several days, having discovered it, I found that the coast ran towards the north, to my great disappointment. From thence, sailing along it to ascertain if I could find any gulf to run into, I could discover none; and thus, having proceeded as far as 56° under the pole, and seeing that here the

---

[1] "In Ramusio's *Collection of Voyages* an anonymous writer puts into the mouth of Sebastian Cabot more or less autobiographical narrative, in which there are almost as many blunders as lines. . . . It is to Ramusio's narrative, moreover, that we owe the ridiculous statement—repeated by almost every historian from that day to this—that the purpose of the voyage of 1498 was the discovery of a 'north-west passage to the coast of Asia'" (Fiske, vol. ii. pp. 8, 9).

coast trended towards the East, I despaired of discovering any passage, and after this turned back to examine the same coast in its direction towards the equinoctial, always with the same object of finding a passage to the Indies, and thus I reached the country at present named Florida, where, since my provisions began to fail me, I took the resolution of returning to England.

"'"On arriving in that country I found great tumults, occasioned by the rising of the common people and the war in Scotland; nor was there any more talk of a voyage to these parts. For this reason I departed into Spain to their most Catholic Majesties, Ferdinand and Isabella,"'" etc.

Inasmuch as the name of the person who is said to have related what he had heard from Sebastian Cabot is not given, this narrative is not entitled to be considered as above suspicion. A casual glance at the relation clearly points out that the details may have been slightly altered in transmission between the anonymous "Mantuan gentleman" and Ramusio. Several years must have elapsed between the date of the alleged interview between Sebastian and the "Mantuan gentleman." Then, again, it is not certain that Ramusio wrote down the statement at the time it was made. In all probability the memory of Ramusio served him very well, but most persons know how difficult it is to remember the exact details of a conversation. "I do not pretend," says Ramusio, "to write his discourse with as full details as I heard it, for that would require other skill and memory than I possess; still, I will try to give a summary, or, as it were, the heads of what I can remember."—"Il quale ragionamento, egli dice, non mi Casta l'animo di potere scrivere cosi particalarmente com'io lo udì, perchè vi sariadi bisogna altro ingegno, et altra memoria, che non è la mia, pur mi sforzerò sommariamente e come per capi di recitar quel che mi potrò ricordare." Ramusio, in referring to another matter, acknowledges that his memory was not quite a perfect record. "With regard to the Mediterranean Sea, I seem to remember that he touched upon I know not what voyage that might be made upon it with great profit, but to what place has entirely escaped my memory."—"A proposito del Mar Mediterraneo mi par ricordare che toccasse anche di non so che viaggio che si potria fare in quello di grandissimo proposite, ma a che parte emmi al tutto fuggito dalla memoria." We cannot regard it as more than second-hand evidence of a very weak description. We find that the Anonymous says that Sebastian was looked upon as "a Venetian born," and that he corroborates Martyr's statement as to having been taken to London when he was very young.

Martyr.	The "*Mantuan Gentleman.*"
"Being yet but in manner an infant, his parents carried with them into England, having occasion to resort thither for trade of merchandise," etc.	"He informed me that his father, many years ago, having left Venice to dwell in England, to follow the trade of merchandise, had taken him to London while he was yet very young."

As to the number of ships, the Anonymous corroborates Martyr.

Martyr.	The "*Mantuan Gentleman.*"
"He (Cabot) therefore furnished two shippes in England at his own charges."	"I imparted my ideas to the king, who immediately commanded two caravels to be furnished with all things necessary for the voyage, being much pleased therewith."

But in the account given by the Anonymous we are told that this voyage took place in 1496, and that at that time his father (John Cabot) was actually dead. Under the circumstances, there seems to be no alternative but to dismiss this unintelligible story from a place in a serious history. These second-hand relations of events should be carefully studied, and placed in juxtaposition with the accounts of the voyages given by John Cabot to the various persons who placed his statements upon record.

It is worthy of note that Peter Martyr records the fact that it was doubted by some Spaniards that Sebastian Cabot was the discoverer of the region called Baccalaos. "Ex Castellanis non desunt, qui Cabothum primum finisse Baccalaorum, repertorem negent tantumque ad occidentem tetendisse minime assentientur." (Some of the Spaniards deny that Cabot was the first finder of the land of Baccalos, and affirm that he went not so far westward.)

And it is also worthy of note, when we come to consider all the evidence as to whether or not Sebastian was with his father in the voyage of 1497, that the Drapers' Company, in 1521, in an address to the king, said that Sebastian Cabot "was never in that land himself," while "he makes report of many things as he hath heard his father and other men speak in times past."

Dr. Samuel Edward Dawson, in some remarks as to the discovery in 1497 by the *Matthew of Bristol*, with a crew of eighteen men, says: "In consideration of this discovery made by John Cabot, King Henry VII. granted new letters-patent, drawn solely to John Cabot, authorising a second expedition on a more extended scale and with fuller royal authority, which letters-patent were dated February 3rd, 1498. That this expedition sailed in the spring of 1498, and had not returned in October . . . [are] points [which] are now fully supported by satisfactory evidence, mostly documentary and contemporary. As for John Cabot, Sebastian said he died, which is one of the few undisputed facts in the discussion; but if Sebastian is correctly reported in Ramusio[1] to have said that he died at the time when the news of Columbus's discoveries reached England, then Sebastian Cabot told an untruth, because the letters-patent of 1498 were addressed to John Cabot alone. The son had *a gift of reticence concerning others*, including *his father* and brothers, which in these latter days has been the cause of much wearisome research to scholars." Dr. Dawson also says: "During the whole of the first voyage John Cabot was the commander; on the second voyage he sailed in command, but who brought the expedition home, and when it returned, are not recorded. It is not known how or when John Cabot died, and although the letters-patent for the second voyage were addressed to him alone, his son Sebastian, during forty-five years, took the whole credit in every subsequent mention of the discovery of America. This antithesis may throw light upon the suppression of his father's name in all the statements attributed to or made by Sebastian Cabot. . . . He was marvellously reticent about his father. The only mention which

[1] "Discourse of the Anonymous Guest at the House of Frascator Ramusio," *Navigazioni et Viaggi*, vol. i. fol. 374D, 3rd ed., Venice.

occurs is on the map, seen by Hakluyt, and on the map of 1544, supposed, somewhat rashly, to be a transcript of it. There[1] the discovery is attributed to John Cabot and to Sebastian his son, and that has reference to the first voyage. . . . Sebastian manifested no concern for any person's reputation but his own. He never once alluded to his two brothers who were associated in the first patent, and the preceding slight notice of his father is all that can be traced to him,[2] although contemporary records of unquestionable authority indicate John Cabot as the moving spirit, and do not mention the son. . . . What we are concerned to solve is the historical problem: Who first discovered the mainland of America? For that reason John Cabot and his little vessel, the *Matthew of Bristol* have to us a paramount interest. In this portion of my paper, then, Peter Martyr, Gomara, Ramusio, and Hakluyt are of minor importance. I am to concern myself first with those Spanish and Italian envoys, whose letters and despatches from England in the same year are almost the only contemporary evidence we possess of John Cabot's achievement. As these were all written before the return of the second expedition, in studying them we are sure of having the only extant information concerning the first voyage absolutely free from any inter-

[1] It may or may not be Sebastian Cabot's map. The evidence as to the authorship is merely conjectural. There exists no authentic proof that the inscriptions on the map were placed thereon by Sebastian Cabot.

[2] This certainly depends upon whether the authorship of the legends on the so-called Cabot map can be traced to Sebastian. In fairness, however, the inscription on the portrait of Sebastian should also be mentioned.

mixture with the details of the second." Dr. Dawson has shown, in his discussion of the various important points at issue in the Cabot history, that he possesses a singularly apt method of leading up to and offering a solution of the complicated questions, which, in consequence of what Sebastian Cabot said, or it may be what he left unsaid, have caused so much difficulty to those who are desirous to get at the truth. Dr. Dawson's monograph, which was published in 1894, together with an article written by him which is included in a recently published pamphlet,[1] entitled "The Discovery of America by John Cabot in 1497," etc., deserves the best attention of every student of American history.

In concluding the notice of the accounts related by Peter Martyr, Galvao, Gomara, and Ramusio, the following questions are presented before us for our serious consideration. First, was Sebastian Cabot with his father, either in the voyage of 1497 or in that of 1498? Secondly, did he wilfully suppress the fact that it was his father who was the real discoverer? Thirdly, did he trade upon the imperfect knowledge he had gleaned as to the voyages of 1497 and 1498, or either of them, from his father?

These questions are put as the result of a very careful study by the questioner of all the documentary evidence it is possible to obtain. The answers must be left to the readers of this volume, who are advised to keep their minds open until after they have read its last page. The final decision should not be arrived at until the whole

[1] *Ottawa*, for sale by James Hope & Sons, 1896.

of the difficulties and entanglements of the Cabot history have been carefully examined. "Great surprise," says Biddle, "has been expressed that [Sebastian] Cabot should have left no account of his voyages, and this circumstance has ever been urged against him as a matter of reproach." Perhaps it is better to say that it is a great pity, both for the sake of Sebastian and the public, that, so far as the allegations as to the agency of Sebastian Cabot in the voyages of 1497 and 1498 are concerned, we are left to judge as to the truth or otherwise from statements made at second-hand.

CHAPTER VI

In the year 1521 we find that Sebastian Cabot had made terms with King Henry VIII. for taking command of an expedition. As a matter of fact, we cannot tell for certain whether the expedition ever sailed; it is certain, however, that if it actually sailed, Sebastian Cabot took no part whatever in it. But the records of the proceedings connected with the negotiations tend to throw some very important side-lights on the history of Sebastian Cabot.

Sir Robert Wynkfeld and Sir Wolston Brown, two members of the council of Henry VIII., called upon the wardens of the various livery companies of London to furnish five vessels "for a viage to be made into the newe found Iland," which was to be placed under the command of "one man callyd as understoud Sebastyan." It is certain that this means that arrangements of some kind—whether of a complete nature or subject to some condition, must be left to conjecture—had been made with Sebastyan Cabot, whose surname was suppressed. At that time he was in the employ of Spain. The wardens of the drapers and of the mercers took exception to the proposed expedition on the ground, as they alleged, that the king and his council "were not duely and substancially enformed in such manner as perfite knowledge myght be had by credible reporte of maisters and mariners *naturally born within this Realm of England*,[1] having experience and excersided in and about the forsaid Iland." The report also says: "And we thynk it were too sore a venture to joperd v shipps with men and goods unto the said Iland uppon the singuler trust of one man, callyd, as we understand, Sebastyan, which Sebastyan, as we here say, was never in that land hym self, all if he maks report of many things as he hath hard his father and other men speke in tymes past."

The substance of Sebastian's negotiations with England, at a time when he was receiving considerable pay as pilot-major in Spain, seems to point to the fact that he was making capital out of his alleged knowledge, that some further important discovery was within the realm of fact. At this period he was certainly looked upon by some Spaniards as a born Englishman, and, judging by his subsequent intrigues with Venice, we must receive any representation made by him regarding his birthplace with suspicion.[2] It is certain he was a man who would not hesitate to make any number of misrepresentations when it suited his purpose to do so. We are much puzzled when we find that he did not take part in a projected enterprise, which was, in accordance with negotiations carried on with Cardinal Wolsey and the king's council, in course of preparation. Did he use the fact that the English were negotiating with him for his services for any ulterior purpose? It is not at all improbable that it was only part of a plan to enhance the value of his

---

[1] This is evidently a hit at Sebastian Cabot's supposed nationality.
[2] Of course, they may have had no good cause for their belief that he was not a natural-born Englishman.

services in the eyes of the Spanish Court. We are still further puzzled when we find, as a fact, that in 1522 he was intriguing with the Council of Ten of Venice to sell to the republic a piece of secret information. He represented that he was acquainted with a north-west passage to the Indies. In his negotiations with Venice it will be seen that he refers to his English negotiations, and, in M. Harrisse's words, we find that he represented that, "Cardinal Wolsey had made great efforts to induce him to take the command of an important expedition to discover new countries, 30,000 ducats having actually been obtained for equipping the fleet: 'Hor ritrovandomi ja tre anni, salvo il vero, in Ingilterra, quel Reverendissimo Cardinal mi volea far grandi partiti che io navigasse cum una sua armada per discoprir paesi novi la quale ora quasi in ordine, et haveano preparati per spender in casa ducati 30 m.'"[1]

It strikes one as a most extraordinary coincidence that his idea of a passage to the Indies by the northwest was first disclosed at a time when the southwest route was actually suggested or delineated on a globe, and at a time, too, when Magellan's proposals for circumnavigation were in actual existence.[2] The

---

[1] C. Bullo, *La vera patria di*, p. 64, and Jean et Sebastian Cabot, *Nicolo, de' Conti e di Giovanni Caboto*, doc. xxviii. p. 348; *Studj e Documenti Chioggia*, 1880.

[2] Magellan returned to Portugal from Morocco in 1514, and at once devoted himself to scientific researches in connection with cosmography and navigation. In consequence of the existence of the Treaty of Tordesillas, and of the papal bulls, Portugal had no interest in discovering either a south-west or a north-west passage to the Indies; on the contrary, inasmuch as the Spaniards were prohibited by the terms of the agreement between Spain and Portugal, which had been ratified by the papal authority, from sailing to the Indies by the way of Good Hope, it was to the interest of Portugal to throw obstacles in the way

fact that the circumnavigation of the globe, in accordance with the theory of Magellan, had become an accomplished fact at the time Sebastian sent his communication to Venice, should not be entirely lost sight of. The brave Portuguese lost his life in the course of his marvellous voyage. He was killed in a fight with the natives of the island of Matan, in April 1521, after a most desperate encounter, in which he proved himself almost insensible to danger. When he was disabled and laid low, the natives "threw themselves upon him with iron-pointed bamboo spears and scimitars, and every weapon they had, and ran him through—our mirror, our light, our comforter, our true guide—until they killed him."[1] On the 6th of September 1522, the *Victoria*, one of the five vessels which took part in Magellan's expedition, arrived in the Guadalquivir, and the story of the circumnavigation of the globe by a south-west passage was then made known. Mr. Fiske[2] describes this voyage "as the greatest feat of navigation that has ever been performed, and nothing can be imagined that would surpass it except a journey to some other planet. It has not the unique historical position of the first voyage of Columbus, which brought together two streams of human life that had been disjoined since the Glacial period. But as an achievement in ocean navigation, that voyage of Columbus sinks into insignificance by the side of it. ... When we consider the frailness of the ships, the immeasurable extent of the unknown, the

of any proposal for the discovery of another route. As a consequence, Magellan, a Portuguese, very reluctantly offered his services to Spain, and they were accepted.

[1] Guillemard's *Magellan*, p. 252.
[2] Vol. ii. p. 210.

mutinies that were prevented or quelled, and the hardships that were endured, we can have no hesitation in speaking of Magellan as the prince of navigators." This little digression has been made for the purpose of pointing out that it was just at the period when the survivors of Magellan's expedition arrived in Spain that Sebastian Cabot opened his negotiations as to the " North-West Passage " with Venice.

It is now proposed to give the correspondence relating to Sebastian Cabot's intrigue with Venice during the time he was in the employment of Spain.

DESPATCH of the Council of Ten to Gaspar Contarini, Venetian Ambassador to Spain, 27th September 1522.

"Oratori nostro apud Cæsaream et Cattolicam Maiestatem.

"Zonze l'altro giorno de qui uno Don hierolamo di Marin de Bucignolo Rhaguseo, quale venuto alla presentia delli Capi del Consiglio nostro di Dieci Disse esser sta mandato per uno Sebastian Cabotto, che dice esser di questa città nostra, et al presente habita in Sybilia, dove par habbi provvision da quella Cesarea et Cattolica Maestà per suo pedota major in le navigation del discoprir terre nove. Et per nome di quello referi quanto per la insertia deposition sua vederete, dalla quale ancorchè ne appari non poter prestare molta fede, pure per esser de la importantia le non havremmo dovuto refiutare la oblation ne fa epso Sebastian de poter venir de qui alla presentia nostra, per dichiarirne quanto li va per mente in la materia propostane. Unde siamo sta contenti che el ditto Hierolamo li rescrivi nel modo che per le sue incluse vederete; volemo adunque et noi detti capi del consiglio nostro dei Dieci ne commettemo, che cun ogni diligente ma cauta forma, provriasi di intender se il predetto Sabastian fusse in quella corte aut per venirli de breve, nel qual caso faciano venirlo ad voi, et consignarli dette lettere a lui directive, le quali per ogni bon rispecto haveriamo fatto allegar ad altre indriciate al fidelissimo servitor vostro, che pur staranno in le presenti. Ne in lui dimonstrarete saper alcuna cosa di tal materia, nisi in caso che el se scoprisse cun voi, nel qual, siamo ben contenti li dichiariate el tuto, cun veder de sottrazer quel più potersi del sentimento suo, et quando vedesse el si movesse cun bon fondamento, et sensibile, lo conforterete ad venir di qui, perche non solum siamo volenti ch'el venga sicuramente, ma lo vederemo molto volentieri. Quando autem el non fusse di li in corte, et nunc per venirle, ma si ritrovasse in Sybilia, darete ogni opera di mandarli tutte lettere per via che siate sicuro le gel capitino in mano propria. Demostrando a quello per cui le mandaste, che vi siano sta inviate da alcun vostro particolar de qui, et di ogni sucesso ne darete adviso ad detti Capi del Consiglio nostro di Dieci. Demum travendo nui ricevuto novamente lettere dal capitano general de 5 dell' instante di Candia cun advisi de la cose da Rhode, vi mandiamo juxta il solito li summarij, accio li comunichiate de more a quella Cesarea et Cattolica Maestá Magnifico Gran Cancellier, Reverendo Episcopo de Valenza, et altri che vi apparerano.

"(Lecta universo Collegio.)
"IULIANO GRANDONICO, C.C. ✠
"ANDREUS MUDESCO, C.C. ✠
"DOMINICUS CAPELO, C.C. ✠

"Le ultime che habbiamo da voi sono di 14 del presente alle qual non dovrete far alcuna risposta[1] (Capi del Consiglio dei X. Lettere Sottoscritte, Filza N. 5, 1522)."

[TRANSLATION][2]

"27th September 1522.

"To our Orator near the Cæsarean and Catholic Majesty.

"Since the other day one Don Hierolamo de Marin de Bucignolo, a Ragusan, who came before the presence of the chiefs of our Council of Ten, said that he was sent by one Sebastian Cabotto, *who declares that he belongs to this our city,*[3] *and now resides in Seville,* where he has the appointment from that Cæsarean and Catholic Majesty of his chief pilot for the discovery and navigation of new lands. And, in his name, he referred to an accompanying disposition as his credential, touching which, although we do not see that we can place much trust in it, yet, as there may be some importance in it, we have not thought fit to reject the offer of the same Sebastian to come to our presence to say what he has in his mind respecting this matter. Hence we are content that the said Hierolamo should write to him according to the tenor of what you will see in the enclosed. We

---

[1] Rawdon Brown's English translation has, "To which you will perhaps receive no further reply."
[2] This correspondence with the Venetian ambassador in Spain is preserved at Venice. It was printed by Mr. Harrisse, for his work on the Cabots; and it has been translated from his text for the Hakluyt Society, with his permission.
[3] Venice.

therefore desire, and we, the said Heads of our Council of Ten, instruct you that, with all diligence, but with due caution, you shall take means to find out if the aforesaid Sebastian is in the Court or about to come there shortly, in which case you are to procure that he shall come to you, and you are to deliver to him the said letter, which we have arranged to send by another way to your very faithful servant, that it may reach you presently. You should endeavour to find out something of the matter in hand in the event of his being disposed to be open with you, in which case we are well content to leave it to you to ascertain his sentiments. When you see him, you should move him with sound reasoning, and encourage him to come here; for we are not only desirous, but anxious, that he should come to us securely. If he should not be at Court, nor about to come, but returned to Seville, take care to send all letters by a safe channel, so that they may reach him. Let him know by whom they are sent, that they come from his own friends here, and under any circumstances report everything to the said Heads of our Council of Ten. Having just received letters from the Captain-General of Candia with news touching the affairs of Rhodes, we send you a summary, that you may communicate it to that Cæsarean and Catholic Majesty, to the Magnificent Grand Chancellor, to the Reverend Bishop of Valencia, and to others in your discretion.

"JULIANUS GRADOVICO, C.C.
"ANDREUS MUDESCO, C.C.
"DOMINICUS CAPELO, C.C.

"*Recompense granted to the Ragusan.*

"1522, September 27.—In the College of the Lords. the Heads of the most illustrious Council of Ten.

"That it may be ordered to the Chamberlain of our Council of Ten, that from the moneys of their treasury there be disbursed a gift of 20 ducats to the Lord Hieronimo de Marin, a Ragusan, for good cause."

(The order given.)

The declaration of Sebastian Cabot as to his birthplace is of the most emphatic character. He sent word to the Council of Ten of Venice, by the Ragusan, Don Hierolamo, that he was a native of Venice. If there were no other facts to guide us to a conclusion, his statement would probably be deemed conclusive. Since the proposal rests (as Sebastian says) upon a desire to benefit his native land, and since the negotiation was secret and fraught with perilous consequences, it is difficult to believe that he was not at that time under the impression, whether rightly or wrongly, that he was born in Venice. To those who know anything of the history of Venice or of the history of the Council of Ten, with their machinations, their secret spies, and their marvellous methods of obtaining information, it must immediately occur to them that Sebastian Cabot would have hesitated before making an attempt to deceive them. With regard to the value of the alleged secret of navigation, it will be seen that the Council of Ten attached no very great importance thereto, but, with characteristic caution, they waited for further information before coming to a decision.

DESPATCH of Gaspar Contarini to the Senate of Venice, 31st December 1522.

"Serenissime Princepe et Excellentissime Domini,—

"La terza vigilia di natale cum la debita riverentia mia ricevi le letteré di Vostra Serenità date fino adi 27 septembrio per le quali quella mi significa la expositione fatali da Hieronimo Ragusei per nome di Sebastian Caboto et commettemi che essendo qui a la Corte io li debba apresentar quella lettera et facendomi lui moto alcuno, che io li debba aprir il tuto et parendo le cose proposte da lui factibile che io lo exhorti a venir a li piedi di Vostra Serenità. Hor per dar executione a prefate lettere, feci dextramente intender se costui era a la Corte et inteso chel era qui, et la stantia sua, li mandai a dir che el secretario mio li haveva da dar una lettera inviatale da un suo amico et che volendo el se transferisse allo allogiamento mio. Costui inteso questo rispose a quel servitor mio che el veniria et cussi la vigilia di Natale venne al hora de disnar. Io ritiratomi con lui, li detti la lettera, lui la lesse et legiendola si mosse tutto di colore. Da poij letta, stete cussi un pocheto senza dirmi altro quasi sbigotito et dubio. Alhora io li dissi quando che el volesse risponder a dicte lettere over farme intender qualche cosa che el volesse che io scrivesse a chi me l'havea inviata che io era prompto a farli aver bon recapito. Lui assecurato alhora me disse. Io già parlai a lo ambassator della Illustrissima Signoria in Ingelterra per la affectione che io ho a la patria cum queste terre novamente trovate de la quale io ho modo di dar gran utile a quella terra, et hora di questo n i vien scripto, come dovete saper anchor vuj, ma vi prego quanto posso che la cosa sij secreta perche a me anderebbe la vita. Io alhora li dissi che io sapeva il tutto molto bene et disseli come il Raguseo era stato al Tribunal de li Exellentissimi Signori Capi et che da quel Magistrato secretissimo io havea habuto adviso del tutto et che per lui mi era sta inviata quella lettera, ma perché havea meco a pranso alcuni gentilhuomini che non era commodo che in quel hora parlassemo insieme, ma la sera al tardo ritornado più comodamente ad longum ragionassemo insieme, et cussi partito, la sera ritornò circa ad un hora di nocte, et rechuisi soli in la mia camera me disse : *Signor Ambassator per dirve il tuto io naqui a Venetia ma sum nudrito in Ingelterra* et poij veni al servitio di questi Re Catholici de Hispania, et dal Re Ferdinando fui facto Capitano cum provisione di 50 m. maravedis, poij fui facto da questo Re presente piloto major cum provisione di altri 50 m. maravedis, et per adiuto di cose mi da poij 25 m. maravedis, che sono in tutto 125 m. maravedis, possono valer circa ducati 300. Hor ritrovandomi ja tres anni, salvo il vero, in Ingilterra, quel Reverendissimo Cardinal mi volea far grandi partiti che io navigasse cum una sua armada per discoprir paesi novi la quale era quasi in ordine, et haveano preparati per spender in essa ducati 30 m. Io li risposi che essendo al servitio di questa Maestà senza sua licentia non lo poteva servire ma che havendo bona licentia di qui io el serviria. In

quelli giorni ragionando cum uno frate Stragliano
Collona veneto cum il quale havea amicitia grande,
mi fu dicto dal prefacto frate: *Messer Sebastiano vui
vi affaticati cussi grandemente per far beneficio
a genti externe non oi aricordate della vostra
terra*, non seria possibile che etiam lei havesse
qualche utilità da vuj. Allhora io mi risenti tutto
nel core et li risposi che penseria sopra ciò Et
cussi ritornato a lui il giorno seguente li dissi
che io haveva modo di far quella Città partecipe
di questa navigatione, et dimostrarli via per la
quale era per haver grande utilità, come è il
vero che io l'ho ritrovato et cussì perchè servendo
el Re d'Angeltera non poteva più beneficiar la patria
mia, io scrissi alla Maestà Cesarea che non me desse
per niente licentia che servisse il Re de Engelterra
perchè li saria de danno grande, immo che subito me
rivocasse, et cussì rivocato et ritornato essendo in
sibilla contraxi grande amicitia cum questo Raguseo,
il quale hora mi scrive, dicendomi lui che el dovea
transferirse a Venetia, mi slargai cum lui et li comissi
che questa cosa non la dovesse manifestare ad altri
che ali Capi di X. et cussì mi jurò Sacramento. Io
li respusi prima laudando grandemente l'affecto suo
verso la patria, poij li dissi chel Raguseo era stato a
li Excellentissimi Signori Capi, et che io da quel
Magistrato havea habuto lettere supra questa materia
et commissione che dovese essere cum lui et intender
il modo che lui se havea immaginato et significarlo a
Sue Excellentissime Signorie et che poij lui potria
andarli in persona. Ma rispose che lui non era per
manifestar il pensier suo ad altri che a li Excellentissimi Signori Capi, et chel era per transferirse a
Venetia, richiesta prima licentia da Cesare cum questa

excusatione di la ricuperatione di la dote di sua madre, di la qual cosa se faria che lo episcopo di Burgos et il magnificio Cancellier me parleriano et me instariano che io scrivesse in favor suo a la Serenita Vostra. Io li dissi che volendo venir lui a Venetia io laudava questo modo che il mi diceva di chieder licentia, etc. Quanto poij chel non mi volesse manifestar il pensier suo, che io non poteva voler puì di quel che lui volea, ma che ben mi pareva di dirli queste parole et cussì dissi che in ogni deliberatione bisognava considerar due cose, l'una era se quella impresa a la quale l'homo se metteria cum utilita, poij sel era possibile, et che questa impresa de la qual ragionavano io era certo che riuscendo l'havea esser utile. Ma che quanto alla possibilità io era molto dubbio perchè mi havea pur dilectato un pocho de geographia, et considerando il sito di Venetia, io non ritrovava via alcuna a questa navigatione perchè el bisognava over navigar cum navilij facti a Venetia over farli far for di stretto, in altro loco; facendoli a Venetia era necessario uscir for del stretto de Zibilterra per venire nel Oceano, al che havendo contrarij il Re di Portogallo et il Re di Spagna era impossibile che la cosa riuscisse. Facendo li navilij for di Venetia non se potevano far se non a la volta del mar oceano de mezogiorno, ne altro loco era se non il mar rosso, al che ne erano infiniti contrarij perchè prima bisognava haver intelligentia cum el sig. Turcho, poij lì per la penuria de li legnami era impossibile far navilij. Poij quando ben si facesseno essendo le fortezze et armate di Portogallo, non era possibile continuar quella navagatione. Poij chi volea fabricar navili qui supra l'oceano septentrionale discorendo da la Spagna a la Daha et poij più in la anchora, io non li vedeva modo, maxime essendo la Germania a la obedienta del Imperatore. La via poij di condure merce da Venetia quelli navilij, et da li navilij le spesie et ultre cose a Venetia, io non li vedeva via alcuna, tuta volta perchè essendo lui valenthuomo in questa materia, io mi riportava a lui. Me rispose vuj avete ben discorso, et in veritá ne cum navilij facti a Venetia ne etiam per la via del Mar rosso io non vedo modo alcuno. Ma ce altra via non solum possibile ma facile et di far navilij et de condur merce da Venetia al porto, et dal porto a Venetia spetie, oro et altre cose che io so perchè io ho navigato tutti quelli paesi et so ben il tuto, immo vi dico che non vulsi tor il partido de il Re de Engelterra per beneficiar la patria, perchè se tolleva quel partido non restava poi via alcuna per Venetia. Io strinsi le spalle et benche a me la cosa pari impossibile, pur non volsi dissuaderlo chel venisse a li piedi di Vostra Celsitudine, ne anche el suasi perche la possibilità e molto più ampla de quel che l'homo spesse fiate crede. Costui poij qui ha grande fama, et cussì alhora se partì. Il giorno poij di San Zuane la sera vene a trovarme per far riconzar alcune parole in le letere del Ragueso, delle qual dubitava che costoro non prendesseno suspecto, et cussì da uno nostro veronese mio intrinseco fu rescripta et riformata la lettera. Lui ragionando cum me de molte cose di geographia fra le altre me disse uno modo che l'havea observato per la via del bossolo di conosser la distantia fra due lochi da levante al ponente, molto bello ne mai più observato da altri, come da lui venendo Vostra Serenità potrà intender. Poij ragionando pur cum lui circa la materia principal nostra et dextramente ripetendoli io le difficultà me disse et io vi dico che la via et il modo è facile. Anderò a Venetia a mie spese, me undirano ne piacendoli el modo per me excogitato, io mi ritornerò pur a mie spese, et fecemi instantia che io tenesse la cosa secreta. Questa è stata la executione che io ho facto. Vostra Serenità la udirà, et cum la sapienta sua farà quel iuditio che li parerà " (*Vallijoleti, Die ultimo,* Decembris, 1522).

[TRANSLATION]

" Most Serene Prince and Most Excellent Lords,—

" On the third vigil of the Nativity, with due reverence, I received the letter from your Lordships, dated the 27th September, by which is explained to me the proposal of Hieronimo, the Ragusan, in the name of Sebastian Caboto, and I am instructed, if he is at the Court, to give him that letter, and to make certain proposals to him, opening the whole business and exhorting him to come to the feet of your Serenity. In order to execute these instructions, I dexterously ascertained whether he was at the Court, and, this being so, I sent to say that my secretary had to deliver a letter sent by a friend of his, and that if he wished to receive it, he should come to my lodgings.

" He understood this from my servant who went to him, and came on Christmas Eve at the hour of dinner. I withdrew with him, and gave him the letter, which he read, and, in reading it, he lost all colour. Having read it he put it in his pocket without speaking to me, and looked frightened and amazed. I then said to him that, when he should desire to answer that letter, he should tell me what he wished, and that I would write to those who had sent it, for that I should be prompt in making the business end well. Having been reassured he spoke to me: 'I had already spoken to the Ambassador of the most illustrious Seigneury in England, owing to the affection I have for the fatherland, when those newly-found lands could be made of such great utility to my country; and now, as regards what has been written to me, you ought to know all; but I pray you that it may be kept secret, for it is a matter on which my life depends.' I then told him that I knew about it very well, and how the Ragusan was brought before the most excellent Chief Lords, and that I have received intelligence of all that was sent in that letter from the most secret magistrate. But, as some gentlemen were coming to dine with me, it was not convenient to discuss the business further at that time. It would be better if he would return in the afternoon, when we might confer more fully. He then went away and returned at night, when I received him alone in my room. He said to me: '*Lord Ambassador, to tell you all, I was born in Venice, but was brought up in England*, and afterwards entered the service of this Catholic King of Spain, and was made captain by King Ferdinand, with a salary of 50 m. maravedis. I was then made Chief Pilot by this King, with another 50 m. maravedis, and, to help my expenses, was given 25 m. maravedis, making in all 125 m. maravedis, which may be reckoned at nearly 300 ducats. Having returned to England three years ago, that most reverend Cardinal wished that I would undertake the command of a fleet of his to discover countries, which fleet was nearly ready, he

being prepared to expend upon it 30 m. ducats. I
replied that, being in the service of this Majesty, I
was not able to undertake it without his permission.
At that time, conversing with a Venetian friar named
Stragliano Collona, with whom I had a great friendship, he said to me : " Messer Sebastian, you are very
anxious to do great things for foreigners, do you not
remember your own country ? Is it not possible
that you might also be useful to it ?" I felt this n
my heart at the time, and replied that I would think
it over. Having returned to him on the following
day, I said that I had a way by which that city[1]
might participate in these voyages, and I showed
him a way which would be of great utility. As by
serving the King of England I *should not be able to
serve my country*, I wrote to the Cæsarean Majesty,
that he should not, on any account, give me permission to serve the King of England, because there
would be great injury to his service, but that he
should recall me. Having returned to Seville, I
formed a great friendship with this Ragusan who
now writes to me, telling me that I ought to transfer
my services to Venice. I have opened myself to
him, and I charged him that the affair should not be
made known to anyone but the Heads of the Ten,
and he swore this to me on the sacrament.' *I
answered him first by praising his affection for his
native land*, and then said that the Ragusan had been
to the most excellent Chief Lords, that I had received
letters on the subject, and that now they should be
informed of the details of his plan, and that the time
was come for him to present himself before your
most excellent Chief Lords, and that he must there-

[1] Venice.

fore proceed to Venice. He replied that it would first be necessary to obtain permission from the Emperor, *on the plea that he wished to recover the dowry of his mother*, on which affair he would speak to the magnificent Chancellor and the Bishop of Burgos, if I would write in his favour to your Serenity. I answered that, as he wished to go to Venice, I commended the way in which he proposed to obtain leave. As I did not wish to expose his scheme, not wishing to do more than he desired, I thought it well to say this much, adding that in any deliberation he ought to consider two things—one was, that the proposal should be useful; and the other, that its utility could be secured. But with regard to the possibility of such an issue I am doubtful; for I have some slight knowledge of geography, and, considering the position of Venice, I can see no way whatever by which she can undertake these voyages. It would be necessary to sail in vessels built at Venice, or else they must be built outside the Strait. If they are built at Venice they will have to pass the Straits of Gibraltar to reach the ocean, which would not be possible in face of the opposition of the King of Portugal and the King of Spain. If they are not built at Venice, they can only be built on the shore of the western ocean, for they cannot be constructed in the Red Sea without infinite trouble. First, it would be necessary to make an agreement with the Turk; and, secondly, the scarcity of timber would make it impossible to build ships. Even if they were built, the forts and armed vessels of the Portuguese would make it impossible to continue that navigation. Nor can I see any possibility of building ships on the western ocean, Germany being subject to the Emperor; so that I can perceive no way whatever by which merchandise could be brought to Venice from those ships, or from the ships to Venice; but, he being an expert person in such matters, I merely made these observations in deference to him. He replied there was much in what I said, and that truly nothing could be done with vessels built in Venice or in the Red Sea. But there was another way, which was not only possible but easy, by which ships might be built, and merchandise be carried from the port of Venice, and from Venice to the port, as well as gold and other things. He added: 'I know, because I have navigated to all those countries, and am familiar with all. I told you I would not undertake the voyage for the King of England, because that enterprise would in no way benefit Venice.' I shrugged my shoulders, and, although the thing appeared to me to be impossible, I would not dissuade him further, so as not to discourage him from presenting himself to your Highnesses, and I considered that the possibilities are much more ample than is often believed. This man has great renown, and so for the present we parted. On the evening of St. John's day he came to see me, to look at some words in the letter of the Ragusan, doubting whether they might arouse suspicion, and so the letter was rewritten and corrected. He then discussed many geographical points with me, and told me of a method he had observed of finding the distance between two places east and west of each other, by means of the needle. It is a beautiful discovery, never observed by anyone else, as he will be able to explain when he comes before your Serenity. And reasoning with him on the principal business,

I dexterously repeated my objections; but he repeated that the way was easy. 'I will go to Venice, at my expense,' he said; 'they will hear and be pleased with the plan I have devised; I will return at my own expense,' and he urged me to keep the matter secret. Such is the arrangement that I have made. Your Serenity will hear, and your wisdom will decide on what shall appear best."

"*Valladolid*, 31 *December* 1522."

It is quite possible for persons, whether Italians or English, to attach too much importance to the question of Sebastian's birthplace. Those who are anxious to state as a fact that Sebastian was born in Bristol must be staggered with the statement that their hero, in 1522, declared most positively that he "was born in Venice, but was brought up in England." And this declaration follows his statement, previously forwarded to Venice by his agent, that he was a native of that city. It is beyond the possibility of doubt that he did represent himself to be a Venetian, and his further explanation as to what had taken place between himself and the Venetian friar forms additional proof of the fact. He reiterates the statement as to his birthplace in giving Contarini his reasons for not completing his negotiations with Henry VIII. "As by serving the King of England I should not be able to serve my country, I wrote to the Cæsarean Majesty[1] that he should not, on any

---

[1] The purport of this statement is, that while he was in London negotiating with King Henry VIII. or his council for a voyage of discovery, he wrote to the King of Spain asking him to recall him (Sebastian) to Spain.

account, give me permission to serve the King of England, because there would be great injury to his service, but that he should recall me." Here is a beautiful example of the wiles and guiles of the artful Sebastian. In England, as we shall presently see, he represented himself, or allowed people to regard him as, an Englishman. In his negotiations with Cardinal Wolsey and the council, he probably intimated that he knew of a new route—a north-west opening—to the Indies. It should be remembered that the knowledge at that time in England as to the position of "the Indies," and as to the extent of the continents of North and South America, was of a very hazy description. Simultaneously with his intrigues with the English, he, with a view to enhance the value of his services in Spain, wrote to the Spanish King telling him of the desire of the English for his services, and intimating that it was his (Sebastian's) wish to be recalled to Spain, because an engagement in England would greatly injure the interests of the Spanish King. We have previously seen that arrangements were actually made for an English expedition, which was probably prepared for the navigation of the mythical North-West Passage. And now we know that the whole scheme, for which preparation had been made, was frustrated by the duplicity of Sebastian. But this cunning intriguer had the audacity to tell the Venetian Ambassador, that he had asked the King of Spain to recall him on the ground that Spanish interests might be prejudiced. He was clearly deceiving the King of Spain. The alleged reason for his wishing to obtain employment in England, which was supposed by the English King to be Sebastian's birthplace, was, that he was anxious to serve his native country. He now represents that he belongs to Venice. "As by serving the King of England, I should not be able to serve *my country*." And this is alleged to have been the result of a conversation with a Venetian friar whom he met in England, and who had asked him to remember his "own country" (Venice.) "Is it not possible that you might also be useful to it?" asked the Venetian friar. "I felt this in my heart at the time, and replied that I would think it over. Having returned to him [the Venetian friar], on the following day, I said that I had a way by which that city [Venice] might participate in these voyages, and I showed him a way which would be of great utility."

In the year 1547, the Privy Council of Edward VI. accepted Cabot's offer to enter the English service. On the 9th of October in that year a warrant was issued to Sir Edmund Peckham, high treasurer of the Mints, "for the transporting of one Shabot (*sic*) as Pilot to come out of Hispain to serve and inhabit in England." Harrisse[1] explains that Cabot was engaged for more than ten years in underhand dealings with the English ambassador at the Court of Spain, proffering his services to England. It appears that so far back as the 28th of November 1538, Sir Philip Hoby, on his leaving Spain for England, made the following memorandum : " To remember Sebastian Cabote. He hath here but 300 ducats a year, and he is desirous, if he might not serve the King,[2] at least

[1] Pp. 320, 321.   [2] Henry VIII.

to see him, as his old master. And I think therein. And that I may have an answer in this."[1] On the 6th January 1548-49, Edward VI. granted Cabot an annuity of £166, 13s. 4d., "but not the title or office of pilot-major of England, as is generally believed."[2] It appears that at the time Cabot was arranging terms with the council of Edward VI. he was merely on leave of absence from Spain, he having appointed as his deputy one Diego Gutierrez. On the 29th of January 1549-50, we find that the Spanish ambassador in London requested that the Lords of the Privy Council of Edward VI. would, as soon as possible, give him an answer to a request of the Spanish King to send Cabot back. On the 21st of April 1550, Sir Philip Hoby conveyed an answer to the effect that "Cabot was not detained in England by them, but that he of himself refused to go either into Spain or to the Emperor, and that he being of that mind, *and the King's subject*, no reason nor equity would that he should be forced or compelled to go against his will." But Sebastian's desire for intrigues led him once more into a correspondence with Venice. We have seen that, in the year 1550, he was described as an Englishman, "King's subject." It is recorded in the Venetian archives, that in September 1551 he had again proffered his services to the maritime republic, and, whatever may have been the nature of the communication, it is certain that the

---

[1] Harrisse, p. 318. Gairdner, *Letters and Papers, Foreign and Domestic, of the reign of Henry VIII.*, vol. xiii. pt. i.; vol. ii. No. 974, p. 415.

[2] Harrisse, p. 321. Biddle, *Memoir of Sebastian Cabot*, p. 305.

CABOT'S DISCOVERY OF NORTH AMERICA 233

Venetians regarded him as a native of Venice. The extraordinary fact, founded upon the unimpeachable evidence of the Venetian archives, is that the communications from Sebastian Cabot were transmitted through Giacomo Soranzo, the Venetian ambassador in London, to the Council of Ten of Venice, and that they were remitted by the council to *Ramusio, the historian*, who was at that period its secretary. And the same mysterious dealings between the parties to the intrigue which had characterised the former communications, made when Sebastian was in Spain, were yet again resorted to.

DESPATCH of the Council of Ten to Giacomo Soranzo, Venetian Ambassador in England.[1]

"By your letters of the 17th of last month to the heads of our Council of Ten, we have understood what you have deemed it necessary to report respecting our most faithful Sebastian Caboto, which has been very agreeable to us, and we approve of your diligence in obtaining special information respecting his quality and condition. In reply, we say that you should inform him that this, his offer, is most gratifying, using the best words that your judgment suggests. As to the request that has been made to you by those Lords touching the credit he claims, and the recovery of goods, you can reply that we desire to do all we can to make things agreeable to that Majesty and to their Lordships; but, as Caboto is not known to anyone here, it will be necessary that he himself should

[1] *Calendar of State Papers (Venice)*, v., No. 711, p. 264.

come personally to justify his claim, the matters of which he speaks being of very old date, and we have now replied to the magnificent ambassador of that Majesty, in conformity with your letter; therefore, explain all this to Caboto. On this ground he might ask and obtain permission to come, and you should see that he has the means to come here as soon as possible. You should endeavour, using the same method, to gather further information from him respecting those important particulars that you have been able to report hitherto, as well as his designs touching this navigation, transmitting all details to the heads."

We must now resume the correspondence of the years 1522 and 1523.

Despatch of Gaspar Contarini to the Senate of Venice.

"Serenissime Princeps et Excellentissimi Domini.

"Quel Sebastian Cabot del quale vostre Excellentie me imposé a parlarli circa le cose de le spiziarie et da me cussi exequito como per mie di X. zener li significai, è stato più volte da poij ad me sempre facendomi intender la disposition sua esser di venir exeguir quanto l'havria in animo di operar per Vostra Celsitudine in tal materia de specie. Tandem hozi venuto ad trovarmi, se ha risolto non poter per hora dimandare licentia dubitando che non lo tolesseno per suspecto che el volesse andare in Engelterra, et che però li era necessario anchor per tre mesi scorer, qual passati al tuto era per venir a li piedi di Vostra

Illustrissima Signoria, pregandola che interim la vogli scriver una lettera in la forma de l'altra li fu mandata et solicitarlo a venir de li a Venetia per expedir le cose sue a cio monstrandola, de qui li fusse più liberamente concesso licentia. Scrivo a Vestra Celsitudine quanto che lui Sebastiano mi ha dichiarito et ricercato, quella disponerà quanto li piacerà.

"*Vallijoleti, Die* 7 *Martij* 1523."
(Carte 289 tergo. Lettere, Contarini citate.)

[TRANSLATION]

" Most serene Prince and most excellent Lords.

"That Sebastian Cabot, with whom your Excellencies instructed me to speak on the subject of the spice countries, and respecting whom I reported, has been to me several times, always giving me to understand that his wish is to come to Venice, and to work in the interests of your Highnesses in that matter of the spiceries. At length, he sought me to say that he could not now seek permission to go, doubting whether it might not be suspected that he wished to go to England, and that he would be absent three months. After that, he would come to the feet of your most illustrious Lordships, praying that meanwhile a letter might be written in the form of the other that was sent, asking him to come to Venice to expedite his private affairs. Thus leave would be more easily obtained. I write to your Highnesses to report what this Sebastian has said, respecting which steps will be taken as seems desirable.

"*Valladolid, 7th day of March* 1523."

DESPATCH of the Council of Ten to Gaspar Contarini.[1]

"28 Aprile 1523.

"Ser Casparo Contareno.

"Oratori nostro apud Cesaream Maiestatem.

"Ricevessimo in questi giorni passati le vostre direttive a li Capi del Consiglio nostro dei Dieci, de ultimo Dicembre prossimo preterito, per le quali intendessemo tutto il colloquio havuto cum Sebastiane Cabotto ne la materia de la specie, nel che in vero cum summa prudentia, et bon modo vi sete governato, et non potemo, se non grandemente commendare il studio et diligenza vostra. Dapoi habiamo riceputo altre vostre de 7 Marzo preterito, per le qual vedemo la risolutione in ch'era rimasto esso Sebastiano, de non poter venir qui fino a tre mesi; et che poi al tuto l'era per vinir, rechiedendo chel se li faci de qui scriver una lettera in la forma delle precedenti per le cose sue, aciò che cum quella al tempo predicto possi licitamente partirsi de lì. Unde per satisfactione sua habiamo fatto far una altra lettera in nome di quello Hieronymo de Marino de Rhagusi, che qui vene ad farne la relatione di tal cose et mandovela qui inserta nel mazzo del Circunspecto Secretario vostro, si come fu facto delle precedenti, la qual consignarete al dito Caboto semotis arbitris, suadendolo che el se ne vengi qui, si come el vi ha promesso de far, perché sempre el sarà ben veduto da noi : et cusi eseguirete dandone adviso a li capi antedicti, et se al zonzer de queste il prefacto Cabotta non se retrovasse de lì in Corte, mandereteli la lettera sua dove el se ritrovera. Tutta via per mezo fido et securo si che la ge capiti in mano ; denotandovi che il dito Hieronimo Marino al presente

[1] Brown, N. 699, vol. iii.

non se retrova qui in Venezia, ne sapemo dove el sii, ancor che le lettere de esso Hieronimo apparino date qui in Venezia. Il che dicemo per vostra instructione.

"Andreas Foscarenus, C.C. Xm.
"Jacobus Michael, C.C. Xm. subscrip.
"Andreas Fosculus, C.C. Xm. subscrip.
"Lecta Dominis Sapientibus utriusque manus semotis ceteris et etiam Dominis Consiliariis.
"Lecta Dominis Capitibus."

[Translation]

"Lord Gasparo Contarini, our Orator near the Cæsarean Majesty. 28th April 1523.

"We have received, a few days since, your despatches addressed to the chiefs of our Council of Ten, dated the last of December, in which you report all the intercourse you have had with Sebastian Cabotto on the subject of the spices, and we cannot refrain from highly commending the prudence and judgment with which you have conducted the negotiation. We have also received your despatch of March 7th, from which we learn the resolution of the said Sebastian not to come here for three months; and that he requests a letter may be written on the subject of his own affairs, whereby leave may be more easily obtained. We have, therefore, caused another letter to be prepared in the name of that Hieronimo de Marino from Ragusa, who came here to make the proposal; and we have ordered that it be placed in the bundle of your circumspect secretary, like the last, to be delivered to the said Cabotto, telling him that he should come here in accordance with his promise, as he will always be welcome by us. Let the said Cabotto be informed of this, and, if he is not at Court, the letter should be forwarded to him. Take care that it reaches him. The said Hieronimo Marino *is not now to be found here in Venice, nor do we know where he is*, but the letters of this Hieronimo arrive here. Receive what we say as your instructions.

      "ANDREAS FOSCARENUS, C.C.
      "JACOBUS MICHAEL, C.C.
      "ANDREAS FOSCULUS, C.C."

LETTERÆ SCRIPTÆ nomine Hieronymi di Marino Rhagusor ad Sebastianum Caboto in Hispaniam existentem.

"Spectabile Messer Sebastiano,—Za alcuni mesi zonto che io fui qui in Venetia vi scrissi quanto haveva operato per inquirir dove si trovano de li beni vostri, nel che io hebbi bone parolle in cadauno loco, et mi fu dato bona speranza de recuperar la dote di vostra madre, et ameda, unde non dubito che si vui fosti venuto qui haveresti za conseguito quanto ó il vostro desiderio; et per tanto per lo amor vi porto, et per il beneficio, et utile ve sio exhortar ad non vi manchar a vui medesimo, ma transferirve qui a Venetia, dove non dubito impetrarete il tutto, et non tardarete ad venir qui, perché la ameda vostra ó molto vecchia, et mancando lei, haveresti poi grandissma fatica a inquirir et recuperar il vostro; peró ve conforto ad mettervi in camino più presto potete. Altro non vi dico per tora a vui mi offro per sempre.

"Vostro Hieronimo de Marino.

"*Venetiis, die* 28 *Aprilis* 1523."
(Capi del Consiglio de'Dicci. Lettere sottoscritte, Filza, No. 6, 1523.)

TRANSLATION of the Forged Letter from Jerome the Ragusan to Cabot.

"VENICE, *April* 28, 1523.

"Respectable Master Sebastian,—

"It is some months since I came to Venice, and I wrote to you an account of what I had done to inquire where your goods are to be found, that I received good words on all hands, and was given good hope that I should recover the dower of your mother,[1] so that I have no doubt, if you could come, you would obtain all your desires. For the love I bear you, and for your own welfare and benefit, I exhort you not to be false to yourself, but to come here to Venice, where I doubt not, you will obtain everything; so do not delay in coming here, for your *ameda* is very old, and failing her there will be very great trouble in recovering your property. Set out as soon as possible, so no more at present.— I am, always yours, HIERONIMO DE MARINO."

DESPATCH of Gaspar Contarini to the Senate of Venice, 26th July 1523.

"Serenissime Princeps et excellentissimi Domini, Cum la posta venuta de Italia per qui, come in le

[1] "et ameda." (?)

comune facio mentione per via da Roma, ricevi cum la solita riverentia mia lettere sue de 23 April per le qual Vostra Serenità dandome adviso dil ricever de le mie scripteli circa la executione facta cum Sebastiano Caboto, etc., me subgionge che iterum la invia altre lettere a lui Sebastiano a nome di quel Hieronimo de Ragusi iuxta la richiesta sua et cussi ho ritrovato in le publiche esse lettere. La bona sorte volse, che essendo lui Sebastiano in Sibilia due giorni da poii il ricevir de le lettere, ritornò de qui al qual consignato le sue lo exortai a venirsene de li. Disseme che in altro non era il pensier suo et a questo fine era venuto de qui. Da poij mi ha parlato dicendo chel procura cum questi del consiglio Cesareo di haver licentia di conferirse de li, et che etiam parlino a me in commendatione sua. Questo é quanto ho da lui, de quanto seguirà Vostra SERENITÁ NE SARÀ ADVISATA.

"*Vallijoleti, die 26 Julij* 1523."
(Carte 302, Lett. Contarini cit.)

[TRANSLATION]

"Most Serene Prince and most excellent Lords,—

"By the post arrived from Italy coming by way of Rome, I received with due reverence your letter of April 23rd, in which your Serenity informed me of the receipt of my letters reporting the negotiation with Sebastian Cabot, and adding that other letters have been sent to Sebastian in the name of Hieronimo of Ragusa with reference to his request. By good luck Sebastian was in Seville when he received the letters, and he returned here on being exhorted to come. He told me he had no other thoughts, and with that object he had come; adding that he had sought permission from the Cæsarean Council to confer with me, and they have also spoken to me in his commendation. I will advise your Serenity of what may happen next.

"*Valladolid, 26th day of July* 1523."

This correspondence gives us a delightful insight into the intricacies pursued by the wily Italian school of diplomacy of the period. The Venetian Council of Ten had at its disposal, and employed in the secret service of Venice, some of the most highly-educated men which the Renaissance had produced. Contarini, for example, who was born in Venice in 1483, was a man who was possessed of deep learning and of a variety of accomplishments. He belonged to a patrician family that had grown rich through commerce. He was an apt scholar, and his environments led him towards a practical application of the benefits he had received from a liberal education. In the Venetian Senate he was a marked success, and in consequence of his great abilities he was appointed Ambassador to Charles v. of Spain. A perusal of his despatches afford only slight evidence of his great ability. Peter Martyr d'Anghiera, the historian, had recourse to him for the purpose of solving any questions of unusual difficulty in geographical or cosmographical matters.[1] Contarini served the

[1] A Spanish ship arriving at one of the Moluccas found that it was Thursday, whereas the Spaniards' calculation showed that it ought to be Wednesday; and they were all sure that there was no error in their calculation. From this they came to suspect that the course of time from our shores to those regions must have caused the difference. Peter Martyr, having to relate this matter in his *Decades*, did not know what to think about it, and to put himself at ease he had recourse to the great learning of Contarini: "Quando ad Gorgones

Republic of Venice as Ambassador to Pope Clement VII. From another occupant of the papal chair (Paul III.) he received such flattering assurances of the high respect in which he was held that he was offered, and ultimately induced to accept, a cardinal's hat. He hesitated for a long time before entering the Church, and his objections were not satisfied until some pressure was brought to bear upon him by his own Venetian fellow-citizens. The offer was made to him at a period when a struggle —one of the most momentous importance—was being waged in Germany against the power of Rome. He worked indefatigably in endeavouring to bring about a reconciliation between the conflicting interests. In conjunction with several other Church dignitaries, notably Cardinals Pole, Sadolet, and others, he propagated ideas for the reform of the abuses of the Romish Church, with a view to conciliate the formidable opposition which had arisen. So far as can be gathered from contemporary records, his great knowledge of the world prompted him to lean towards the reformers, and we have practical proof of the bent of his mind in his "Relation" to Paul III. against the abuse of compositions, and the sale of spiritual favours. In the year 1541 he attended the Conference of Ratisbon. His diplomatic knowledge was of little avail, however, against the great struggle which was then proceeding. The French Court

navis hæc regressa fuit, diem fuisse Mercurii arbitrabantur, Jovis esse repererunt. Unde diem unum in eo discursu aiunt sibi ablatum, ea trium annorum intercapedine. . . . Agitatus ea cura conveni Gasparem Contarinum, oratorem apud cæsarem pro sua illustri Republica Veneta, omni litteratum genere non mediocriter eruditum" (*Dec.* v. cap. 7). It is needless to say that I relate this anecdote merely as a proof of Contarini's learning, and of the estimation in which he was held on questions of cosmography.—Tarducci, pp. 290, 291.

threw all sorts of obstacles in the way of a reconciliation between the Catholics and the Protestants of Germany, not on religious grounds, but because it was so apparent that the *rapprochements* of the contending parties would be the means of strengthening the temporal power of Charles v. It was deemed advisable on the part of France to fan the flames of religious fanaticism. Contarini's mission to Germany was a great strain upon his health. He was subsequently appointed by the pope as ambassador, just on the eve of the Council of Trent, but died shortly after his appointment. His death took place at Bologna in 1542.

CHAPTER VII

Mr. Harrisse says :[1] "As the reader has seen, the letters-patent of 1496 were granted to John Cabot and his three sons; but no documentary proof whatever has yet been adduced to show that any of them accompanied their father in his first trans-atlantic voyage. The only circumstance which may be cited on the subject would rather prove the reverse. Pasqualigo, in describing John Cabot's return, says: ' E ali dato danari fazi bona ziera fino a quel tempo e con su moier venitiana e con so fioli a Bristo :— And [the King] has given him money wherewith to amuse himself till then [the second expedition]; and he is now at Bristol with his Venetian wife, and with his sons.'"

With regard to the claim made on behalf of Sebastian Cabot, that he was the discoverer of the north continent of America in 1497, Mr. Harrisse says : "The belief rests exclusively upon statements from his own lips, made at a time, under circumstances, in a form and with details, which render them very suspicious." The evidence seems to justify Mr. Harrisse's suggestion that "the belief" did originally arise from a statement made by Sebastian Cabot; at the same time, every person should form an independent judgment as to the

[1] P. 48.

comparative agency of John and Sebastian Cabot in the voyage of discovery in 1497. Bearing always in mind the important fact—which many persons regard as the key-note to all the difficulties—that the evidence now before us, which has been exhumed from foreign archives, was not known to the early historians, we will now refer to certain MS. English chronicles, maps, histories, etc., with a view to ascertain to what extent they throw light on those points of historical interest which yet remain unsettled or unsolved.

In the Cottonian MSS., preserved in the British Museum, there is a chronicle bearing this title: " Chronicon regum Angliæ et series maiorum et vicecomitum Civitatis London ab anno primo Henrici tertium ad annum primum. Hen. 8$^{vi.}$"[1]

"In Anno 13, Henry VII.

"This yere the King at the besy request and supplicacion of a straunger venisian, which by a cæart made hym self expert in knowyng of the world caused the Kyng to manne a ship w^t vytaill and other necessairies for to seche an Ilande wheryn the said straunger surmysed to be grete commodities: w^t which ship by the Kynge's grace so Rygged went 3 or 4 moo owte of Bristowe, the said straunger beying Conditor of the said Flete, whereyn dyuers Merchaunts as well of London as Bristow adventured goodes and sleight Merchandises, which departed from the West Cuntrey in the begynning of somer but to this present moneth came never knowlege of their exployts."

This chronicle, which purports to refer to events which took place between the first year of Henry VII.

[1] MS. Cott. Vitellius, A. xiv. f. 173.

and the first of Henry VIII., speaks of an event which is said to have happened in the thirteenth year of Henry VII. This entry is typical of the hopeless muddle which the history of the two voyages of John Cabot was in prior to the year 1831.[1] Up to that date the chroniclers and historians, whether contemporary or subsequent, knew only of one voyage.[2] In writing as to this chronicle, Mr. Henry Harrisse says: "Mr. Gairdner, of the Public Record Office, who kindly re-examined that manuscript at our request in 1881, and who is one of the highest authorities on such historical matters, reported that the Chronicon is a perfectly trustworthy source of contemporaneous information, its earlier portion derived from a common source with several other London chronicles, such as Gregory's;[3] whilst the latter part has something in common with Fabyan, but containing a good deal for the reign of Henry VII. not to be found anywhere else in print. So much for the intrinsic and paleographic proofs of its authenticity" (Harrisse, *John Cabot*, etc., London, 1896, p. 128).

We should not accept too readily any statement which suggests that this chronicle is a contemporary record in the truest sense. It is an anonymous compilation, so far as we can ascertain, and it is impossible for anyone to say within a score or so

---

[1] The date of the publication of Biddle's Memoir of Sebastian Cabot.

[2] An exception to this statement may, perhaps, be made in favour of Hakluyt, who seems to have discovered the two grants of letters-patent by King Henry VII. But Hakluyt's information was not put before his readers as clearly as it should have been. In justice to Hakluyt and other chroniclers, it should never be forgotten that access to the archives of foreign countries was completely barred, and that the English Rolls were practically inaccessible.

[3] Published by M. Gairdner, in the collections of a London citizen.

of years when the entries were first made. These entries may have been largely taken from a previous record. The information contained in it may or may not be strictly beyond suspicion. In all probability it is a very honest production,—that is, a compilation made by a person who was desirous of honestly chronicling events of importance which, in the opinion of the chronicler, it was desirable should be handed on to succeeding generations. And we must always bear in mind, in connection with MS. chronicles, that they may contain entries of events, particulars whereof have been obtained from other persons, and therefore may record facts not strictly within the personal knowledge of the chronicler. A most casual glance at the entry in this chronicle will convince one that it was written by a person who probably knew of one voyage only, namely, that of the year 1498. The accurate information we possess as to the details of the two voyages leaves us no alternative but to say this. The name of Cabot is not referred to: and, as a matter of fact, his name is never mentioned by an English chronicler for at least half a century after the date of his voyage of discovery: outside the official rolls his name cannot be found. Campbell, in *Lives of the Admirals*, very properly says: "John Cabot was the real discoverer, of which honour he ought not to be despoiled, even by his son."

We will now proceed to discuss an event, than which, in the evolutionary process through which the Cabot history has proceeded, none is of greater importance.

In the year 1582 Richard Hakluyt published

the first edition of his celebrated work as to voyages relating to the discovery of America. It may be as well to here relate a few particulars of Hakluyt and of his publications. He was born in, or about, the year 1552, and after an early education at Westminster School, was, in 1570, elected to a studentship at Christ Church, Oxford, where he graduated B.A., 19th February 1574, and M.A., 27th January 1577. In the year before mentioned (1582), he, as the result of much study of the various chronicles and histories containing information to guide him, published *Divers Voyages touching the Discovery of America*, full particulars whereof will be presently given. His next collection of information was described as *A particular Discourse concerning Western Discoveries*, written in 1584, but first printed in 1877, in the Collections of the Maine (America) Historical Society. A copy of this MS. work presented to the Queen, procured him the reversion of a prebendal stall at Bristol, to which he succeeded in 1586.[1] In 1589 he published *The principal Navigations, Voyages, and Discoveries of the English Nation made by Sea or over land to the most remote and furthest distant quarters of the Earth, at any time within the compass of these 1500 years*. This volume was the germ, or, as it is commonly called, the first edition, of the much larger work which he published some ten years

[1] Canon Ainger now occupies the stall in the Bristol Cathedral formerly in the possession of Richard Hakluyt. This information is given upon the authority of Mr. W. W. Hughes, the chapter-clerk, who is an active member of the Cabot Celebration Committee at Bristol. Hakluyt, who returned from a European journey in quest of geographical information in 1584, exhibited in person before the Chapter of Bristol the Queen's mandate for the reversion of the Prebend on the 24th May 1585 (*Encyclop. Brit.* pp. 378, 379).

later, under a title almost identical in its general statement, but differing in its details (3 vols. sm. fol. 1598–1600). It should be mentioned that Hakluyt, in April 1590, was appointed to the rectory of Wetteringsett, in Suffolk. In May 1602 he was appointed prebendary of Westminster, and archdeacon in the following year. He died in 1616 (*Encyclopædia Britannica*, pp. 378, 379).

Hakluyt's first work, published in 1582, was dedicated to "The Right Worshipful, and most virtuous gentleman, Master Philip Sydney, Esq." Zouch, in his *Life of Sir Philip Sydney* (p. 317), refers to Hakluyt as follows :—" His incomparable industry was remunerated with every possible encouragement by Sir Francis Walsingham and Sir Philip Sydney. To the latter, as a most generous promoter of all ingenious and useful knowledge, he inscribed his first collection of voyages and discoveries, printed in 1582."

The following description of the rare little work is given in one of Mr. Bernard Quaritch's catalogues :—

"Hakluyt's voyages. The excessively rare original collection. Divers | voyages touching the discouerie of | America, and the Ilands adjacent | vnto the same, made first of all by our | Englishmen, and afterwards by the French- | men and Britons : | And certaine notes of aduertisements for obserua- | tions.
. . | . . | With two mappes annexed hereunto
. . | . . . | . | Imprinted at Lon- | don for Thomas Woodcocke, | dwelling in paules Church-yard, at the sign of the blacke beare. 1582.

"Small 4to., 60 leaves of letterpress and 2 folded woodcut maps, one designed by Robert Thorne, the other by Michael Lok." . . .

This little collection of voyages—the first book published by Richard Hakluyt—was expanded seven years' later into a thick folio volume, and the result was to make it so rare that only two perfect copies are now in existence [1] (both in the British Museum); and only four which are not perfect. Of these four, the Bodleian copy has only Lok's map, the two in America have neither map (they are supplied in facsimile), and the present has the original Thorne map, which is the more interesting of the two, as having been designed by himself in Seville in 1527, and sent in that year to Henry VIII.'s ambassador in Spain for transmission to the king.

"Collation and Contents: Title, 1 p.; Names of the late writers of Geographie, 1 p.; Names of certaine late trauailers, 1 p.; A verie late and great probabilitie of a passage by the North-west, 1 p.; Dedication of Sir Philip Sidney, 7 pp,; 1 p. blank; Letters, patents of Henry VII. to the Cabots, in Latin and English, 4 pp.; Notes from Fabian and Ramusio, 3 pp.; 1 p. blank; Robert Thorne's Declaration of the Indies, addressed to Henry VIII. (1527), 5 pp.; The Booke made by Thorne in 1527, 18 pp.; 1 p. blank; Verrazzano's Relation to Francis I., translated, 15 pp.; The Discouerie made by the Zeno brothers, 18 pp.; 1 p. blank; Ribault's Discouerie of Florida, translated by Thomas Hackitt, 20 pp.; 2 pp. blank; Notes given by a Gentleman to Pette and Jackman, sent for the discouerie of the north-east strayte, 12 pp.; Notes to be given to one that prepared for a discouerie . . . 6 pp.; Names of certain commodities growing in part of America, 3 pp.

---

[1] The copy offered for sale by Mr. Quaritch has "the last two leaves and one of the maps in facsimile."

"Parts of this little volume were omitted in the larger publication. For instance, the curious notes concerning the contemporary ownership of Robert Thorne's and Sebastian Cabot's papers; also the accounts of Verrazzano, Zeno, and Ribault. The maps were also omitted. Price, £150."

One of the entries in this volume is the following:—

"This much concerning Sebastian Cabot's discoverie may suffice for a present taste, but shortly, God willing, shall come out in print all his own mappes and discourses drawne and written by himselfe, which are in the custodie of the worshipful Master William Worthington, one of her Majesty's pensioners, who (because so worthie monuments should not be buried in perpetual oblivion) is very willing to suffer them to be overseene, and published in as good order as may be to the encouragement and benefite of our countrymen."

It will be observed that Hakluyt does not say he had actually seen the maps. The above statement is omitted from the subsequent additions of Hakluyt's work.

Hakluyt's publication of 1582 includes the following reference to the discovery of North America by Cabot:—

"A note of Sebastian Gabote's voyage of discoverie, taken out of an old Chronicle, written by Robert Fabian, some time alderman of London, which is in the custodie of John Stow, citizen, a diligent searcher and preserver of antiquities.

"In the 13 yere of King Henrie the VII., 1498.

"This yere the King (by means of a Venetian, whiche made himself very experte and cunning in knowledge of the circuit of the worlde, and Ilandes of the same as by a Carde, and other demonstrations reasonable hee shewed), caused to man and victual a shippe at Bristowe to search for an Ilande, whiche hee saide hee knewe well was riche, and replenished with riche commodities. Which ship, thus manned and victualled at the King's cost, divers merchants of London ventured in her small stockes, being in her, as chief patrone, the said Venetian. And in the companie of the said shippe sailed also out of Bristowe, three or foure small ships, fraught with sleight and grosse merchandizes, as course cloth, caps, laces, points, and other trifles, and so departed from Bristowe in the beginning of May; of whom in this Maior's[1] time returned no tidings."

The heading commences with Hakluyt's addition to some MS. chronicle, which chronicle, he says, was written by Fabyan, and was in the custody of John Stow. Inasmuch as Eden's work[2] was published in 1555, Hakluyt was acquainted with the particulars as to the Cabot voyage given by Peter Martyr[3] and Ramusio[4] respectively, and it is not improbable that his reference to "Sebastian Gaboto's voyage of discoverie" was inserted in the full belief—honestly arrived at—that Sebastian was the real discoverer of America. Stow's collection was published in the year 1580,[5] and his record of the event reads: "This yeare one Sebastian Gabato, a genoas sonne," etc. It will thus be seen that Hakluyt has taken Sebastian's name from the body of the chronicle and placed it in a heading, and has substituted for "a genoas sonne," "a Venetian."

[1] "William Purchas, Maior of London" (1497–1498).
[2] *Ante*, p. 170.   [3] *Ante*, p. 169.   [4] *Ante*, pp. 184, 185, 195.
[5] *The Chronicles of England*, London, 4to, p. 862.

CABOT'S DISCOVERY OF NORTH AMERICA 253

Why did not Hakluyt follow Stow? The remarkable similarity in the accounts given in the three chronicles seem to tempt one to say that they must have had a common origin. This, however, is not a matter of great importance. Hakluyt states, also, that he had obtained information "out of the latter part of Robert Fabyan's chronicle, not hitherto printed, which is in the custody of Mr. John Stowe." And John Stow relates that he had "a continuation by Fabyan himself, as late as the third year of Henry VIII.[1] The most extraordinary part of this story is that Fabyan's Chronicle[2] contains no reference whatever to the event. *In the second of his works*, Hakluyt makes the chronicle read as follows:—" In the 13 yeere of King Henrie the VII., by means of one *John* Cabot, a Venetian," and the same variation appears in his third book. By placing this last account in juxtaposition with that of Stow, the striking alteration made by Hakluyt will at once appear.

JOHN STOW'S ACCOUNT (1580).

In a book written by John Stow, and published in London in 1580, the following information is supposed to relate to a voyage undertaken in the 14th year of the reign of Henry VII. :—" This yeare one Sebastian Gabato, a genoas sonne, borne in Bristow, professing himselfe to be experte in knowledge of the circute of the worlde and Ilandes

[1] Harleian MSS. 538, quoted by Biddle, p. 299.
[2] Robert Fabyan was the author of the *Chronicle of England and France*, otherwise *The Concordance of Stories*. He was born in London about the year 1450. He held several important positions in the Corporation of London. His death occurred in, or about, 1512.

of the same, as by his Charts and other reasonable demonstration he shewed, caused the king to man and victual a shippe at Bristow to search for an Ilande whiche he knewe to be replenished with rich commodities; in the shippe diverse merchauntes of London adventured smal stockes, and in the company of this shippe, sayled out of Bristow three or foure smal shippes frought with slight and grosse wares, as course cloth, caps, laces, points" (*The Chronicle of England, from Brute vnto this present yeare of Christ*, 1580.)

HAKLUYT'S [SECOND] ACCOUNT (1600).

"A note of *Sebastian* Cabot's first discoverie of part of the Indies, taken out of the latter part of Robert Fabyan's Chronicle, not hitherto printed, which is in the custodie of M. John Stow, a diligent preserver of antiquities.[1]

"In the 13 yeere of K. Henry the 7 (by means of one *John* Cabot, a Venetian, which made himselfe very expert and cunning in knowledge of the circuit of the world and islands of the same, as by a sea card and other demonstrations reasonable he shewed), the King caused to man and victuall a ship at Bristow to search for an island which he said he knew well was rich, and replenished with great commodities: which shippe, thus manned and victualled at the King's costs, divers merchants of London ventured in her small stocks, being in her, as chief Patron, the said Venetian. And in the company of the said ship sailed, also, out of Bristow, three or foure small ships, fraught with

[1] Hakluyt, vol. iii. p. 9.

sleight and gross merchandizes, as course cloth, caps, laces, points, and other trifles, and so departed from Bristow in the beginning of May, of whom, in this Maior's time, returned no tidings" (*Voyages, Navigation*, etc., collected by Richard Hakluyt, preacher, and sometime student of Christ Church in Oxford . . . 1600).

Quoting the words of the "Chronicon," yet preserved in the British Museum, as follows:—
"This yere the Kyng, at the besy request and supplication of a Straunger venisian, which by a cœart made by hymself expert in knowying of the world" . . . Harrisse says: "Hakluyt's first account (1582) is certainly more in accordance with the above text than is that of Stow, and as he expressly states that he took it from the copy of Fabyan, then in the possession of Stow, we are bound to infer that Stow's copy of Fabyan did not contain the words, 'Sebastian Gabato, a genoas sonne,' and that these are an interpolation made by Stow himself." Francesco Tarducci says: "Stow's collection was also published after his death, and there we find the same narrative precisely as it is given by Hakluyt; but in the single point where the two editions differ, . . . Stow's collection is at variance with both. . . . It is clear that the original account of the old chronicle has been falsified. By whom? Before answering, let me briefly recall to the reader's memory who Hakluyt and Stow were, for a knowledge of their persons and characters may aid us to take a few steps in the obscurity of this question.

"Hakluyt[1] . . . was the greatest writer and

[1] Dr. S. E. Dawson says: "Hakluyt is the pioneer of the literature of English discovery and adventure—at once the recorder and

collector of memoirs relating to the voyages and navigations of discovery made by the English in the northern seas. . . . As to his collection, it is still among the best, not of England only, but of the whole world. The appreciation of the English for this collection, especially of navigators and discoverers, is shown by the facts that in his lifetime Bylot, who had Baffin[1] for his pilot, gave the name of Hakluyt to an island in Baffin's Bay. Hudson, whose name is borne by the great inland sea of North America, called a cape off Spitzberg after Hakluyt, whilst he was still living; and finally, during his lifetime also, a river discovered by English navigators in 1611, near Petschora, was called by his name." He then goes on to say that Stow " was born of poor parents," that in pursuing his researches he was severely handicapped by his poverty. " Short of means, he made long journeys afoot to hunt over and ransack colleges and monasteries, and no matter how worn and torn might be the rags of old papers which he found, he kept all, reviewing, connecting, copying, comparing, annotating with truly wonderful ability and good sense. Arrived at fourscore years, and no longer capable of earning a livelihood, he applied to the king, and James I., consenting to his petition, granted to the man who had saved treasures of memoirs for English history, the favour of wearing a beggar's garb and asking alms at church doors.

inspirer of noble effort ; . . . if discrepancies are met with in a collection so voluminous, it is not surprising, and need not be ascribed to a set purpose; for Hakluyt's sole object in life seems to have been to record all he knew or could ascertain of the maritime achievements of the age."

[1] Hence " Baffin's " Bay.

In this abject state, forgotten and despised, he died two years later in 1605. Which of the two would be likely to lay his rash hands on the old chronicle attributed to Fabyan, the learned Hakluyt, or the devoted Stow? Both; and each in good conscience according to the different point of view from which he regarded the matter." The real truth is that both writers had probably met with information which, in good faith, they turned to account by making a slight variation in the reading of the old chronicle. At that period the contemporary documents were not known to be in existence—such as, for example, the despatches of the foreign ambassadors, which, since their comparatively recent publication, have put it beyond doubt that John Cabot was the sole leader of the expedition which set out from Bristol and eventually discovered the north continent of America. The chroniclers were therefore restricted to the meagre material afforded by the letters-patent, MS. notes, etc., and possibly the impecunious Stow might not have been able to procure a view of the State papers, and may not have known of the existence of the two grants of letters-patent. On the other hand, we have evidence that Hakluyt had not only access to the rolls, but that he made copies of the letters-patent relating to the Cabot voyages. It is not unreasonable to assume, therefore, that so far as Hakluyt is concerned he thought he was perfectly justified in adding the name of John Cabot to the entry found in the chronicle.

It is extremely doubtful whether poor Stow ever had excess to the patent rolls. When Richard Biddle was compiling his Memoir, which was first published in 1831,[1] he experienced the greatest difficulty in finding the document in which the name of John Cabot appeared. At p. 78 of his Memoir he says :—

"The manner in which the precious document referred to, and others of a similar kind, are kept, cannot be adverted to without an expression of regret. They are thrown loosely together, without reference even to the appropriate year, and are unnoticed in any index or calendar. It required a search of more than two weeks to find this patent of 3rd February, 1498, although the year and name of its date were furnished at the outset. . . . An extraordinary compensation is claimed at the Rolls Chapel on account of the trouble attending a search amidst such a confused mass. For *finding* the documents, two guineas were demanded in addition to the cost of copies. The applicant is informed that the charge must be paid whether the document be discovered or not; so that the officer has no motive to continue perseveringly the irksome pursuit."

In Richard Biddle's work (p. 42) the following allusions to the chronicles are made :—

"It happens that we can trace the progress of Hakluyt's perversion. The communication from Stow first appears in the *Divers Voyages to America*.

[1] Biddle's work was published in 1831, both in London and Philadelphia, and a second edition was published in London in 1832. The title of the work is as follows :—*A Memoir of Sebastian Cabot; with a Review of the History of Maritime Discovery. Illustrated by Documents from the Rolls, now first published.* The work is unfitted as a guide to persons, other than students of the Cabot history, so far as it deals with John Cabot's discovery, because it does not contain copies of the despatches and other entries relating to the voyage of 1497, which have been since exhumed from foreign archives. But to Richard Biddle we must render our thanks for having been the first writer who explicitly and authoritatively pointed out that there were two early voyages from Bristol, namely, in 1497 and 1498.

etc., published in 1582. When given at that early period, as derived from "Mr. John Stow, citizen," Hakluyt merely changes the words 'a Genoa's son' into 'a Venetian,' without giving any name. *He had not then heard of the patent of February 3, 1498,* naming John Cabot exclusively, for the only document he quotes is the original patent of March 1496, in which both father and son are mentioned, and which describes the father as a Venetian. He struck out, therefore, only what he then knew to be incorrect. Subsequently he received information of the second patent in favour of John Cabot, and in his enlarged work he not only furnishes a reference to that patent, but makes a further alteration of what he had received from Stow. Instead of 'a Venetian,' as in 1582, when he had the memorandum first before him, it becomes 'one John Cabot, a Venetian,' thus effecting, at the two stages of alteration, a complete change of what he had received,—and yet for the statement as thus finally made Fabian and Stow continue to be cited.[1]

"Hakluyt has, incautiously, suffered to lie about the evidence of his guilty deed, which should have been carefully buried. Thus there is retained[2] the original title of the passage: 'A note of Sebastian Cabot's first discovery of part of the Indies, taken out of the latter part of Robert Fabian's Chronicle, not hitherto printed, which is in the custody of Mr. John Stow, a diligent preserver of antiquities.' Now, it is highly probable that all this, with the

[1] It was an unwarrantable liberty for Hakluyt to take in such a matter. It is, however, a singularly apt illustration as to the way in which a perversion of a document is brought about. Hakluyt was a sinner with regard to his treatment of other documents.
[2] Biddle is now alluding to the later edition.

exception of the compliment, was the explanatory memorandum at the head of Stow's communication. It is incredible that Hakluyt himself should prefix it to a passage which does not contain the slightest allusion to Sebastian Cabot. Thus we see that in indicating to the printer the alterations in the new edition, the pen of Hakluyt, busied with amendment at the critical point, has spared, inadvertently, what betrays him by its incongruity with that which remains, and, like the titles of many acts of parliament, serves to show the successful struggle for amendment after the original draft."

The following note as to the patent of 1498 appears in Hakluyt (vol. iii., edition of 1600) :—

[*Billa signata anno* 13 *Henrici septimi.*]

" Rex tertio die Februarij, anno 13, licentiam dedit Ionni Caboto, quod ipse, capere possit sex naues Anglicanas, in aliquo portii, siue portibus regni Angliæ, ita quod sint deportagio 200 doliorum, vel subtùs, cum apparatu requisito, & quod recipere possit in dictas naues omnes tales magistros, marinarios, & sub ditos regis, qui cum eo exires voluerint," etc.

"The king, upon the third day of February, in the 13 yeere of his reigne, gave license to John Cabot to take five English ships in any haven or havens of the realme of England, being of the burden of 200 tunnes, or under, with all necessary furniture, and to take also into the said ships all such masters, mariners, and subjects of the king as willingly will go with him," etc.

In the year 1844 the French Government purchased for 4000 francs a very remarkable planisphere, which had been found in the house of a

Bavarian clergyman. This map is now preserved, and may be seen in the geographical department of the Paris National Library. It purports to have been delineated in 1544—" Plana figura me delineavit, 1544" (Legend xvii.).

It is desirable to give an exact account of the inscription which purports to relate to the discovery of North America on the Mappe-Monde said to have been published in 1544 by Sebastian Cabot.

Mr. Harrisse[1] gives the original Spanish text of the inscription, and of the translation into Latin, as follows :—

[IN SPANISH]

"No. 8. Esta tierra fue descubierta por Ioan Caboto Veneciano y Sebastian Caboto su hijo, anno del nascimiento de nuestro Saluador Iesu ‖ Christo de M.CCCC.XCIIII. a ueinte y quatro de Iunio, por la mannana, ala qual pusieron nombre prima tierra uista, y a una isla grande que ‖ esta par de la dicha tierra, le pusieron nombre sant Ioan, por auer sido descubierta el mismo dia la gente della andan uestidos de pieles de animales, usan en sus guerras arcos, y flechas, lanças, y dardos, y unas porras de palo, y hondas. Es tierra muy steril, ay en ella muchos orsos plancos, y cieruos muy grandes como cauallos y otras muchas animales y semeiantemente ay pescado infinito, sollos, salmones, lenguados, muy grandes de uara enlargo y otras muchas diuersidades de pescados, y la mayor multitud dellos se dizen baccallaos, y asi mismo ayenta dicha tierra Halcones prietos como cueruos, Aguillas, Perdices, Pardillas, y otras muchas aues de diuersas maneras."

[1] Pp. 432, 433.

[IN LATIN]

"No 8. Terram hanc olim nobis clausam, aperuit Ioannes Cabotus Venetus, necnon Sebastianus Cabotus eius filius, anno ab orbe redem = || pto 1494, die uero 24 Julij [Sic[1]] hora 5. sub diluculo quam terram primum uisam appellarunt, & Insulam quandam magnam ei oppositam, Insulam diui Io || annis nominarunt, quippe quæ solenni die festo diui Io || annis aperta fuit. Huius terræ incolæ pellibus animalium induuntur, arcu in bello, sa = || gittis, hastis, spiculis, clauis, ligneis, & fundis utuntur: sterilis incultaque tellus fuit, leonibus, ursis albis, procerisque ceruis, piscibus innume || ris lupis scilicet, salmonibus, & ingentibus soleis unius ulnæ longitudine, alijsquæ diuersis piscium generibus abundat, horum autem maxima copia || est, quos uulgus Bacallios appellat, ad hæc insunt accipitres nigri coruorum similes, aquilæ, perdicesque fusco colore, aliæque diuersæ uolucres. ||"

It appears that Hakluyt knew of an *extract* from a map, which was regarded as a "Map of Sebastian Cabot," which extract was "hung up in the privy gallery at Whitehall." Inasmuch as the "extract" is not, so far as can be ascertained, at present in existence, we have to rely upon the particulars of the inscription which appear in Hakluyt (vol. iii. p. 6).

"Anno Domini, Joannes Cabotus Venetus, et Sebastianus illius filius eam terram fecerunt perviam, quam nullus priùs adire ausus fuit, die 24 Junii, circiter horam quintam bene manè. Hanc autem appellavit Terram primùm visam, credo quod ex mari

---

[1] This discrepancy in the date is not a matter of importance. It is a palpable error.

in eam partem primùm oculos injecerat. Namque ex adverso sita est insula, cam appellavit insulam Divi Joannis, hac opinor ratione, quod aperta fuit eo qui die est sacer Diuo Joanni Baptistæ: Hujus incolæ pelles animalium exuviasque ferarum pro indumentis habent, easque tanti faciunt, quanti nos vestes preciosissimas. Cùm bellum gerunt, utuntur arcu, sagittis, hastis, spiculis, clavis ligneis et fundis. Tellus sterilis est, neque ullos fructus affert, ex quo fit, ut ursis albo colore, et cervis inusitatæ apud nos magnitudinis referta sit: piscibus abundat, iisque sane magnis, quales sunt lupi marini et quos salmones vulgus appellat; soleæ autem reperiuntur tam longæ, et ulnæ mensuram excedant. Imprimis autem magna est copia eorum piscium, quos vulgari sermone vocant Bacallaos. Gignuntur in ea insula accipitres ita nigri, ut corvorum similitudinem mirum in modum exprimant perdices autem et aquilæ sunt nigri coloris."

Biddle has severely criticised this portion of Hakluyt's contribution to the Cabot history, more especially with regard to the English translation which he (Hakluyt) added to the Latin text.

. . . .

In a paper communicated to the Society of Antiquaries, by Mr R. H. Major, F.S.A., the particulars of one of the legends which appeared upon a copy of a map, professing to be by Sebastian Cabot, are referred to as follows:—

"As far back as the year 1594, a German named Nathaniel Kochhaff, but better known by the name of Chytræus, published at Herborn, in Nassau, a little work entitled *Variorum in Europâ Itinerum Deliciæ*, in which he prints a large variety of legends which he met with in his travels. In the year 1556 he saw at Oxford a map professing to be by Sebastian Cabot, containing nineteen inscriptions, which he transcribed and printed. . . . The inscription numbered 8 is as follows :—

"Terram hanc olim nobis clausam aperuit Johannes Cabotus Venetus, nec non Sebastianus Cabotus eius filius, anno ab orbe redemto 1594,[1] die vero 24 Iunii, hora 5, sub diluculo, quam terram primùm visam, & insulam quandam magnam ei appositam insulam D. Johannis nominarunt, quippe quæ solemni die festo Diui Johannis aperta fuit. Huius terræ incolæ pellibus animalium induuntur. Arco in bello, sagittis, spiculis, clauis ligneis & fandis vtuntur, sterilis incultaq, tellus est, leonibus, ursis albis, procerisq, ceruis, piscibus innumeris, lupis & salmonibus & ingentibus soleis vnius vlne longitudine, aliisque piscium diuersis abundat generibus. Horum autem maxima copia est, quos vulgus Bacallios appellat, adhæc insunt accipitres nigri coruorum similes, acquilæ, perdi cesque fusco colore, aliæque diuersæ volucres."

Mr. Harrisse translates the Latin text[2] of the eighth legend into English as follows :—

"This land was discovered by John Cabot, a Venetian, and Sebastian, his son, the year of the redemption of the world, 1494, on the 24th of July [sic], at the fifth hour of daybreak, which [land] they called the first land seen, and a large island opposite the same, [they named] St. John, because it was discovered on the solemn festival of St. John. The

---

[1] The figure "5" is probably either an error of the copyer of the description or of the printer.
[2] *Ante*, p. 262.

inhabitants of that country are dressed in the skins of animals. They use in war bows, arrows, darts, lances, wooden clubs, and slings. It is very sterile ; contains lions, white bears, stags of large size, innumerable fish, namely, seals [?], salmons, large soles an ell long, and abundance of other kinds of fish ; the greatest quantity is called by the common people 'bacallios.' There are hawks black like crows, eagles, dark partridges, and a variety of birds."

Mr. Major also gives a portion of the inscription numbered 17, as follows :—

" Sebastianus Cabotus Dux & Archigubernius sacræ Cæsaræ Catholicæ maiestatis, diui Caroli Imperatoris, huius nominis quinti, & regis Hispaniæ, summam mihi manum imposuit, & ad formam hanc protrahens, planâ figurâ me delineauit, anno ab orbe redempto, natiuitate Domini nostri Jesu Christi 1549, qui me iuxta graduum latitudinem ac longitudinem, ventorum situm, tam doctè, tam fideliter, navigatoriæ chartæ instar, descripsit, Geographi Ptolomæi authoritatem, peritiorumq, Lusitanorum fidem secutus, nec non ex vsu atque industriâ longæ nauigationis, integerrimi viri Joannis Caboti, natione Veneti, atque Sebastiani astrorum peritiâ, nauigandiq, arte omnium doctissimi eius filii, auctorisq, mei, qui aliquotam orbis partem diu nostratibus clausam aperuerunt. . . . At hæc Sebastianus Cabotus, meus autor, occidentalem Oceanum adnauigans, ad æquor quoddam deuenit, & plagam vbi quarta parte Septentrionum iuxta cæciam ventum acus nauigatoriæ lilium illi rectissimè Arctum ostenderet. Quibus decausis & rationibus & tutissimâ nauigandi experientiâ apertissimè constat, defectus

& variationes acûs nauticæ crebro fieri cum Arcti obseruatione."

"Which," says Mr. Major, "I translate thus, without holding myself responsible for the bad construction of the language":—

"Sebastian Cabot, captain and pilot of his Sacred Imperial Catholic Majesty the Emperor Charles, fifth of that name and King of Spain, put upon me the finishing hand, and, projecting me after this form, delineated me in a plane figure, in the year of redemption and of the nativity of our Lord Jesus Christ, 1549;[1] who has described me according to the latitude and longitude of degrees, the position of the winds, so learnedly and so faithfully in the fashion of a sailing chart, following the authority of the geographer Ptolemy and the belief of the more skilled Portuguese, and also from the experience and practice of long sea service of the most excellent John Cabot, a Venetian by nation, and of my author, Sebastian, his son, the most learned of all men in knowledge of the stars and the art of navigation, who have discovered a certain part of the globe for a long time hidden from our people. . . . Sebastian Cabot, sailing into the western ocean, reached a certain sea and region where the lily of the compass needle pointed due north at one quarter north-north-east. For which reasons, and by the safest nautical experience, it is most clearly evident that defects and variations of the compass frequently occur with observation of the north."

[1] The map seen by Kochhaff (*ante*, p. 263) was probably a re-issue of the map which was originally published in 1544. The inscription reads "plana figura me delineavit 1549." The inscription on the orginal issue is given at p. 261 (*ante*).

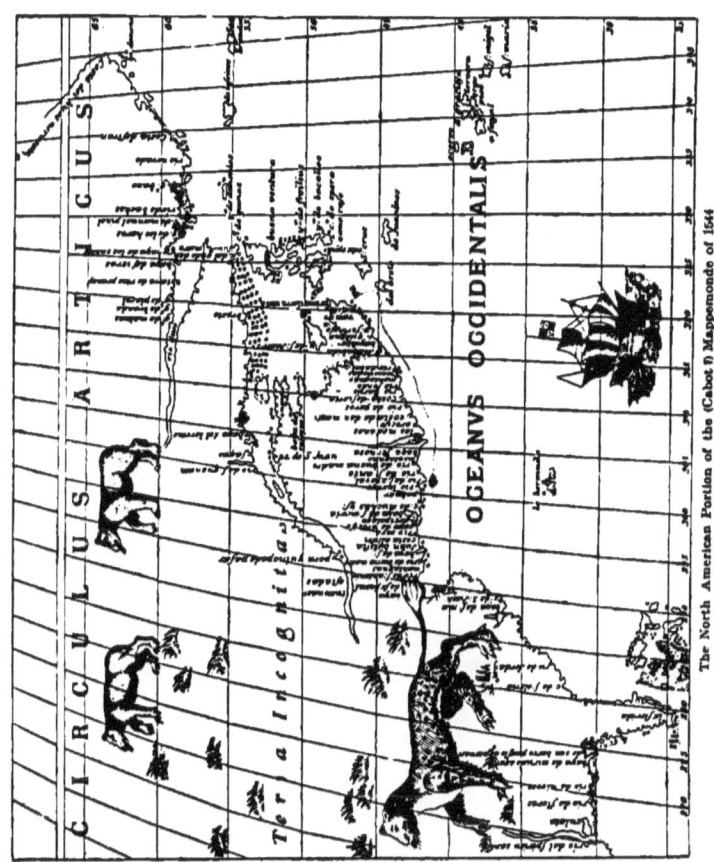

The North American Portion of the (Cabot?) Mappemonde of 1544

The date 1494 has been accepted by many persons as a true record of a voyage which was made in that year by John and Sebastian Cabot. But the best authorities are now agreed that there is an almost entire absence of evidence to support this theory, and that the error is due to a printer's slip in the numerals, which, instead of MCCCCXCIIII. (1494), should read MCCCCXCVII. (1497). M. d'Avezac is the most important writer who has taken this view. He says : " We know this time [1491], appositely, that there then commenced a series of consecutive explorations, which employed, each year, two, three, four caravels, proceeding from the port of Bristol to sail under the direction[1] of John Cabot, the Genoese, for the discovery of the isle of Brésil and of the Seven Cities. This is what the Spanish ambassador, Pedro d'Ayala, sends officially to his Government in a despatch of the 25th of July 1498, on occasion of the departure of a great expedition confided to this Genoese : ' Los de Bristol ha siete annos que cada anno han armado dos, tres, cuatro caravelas para ir à buscar la isla del Brasil, y las Siete Ciudades, con la fantasia deste Genovés.'[2]

"At last, on the fourth voyage of this septennial series, in the month of June 1494, the search is no longer in vain : in one of the legends accompanying the great elliptical Mappe-Monde, published in 1554 by Sebastian Cabot,[3] then grand pilot of Spain, the following indisputable declaration is inscribed both

---

[1] This, with all due deference to M. d'Avezac, is not a literal definition of the position which d'Ayala ascribes to John Cabot in connection with expeditions which sailed from Bristol prior to 1497.
[2] According to the fancy of this Genoese.
[3] This is the map which was found in 1843. There exists not a tittle of evidence to prove that it was published by Sebastian Cabot.

in Spanish and Latin, and is pointed out by an express reference [in the body of the map], for what relates to Tierra de los Bacallaos: 'This land was discovered by John Cabot, a Venetian, and Sebastian Cabot, his son, in the year of the birth of our Saviour Jesus Christ, MCCCCXCIIII (1494), the twenty-fourth day of June (at five o'clock) in the morning; to which land has been given the name of *The land first seen* : and to a great island, which is very near the said land, the name of *St. John* has been given, on account of its having been discovered the same day.'" . . . The writer goes on to say: "I assume it, then, *as a fact to be hereafter uncontested*, as I have always regarded it *as incontestable*, that the first discovery of Cabot was made on the 24th of June 1494. But, during the period of the successive attempts of this intrepid navigator to find a passage to the Indies by the west, the great fact of the Columbian discovery had been accomplished; and in its train had followed the promulgation of the papal bull, adjudging the New World to Spain; and, immediately after, the protestation of Portugal, and the establishment of a line of demarcation, and finally the Treaty of Tordesillas of 7th June 1494. Accordingly, when John Cabot had, in his turn, discovered new countries, he was obliged to acknowledge that it could appertain only to a sovereign to declare them his own, and to confer the *dominium utile* over them on the discoverer; and he had recourse to Henry VII., King of England, to escape from the exclusive pretensions of Spain and Portugal." Having presented this view of the case for perusal, it will be desirable to present other opinions on this so-called Cabot map.

In a very valuable work, entitled *A History of the Discovery of the East Coast of North America, particularly the Coast of Maine,* by J. G. Kohl, of Bremen, there are some extremely important criticisms as to the Cabot map of 1544. Mr Kohl, in dealing with the inscriptions upon the map, expresses an opinion that none of the inscriptions or legends of the map were composed by Sebastian Cabot, and he contends "that these inscriptions were probably interpolated by the editor or publisher of the map, or some person employed by them."

Referring to the inscription No. 17, which asserts that Cabot "hizo esta figura" (made this figure), he asks, "Does the inscription pretend that Cabot himself engraved the map? . . . It is very probable that the inscription means nothing more than that the map was drawn and engraved after some original manuscript map, *supposed to have been made* by Sebastian Cabot."

. . . .

"Oviedo, in the second part of his great work on the *History of America,* which he wrote several years after 1544, mentions the map of Ribero, made in 1529, and of Chaves, made in 1536; but does not allude to a map of Sebastian Cabot as having been published in Spain.

"The copy of the map of 1544, which I am examining, was found in Germany; but several copies of maps ascribed to Sebastian Cabot formerly existed in England, and one is mentioned by Ortelius as having been seen by him in Belgium. These may have been copies, or perhaps different editions, of the map engraved in 1544, as they all have a general resemblance. But, though seen in other countries, not a single copy is known to have existed in Spain, or to have come from there.

"We therefore come to the conclusion that the Cabot map was neither engraved nor published in Spain, but perhaps in Germany or Belgium."

. . . .

"If it should appear probable . . . that this map was not published in Spain, but in some other country, as Belgium for instance, it is rendered extremely doubtful whether Cabot, who was then residing in Spain, had any agency in it. Is it to be supposed that he would direct the work from so distant a country as Spain, examine proof-sheets, correct errors, and do other necessary acts in the publication? This doubt is confirmed by the contents of the map, such as the configuration of the countries, the orthography of the names attached to them, and other circumstances, which go to show that Cabot could not have prepared or inspected the work."[1]

. . . .

"Even Spain itself, and also Great Britain, the countries in which Sebastian Cabot passed the greater part of his life, are very carelessly represented; as, for instance, Ireland is made as large as England and Scotland together. In Spain we find places like

---

[1] Any unprejudiced person who will take the trouble to carefully sift all the evidence we have to guide us as to the birthplace of Sebastian Cabot, his early environments, his character and attainments, will probably come to the conclusion that the only matter connected with the controversy as to Sebastian, which is absolutely free from ambiguity and doubt, is the well-established fact that he was a skilful map-maker. If we regard Sebastian as the author of the map, we have no alternative but to admit that he must have been a very careless, if not untrustworthy, map-constructor.

'Guadelupe' mentioned, but not the important harbour of Corunna. In Great Britain several small places are indicated, but not Bristol—that commercial centre in which the Cabots lived, and from which their exploring expeditions proceeded.

"In connection with Bristol I may also observe, that this map gives to Iceland the longitude of the Shetland Islands, and places it directly north instead of north-west of Scotland. The route from Great Britain to Iceland had been, from time immemorial, familiar to British ships in their yearly traffic. That Iceland was situated north-west and not north of Great Britain must have been known in Cabot's time to every sailor in Bristol. How, then, can we account for it that Cabot, on a maritime chart, should have made so great a mistake with respect to an island so well known?

. . . .

"But it is more surprising that the Spanish terms and names are corrupted and disfigured in such an extraordinary way that sometimes it is nearly impossible to make out what the author means. I will give some instances: 'España' is called 'Hispaia'; the island 'S. Miguel,' 'S. Migel'; the island 'S. Juan Estevanez,' 'de Juanina' (?); 'Bimini' is written 'binimi'; the Laguna of Nicaragua, 'Laguna de Nicaxagoe.' The Spanish phrase, which occurs on the map, 'por aqui no puede passar' (here one cannot pass), is written 'pora quinopede pasar.' Another Spanish phrase, 'aqui se desembarco Pamfilo de Narvaez' (here landed Pamphilo de Narvaez), is written thus, 'aqui de san barco panflo de narnaez,' etc. Such errors furnish strong proof that Cabot had no agency either in writing the map or correcting it, or in any way superintending its publication, but, on the contrary, that some ignorant compiler had copied an original manuscript in a very careless manner, and had written, in bad Spanish, his construction of the language.

"On this map, in the region of Carolina, a tiger-like animal is drawn, which, with a sweep of his tail, completely covers up, or brushes out, a large section of an important coast. It would appear to be incredible that a distinguished mariner and a mathematician like Cabot should not have been shocked by such a rough and stupid proceeding, and that he should not have corrected the draftsman, who could prefer an elaborate picture of the tuft of a tail to a correct drawing of the coast line. This may suffice for the present in considering the question how far Sebastian Cabot may be regarded as having made this map; or, rather, it may serve to show how utterly improbable it is that it was either originally drawn by him or executed under his direction or superintendence. . . . Whenever he (Sebastian Cabot) is mentioned in the inscriptions, it is with some pompous description like this: 'Navigandi arte astronomiâque peritissimus' (in the art of navigation and in astronomy the most experienced man). Also in the inscription No. 17, where it is stated that the map was made by Sebastian Cabot, he is called 'Astrorum peritiâ navigandique arte omnium doctissimus' (of all men the most learned in astronomy and in the art of navigation). These expressions would appear to go beyond his customary modesty, if we are to believe that it is Cabot himself who here speaks. It looks rather like the recommendation of a map-seller who wishes to procure a large sale under colour of a great name; like the speculator complained of by Humboldt, who had published, against his will, some maps under his name, to which he had contributed nothing else. Such also is the following complimentary expression connected with the above, which runs thus: 'Therefore you may use this hydrographical chart as the most faithful and the most learned mistress (fida doctissimaque magistra) in sailing to any part of the ocean wherever you should have the mind to sail.' I cannot, therefore, but concur in the opinion both of Mr. Bancroft and Mr. Charles Deane, 'that Cabot himself evidently did not write these inscriptions.'"

Mr. Henry Harrisse says:[1] "Considered as a graphic exposition of geographical positions and forms, this planisphere must rank as the most imperfect of all the Spanish maps of the sixteenth century which have reached us. . . . As regards the New World, we are surprised to find how inferior its position and outlines are, when compared with those of the Weimar maps, for instance, although these were constructed fifteen years previous. Labrador and Northern Canada, which, naturally, should be much more exact than in the other charts of the time, are particularly defective. The entire coast of Nova Scotia is 2° too far south, whilst Riberio depicts it, in 1529, a great deal nearer its real latitude. So with the West Indian islands, where Cuba is placed by the Sevillian cartographer between 19° and 23° lat. north, its true place, whilst Cabot inscribes it between 20° and 24°. The east coast for the part

[1] Pp. 285, 287.

corresponding with our Rhode Island, and following the same as far as New York, which is comparatively exact in the Weimar charts (1527, 1529), in Verrazzano's (1529), in the planisphere of the Laurentiana (before 1530), in Wolfenbuttel B (about 1530), etc., etc., is extremely incorrect in Cabot's map, although he must have had in his hands the geographical data brought by Estevam Gomez in 1526.

"If now we examine the regions which he claimed to have discovered (Newfoundland), and those which he has certainly visited (La Plata), we notice with surprise how the shapes and positions are inaccurately and incompletely rendered.

"Breaking up Newfoundland into such a multitude of fragments is certainly more erroneous than representing that vast island as still forming part of the continent, such as we see it depicted in the early charts. Because, in reality, Newfoundland is separated from the mainland by a channel only a few miles wide. . . . On examining the longitudinal inscriptions of the planisphere of 1554, in the belief that they were at least based upon data furnished by Cabot himself, the astonishment is still greater. As Kohl has justly noticed, they are full of legends about sea monsters, people with one foot, or one eye; in short, all the old fables related by Adam of Bremen and other authors of the Middle Ages. In the inscription 'No. VII.' where the La Plata River and Cabot's expedition are described, mention is made of a report, to the effect that in the mountains there are men with faces like dogs, and the lower limbs like those of an ostrich. In No. IX., where the waters of Iceland are described, it is related that there had been seen a fish of the species called 'Moræna,' a veritable sea-serpent, and so colossal that it would attack a vessel and devour the sailors. Spectres or ghosts speaking in the air, are also mentioned in the inscription on Ireland. The inscription 'No. XII' treats of a nation of monsters with ears so large that they cover the whole body, etc. etc." Mr. Harrisse has devoted many pages in endeavouring to afford information as to the several editions of this map, and all interested in the details should consult his valuable work for further information.

In a pamphlet published last year by Dr. Justin Winsor, the well-known American historian, "The Cabot Controversies and the Right of England to North America," by Justin Winsor, Cambridge,[1] [John Wilson and Son, University Press, 1896], the writer says: "The controversy over the date of the voyage of discovery yields more easily to demonstration. Hakluyt, in his preliminary single volume, published in 1589, had cited one of the legends of the Cabot mappemonde (1544), which gave the date in 1494. On the strength of this, before the map itself had been brought to the notice of modern scholars, and notwithstanding Hakluyt later adopted the date 1497, other writers, like Harris and Pinkerton, had accepted the date of 1494, and it has been agreed to in our day by D'Avezac and Tarducci. When Hakluyt, in 1600, made the change to 1497, some years after Lok in his map[2] had given that date, he set a fashion which became more prevalent; and it was adopted by Biddle as

[1] Cambridge, America.
[2] Dr. Winsor is here referring to Michael Lok's map of 1582, upon which an inscription, "J. Cabot, 1497," is placed upon Cape Breton.

the only possible date, in view of the fact that the royal licence for the voyage was issued in March, 1495-96.

"In 1843 the discovery of the only copy of the Cabot map which has been found, and which is now in the Bibliothèque Nationale at Paris, showed that Hakluyt, in copying the legend in 1589, had done it correctly; for the date 1494 was plainly given upon the map. R. H. Major, of the British Museum map department, endeavoured to account for the date 1494 by supposing that in the printer's copy of the legend, the Roman figures VII had been read IIII, because the inclining strokes of the V were not brought together at the bottom. Cumulative evidence, as well as that of the patent, has made it certain to the large majority of investigators that 1497 is the exact date. A conclusive document in support of this date, as well as in proof of the unquestionable agency of the elder Cabot, as against his son's, in the discovery of that year (1497), was found some years ago in the archives at Milan. It is a letter of Raimondo de Soncino, which was originally published in 1865, reprinted by Desimoni in 1881, and was first given in English by Deane in 1883, and later, in another version, by Prowse in 1895."[1] All the important questions which have been raised with regard to the map, its authenticity, etc. etc., are summarised in the following remarks:—

1. It may or may not be Sebastian Cabot's map; at present there is no alternative but to say that there exists no authentic evidence to prove

[1] *Ante*, pp. 143-151.

affirmatively that it was ever issued with his authority; he never said he was its author; and it seems almost certain that he never had a hand in its revision. There is no certainty that he ever saw the planisphere of 1544.

2. There is a probability,[1] but no actual proof, that some portion of the contents of the map may have been originally derived, either from a map made by Sebastian, or from information supplied by him.

3. Until it is proved beyond doubt that Sebastian Cabot was with his father in the voyage of discovery in the year 1497, the map appears to have no bearing on the question at issue, that is, as to the comparative agency of John and Sebastian Cabot.

4. Having regard to the many admitted errors and absurdities which appear upon the map, coupled with the absence of any reliable evidence to prove the agency of Sebastian therewith, it is suggested that it would be unjust to connect him with the map, so far as it purports to be a publication by him, or one issued with his authority.

[1] Dr. Justin Winsor remarks, with reference to the legends on the map, "These inscriptions are further enigmas; for while Sebastian Cabot must necessarily have been the source from which some of the statements are drawn, there are parts of the legends which it is impossible to believe represent such knowledge as he must be supposed to have had. These legends [in Latin and Spanish] are not all a part of the map itself, but most of them are printed on separate sheets of paper and pasted on its margin. A manuscript copy of them in the hand of a learned Spaniard, Dr. Grajales, was found by Harrisse in the Royal Library at Madrid, . . . there does not seem to be evidence that Grajales may not have copied them from another copy or from the printed sheets." (The Cabot Controversies, etc., pp. 12, 13.)

CHAPTER VIII

ON what part of the continent of North America did John Cabot land in 1497? To what extent did he view the coast in the course of his first voyage? It is certain that Cabot, who was a skilful cosmographer as well as an intrepid navigator, set out the result of his voyage upon a map, and also on a globe.[1] Unfortunately, both the map and the globe, so far as we know at present, have perished. But it is now conceded on all hands that the beautiful planisphere of Juan de la Cosa, constructed by him in 1500, the genuineness of which has never been impeached, includes the result of the voyage of 1497. Inasmuch as the Spanish Ambassadors were in possession of the information afforded by John Cabot's own map, it is more than probable that La Cosa had at his disposal the very best evidence obtainable. The map is drawn on an ox hide, 5 feet 9 inches long by 3 feet wide, on a scale of 15 Spanish leagues to a degree, and is now preserved in a glass case in the naval museum at Madrid. It is an exquisite production in colours, and is richly decorated in gold. It is probably the best designed map of the period. Its testimony is all the greater because it was a map made by a skilful cosmographer, from

[1] *Ante*, p. 148.

THE "MATTHEW" SAILING NEAR CAPE RACE
(The outlines of the Cape is not taken from a Sketch published by Dr. S. E. Dawson, of Ottawa.)

authentic information which, in all probability, was better known in Spain than in England. It is fairly certain that the map was kept secret,—at anyrate the details of the map did not appear in any subsequent Spanish map or chart. This map was discovered by Humboldt in the library of Baron Walckenaer in 1832. It was purchased by the Queen of Spain in the year 1853.

The flags throughout the map are marked in the correct colours of the various nationalities. In the highest portion to the west is a small English flag, and an inscription, "Cauo [Cavo] de Ynglaterra" (Cape of England), which, according to some eminent authorities, represents Cape Race. But this is by no means a certainty, although there seems to be considerable evidence to support the conjecture. Dr. Dawson says: "The Cavo de Ynglaterra cannot be taken for any other than that characteristic headland of North-East America, which for almost four hundred years has appeared on the maps under one name in the various forms of Cape Raz, Rase, Razzo, or Race, a name derived from the Latin *rasus*— smooth, shaven, or flat. That the name is expressive and appropriate will be seen from the following engraving from a photograph taken for the Department of Marine of Canada, which has the care and maintenance of the lighthouse upon this historic landmark of the highway between the old and the new worlds."

The termination of the point of the English discovery is marked on La Cosa's map by a legend as follows: "Mar descubierta por yngleses" ("sea discovered by the English.") It will be seen by a glimpse at the map that the last inscription, reading from east to west, before that which shows the sea discovered by the English, is "Cauo [Cavo], descubierto" ("the discovered Cape"). A glance at the map shows that the land coasted by Cabot trends in an eastward direction from the "Mar descubierta por ingleses" to the "Cavo de Inglaterra." The argument put forward by many persons, founded upon this inscription, to the effect that the name "Cavo descubierta" indicates the landfall of John Cabot, is well represented by the words used by Dr. Dawson in his summary of the various views put forward as to the landfall in 1497. "There was no other meaning to the name than the discovered cape; and as this map of La Cosa's was, beyond reasonable doubt, based on John Cabot's own map which Pedro de Ayala, the Spanish ambassador, had from him and promised, in July 1498, to send to King Ferdinand, we have here John Cabot indicating his own landfall in a Spanish translation."[1]

The difficulties connected with any attempt to fix the landfall at any particular spot are now pretty generally recognised. In a report of the Canadian Committee, appointed in May 1895, in relation to the commemoration in 1897 of the discovery of the mainland of North America by John Cabot, the following, amongst other references, deals with the difficulties as regards the landfall :—

"While the committee are of opinion that the greatly preponderating weight of evidence points to the easternmost cape of Cape Breton as the

[1] *The Discovery of America by John Cabot in* 1497, being Extracts from the Proceedings of the Royal Society of Canada, relative to a Cabot Celebration in 1897, etc., p. 16.

landfall of John Cabot in 1497, they would observe that the commemoration now proposed will not commit the Royal Society of Canada, as a whole, to the definite acceptance of that theory. The alternative theory of a landfall on Labrador excludes any possibility of a commemoration there; because no locality on a coast extending over eight degrees of latitude has been specially indicated, excepting Cape Chidley, which is unapproachable because of ice at the time of the landfall, and, if a lower latitude be assumed, the want of means of communication on the coast of Labrador renders it for such a purpose inaccessible. The event to be commemorated is the discovery of the continent of America on the 24th of June 1497—an event of profound importance, the far-reaching consequences of which cannot be overestimated. Such an event the Royal Society of Canada cannot afford to ignore. Nevertheless, although the Society may not definitely decide upon the locality of the landfall, it is fitting that the commemoration should take place upon the Atlantic coast of the Dominion; for, beyond all question, it was along that coast that Cabot sailed, and he did not penetrate into any part of the gulf. . . . It will be remembered that the council of the Royal Society, at the meeting in May last, suggested that a permanent memento of the great achievement of Cabot should be erected upon some point of the Nova Scotia coast. Your committee would remark that no place on the whole Atlantic coast seems so suitable as Sydney. On the brow of the hill overlooking the mouth of the harbour is an ideal spot for such a monument. Standing there, the spectator may look out eastward upon a stretch of ocean, unbroken and uninterrupted, until it washes the western shore of Brittany or extends into the English Channel. This spot is about twenty miles in a direct line from the easternmost point of land in the province. At this remote period it is impossible to locate with certainty, within a few miles, the precise spot upon which the banner of St. George was first planted; and, while your committee believe that the landfall was at the easternmost point of Cape Breton, it is not probable that the exact apex of that point was lighted upon after so long a voyage across an ocean of darkness. Sydney would then, in their opinion, seem to be sufficiently near the landfall, if the Cape Breton theory be adopted, and yet the Society will not be so absolutely bound to that theory as if they were to erect a monument on the Cape itself. The Cape is an unfrequented and forgotten place. No one now lands on a point which was the rendezvous of the fishing fleets of three hundred years ago, and one of two points found on all the maps from 1504 down to the present moment. There are many very well-informed men, even in the maritime provinces, who do not know of a real Cape Breton, which gives its name to the Isle Royale of old Louisbourg days. The overjoyed courtier who, at an anxious period of the old French war, ran to tell King George that Cape Breton[1] was an island, was the prototype of a number of excellent people who are discovering that the island is named after a cape, next to Cape

[1] Cape Breton Island is divided from the mainland by the Strait of Canso. It lies between 45° 27' and 47° 41' north latitude. The inhabitants of Cape Breton Island propose to celebrate the Cabot discovery in June 1897 by building a huge cairn of stones upon Cape North. The distance between Cape North and Cape Ray, Newfoundland, is about 60 miles.

Race, the most ancient, and persistently known to mariners since the veil of the western ocean was lifted. Sydney is the easternmost settlement of any importance on the continent of America, and may, therefore, rightly claim the monument to Cabot."

It will be observed that although the committee are favourably inclined towards the Cape Breton theory,—the chief advocate of which is Dr. S. E. Dawson, a learned Canadian,—yet they have decided not to commit themselves to that theory.

There is very little doubt that Dr. Dawson's researches have been conducted on the lines which should be the guide for all historians. In his theory of the landfall, it is probable that he has come nearer to the actual truth than the others who have propounded theories thereon. At best, however, we are bound to say that the evidence before us is not sufficiently reliable to enable us to point with any degree of certainty to the place where John Cabot planted the English flag in 1497. Having regard to the fact that other eminent authorities have placed the landfall elsewhere, it must be pretty generally recognised that the point is one which it is not easy to settle.

As an example of the difficulties which students of the history of North America meet with in connection with the theories as to the landfall of John Cabot, it is desirable to give some extracts from the work of Mr. Harrisse, who has devoted many of the best years of his life to an intelligent study of all the documents, maps, etc., which could be brought to light, by a lavish expenditure of both time and money. These it is proposed to supplement by some remarks of Dr. Dawson, who possesses all the qualities which fit a man to engage in matters involving researches among ancient records in order to the elucidation of the truth.

Mr. Harrisse says: "When the vessel had reached the west coast of Ireland, it sailed towards the north, then to the east (*sic pro* west), when after a few days, the North Star was to the right: 'Passato Ibernia pùi occidentale, e poi alzatosi verso el septentrione, commenciò ad navigare ale parte orientale, lassandosi (fra qualche giorni) la tramon ana ad mano drita.'[1] After sailing for seven hundred (or only four hundred) leagues, they reached the mainland: 'Dice haver trovato lige 700 lontana de qui terra firma,' says Pasqualigo. 'Lontane de linsula de Ingilterra lege 400 per le cassino de pononte,' reports Soncino.

"Technically speaking, all that geographers can infer from these details is that Cabot's landfall was north of 51° 15' north latitude; this being that of the southern extremity of Ireland. Ireland, however, extends to 55° 15' lat. N. From what point between these two latitudes did he sail westward? Supposing that it was Valencia, and that he continued due west, he would have sighted Belle Isle or its vicinity. But Cabot is said positively to have altered his course and stood to the northward. How far and where did he again put his vessel on the western tack? We are unable to answer this important question, and can only put forward suppositions based upon the following data:—

"The place where he landed was the mainland: 'caphoe in terra firma.'[2] He then sailed along the coast, 300 leagues: 'andato per la costa lige 300.'[3]

[1] Soncino, first despatch.   [2] Soncino, second despatch.
[3] Pasqualigo.

As to the country visited, we find it described as being perfect and temperate: 'terra optima et temperata.' It is supposed to yield Brazil-wood and silk: 'estimanno ehe vi nasea el brasilio e la sete,' whilst the sea bathing its shores is filled with fishes: 'quello mare e coperto de pessi.'[1] . . . Barring the gratuitous supposition about the existence of dye-wood (unless it be sumach) and silk, and taking into consideration that the country was discovered in summer, Cabot's description could apply to the entire northern coast of America. The same may be said concerning the remark about slack tides. It was natural that John Cabot should have been surprised at seeing tides which rise only from two and three-quarters to four feet, whilst in the vicinity of Bristol they rise from thirty-six to forty feet; but this is peculiar to the entire coast from Nova Scotia to Labrador. [Mr. Harrisse gives this statement upon the authority of Mr. Henry Mitchell, the author of the *Survey of the Bays of Fundy and Minas*, for the United States Coast Survey.] There is another detail, however, which is of importance. Cabot, on his return, saw two islands to starboard: 'ale tornar aldreto a visto do ixole.' Those two islands were unknown before, and are very large and fertile: 'due insule nove grandissime et fructiffere.' The existence of islands in that vicinity is further confirmed by the fact that Cabot gave one to a native of Burgundy, who was his companion, and another to his barber: 'uno Borgognone compagno di mess. Zoanne. . . . li ha donato una isola; et ne ha donato una altra ad suo barbero.' What were these large islands? . . . 'La è terra optima et

[1] Soncino, second despatch.

temperata.' The headlands, clad in the pale green of mosses and shrubs, may have conveyed at a distance, to a casual observer, the idea of fertility. As to the climate, it was in June and July that Cabot visited those regions. Now, in Labrador, 'summer is brief but lovely.' He did not see any inhabitants, and therefore we have no specific details enabling us to identify the race of men who inhabited the country. But the needle for making nets, and the snares for catching game, indicate the regular occupation of the Eskimo, whose proper home is from Cape Webeck to Cape Chudleigh; whilst the ingenuity which the making of such implements presupposes, agrees perfectly with the race said 'to have been able, in the manufacture of their tools, to develop mechanical skill far surpassing that of savages more favourably situated.' Nor should we forget 'that, judging from the traditions, they must have maintained their present characteristic language and mode of life for at least one thousand years.' The Eskimos of Cabot's time may therefore be judged by those of to-day. But there is a circumstance in John Cabot's conversation with the Milanese ambassador which is still more convincing. It is evident that the Venetian adventurer and his companion were greatly struck with the enormous quantity of fish which they found in that region. It surpassed anything of the kind they had ever seen, even in the Icelandic sea, where cod was then marvellously plentiful. He dwells at length, and with evident complacency, on that fortunate peculiarity: 'That sea is covered with fishes, which are taken not only with the net, but also with a basket, in which a stone is put so that the basket may plunge into water. . . . They say that they will bring thence such a quantity of fish, that England will have no further need of Iceland, from which a very great commerce of fish, called stockfish, is brought.'

"It is clear that the existence of vast quantities of cod is a circumstance which is applicable to the entire trans-Atlantic coast north of New England. Yet, however plentiful that species of fish may be on the banks of Newfoundland, the quantity is surpassed near the entrance of Hudson's Strait. Modern explorers report that there cod and salmon 'form in many places a living mass, a vast ocean of living slime,' which accumulates on the banks of northern Labrador; and the spot noted for its 'amazing quantity of fish' is the vicinity of Cape Chudleigh, which the above details and other reasons seem to indicate as the place visited by John Cabot in 1497."

Referring to Mr. Harrisse's theory that the landfall of John Cabot in 1497 was in Labrador, at or near Cape Chidley, Dr. S. E. Dawson says: "I cannot sufficiently express my obligations to Mr. Harrisse, for he has made these studies possible to me by his industry and research, and by republishing so many original documents. I have had all the advantages of Mr. Harrisse's learning and labour; but the adventitious circumstance of having been born among the localities under discussion, and therefore familiar with them from boyhood, compels me to see that Mr. Harrisse's judgment upon his materials is misled by the absence of a personal knowledge of the north-east coast of America. The monograph of 1894 pointed out some of the misconceptions which led him astray. This last book affords other instances.

... In going to Cape Chidley he has fallen into a new set of errors. ... Mr. Harrisse, in attempting to disprove his earlier theory of the Cape Breton landfall, says that in June and July navigation all round Newfoundland and the Gulf of St. Lawrence is impeded by fogs, icebergs, and under-currents; therefore Cabot could not have reached Cape Breton at the time stated. Addressing Canadians, it is not necessary to waste time on this astonishing error; but the more wonderful part of it is that *therefore* Mr. Harrisse thinks that northern Labrador was the landfall, as if, while the St. Lawrence was blocked, that coast was free from ice at that season; whereas, while the ports of Quebec and Montreal are crowded with ocean vessels, there is there a procession of icebergs and field ice 1000 miles long, coming down the Arctic current from the north. This is so well known here that in 1886 the Minister of Marine did not send sailing instructions to Captain Gordon until June 22nd, and the steamship *Alert* did not leave Halifax for Labrador until June 24th. He reported that the season was unusually early. He left Blanc Sablon, in the Strait of Belle Isle, on the 29th of June, and steamed along the coast. On the 30th he met large numbers of small icebergs; on July 1st he passed a number of large bergs, one being 170 feet high. On July 2nd he got into field ice, and had to lie on the outer edge of it until the weather cleared. On that day he saw many more bergs, some very close to the ship. He was then sixty miles south of Cape Mugford, north of which point Mr. Harrisse places Cabot's landfall in 1497. He found there heavy field ice, which extended all along the coast to Cape Chidley, packed tight for fifteen miles off the shore, with a 'bordage' of slack ice ten miles farther out. That was an early season, and it was July 2nd; but John Cabot told Soncino that 'the land he found was excellent and the climate temperate, suggesting that Brazil wood and silk grow there.' . . . Among the causes which Mr. Harrisse assigns as contributing to delay Cabot's progress is the supposed fact that, 'in those days, particularly when coasting in unknown regions, anchor was cast at sundown, and sailing renewed again, only with daylight the next morning.' The impossibility of a vessel coasting along northern Labrador, and anchoring out every night on a coast where field ice and enormous bergs are sweeping down with the Arctic current, is evident. No doubt vessels have to run into a harbour or under the lee of an island every night to get shelter, and sometimes they have to make fast to a piece of ice; but this very necessity is another indication of where the landfall could not have been, for there is no trace of such expedients in the records of the first voyage. Another note of the landfall is John Cabot's statement to Pasqualigo, immediately after his return, that he saw *two* islands; whereas there the whole coast is fringed by an archipelago of barren and rocky islands, where trees do not grow. These are shown only on the large charts, and writers not conversant with the coast are misled by the small scale maps in atlases. The coast line is, moreover, 1000 to 4000 feet high, steep and precipitous, with a swell which in calm weather breaks over islands 30 feet high. This formidable and rugged coast, ice-encumbered and frequently lashed with the heaviest seas known to sailors, cannot, in our view, be the land 'with an excellent and temperate climate,' where silk and dye woods grow, as described by Cabot;[1] but Mr. Harrisse dismisses the difficulty by quoting from the *Encyclopædia Britannica* the short but graphic phrase, 'In Labrador summer is brief but lovely.'

"Mr. Harrisse has read books on Labrador, but the want of local knowledge still obscures his conclusions. He finds another proof of the Labrador landfall is the abundance of fish reported by Cabot. This leads him to remark that 'however plentiful codfish may be on the banks of Newfoundland, the quantity is surpassed near the entrance of Hudson's Strait. Modern explorers report that there cod and salmon form in many places a living mass, a vast ocean of living slime, which accumulates on the banks of Northern Labrador, and the spot noted for its amazing quantity of fish is the vicinity of Cape Chidley, which the above details and other reasons seem to indicate as the place visited by John Cabot in 1497.

---

[1] *Ante*, p. 149. There cannot be any doubt as to the meaning of these words,—But do they necessarily refer to that part of the littoral upon which Cabot landed? A consideration of this question opens a flood of controversial matters. And the men who are most experienced in a knowledge of charts, winds, deviations, etc., are just as likely to go wrong as the most inexperienced in nautical knowledge. For example, it is not at all certain that Cabot did not make a pretence of going northward, rather than adopt a northerly course through force of circumstances, with a view to blind the Spanish Ambassador as to his real proceedings. It is clear that several writers have been influenced to a great extent in the matter of the landfall by accepting too readily the idea that Cabot sailed on a northerly course for a considerable distance before he selected a particular parallel of latitude. It might, perhaps, be difficult to prove that Cabot ever had a desire to veil his real intentions; on the other hand, it is not at all certain that the characteristic Italian dexterity for devising expedients was entirely absent.

CABOT'S DISCOVERY OF NORTH AMERICA

"Table showing the approximate mean date of arrival of cod in North-Eastern Newfoundland, Southern and Northern Labrador.

Latitude.	Locality.	Mean Date of Arrival.
°	NEWFOUNDLAND.	
47·30	Conception Bay.	1st June.
48·20	Bonavista Bay.	10th June.
48·30	Notre Dame Bay.	20th June.
50·	Cape St. John to Par Point.	20th June.
49·30	White Bay.	10th June.
51·	Cape Rouge Harbour.	10th June.
51·30	Cape Bauld to Cape Onion. (Over four degrees of latitude.)	20th June.
°	SOUTHERN LABRADOR.	
52·0	Chateau Bay.	20th June.
53·24	Batteaux.	12th July.
54·26	Indian Harbour.	15th July.
54·56	Cape Harrison. (Over three degrees of latitude.)	18th July.
°	NORTHERN LABRADOR.	
55·14	Aillik.	20th July.
54·57	Kypokok.	20th July.
55·27	Hopedale.	20th July.
55·30	Double Island Harbour.	22nd July.
55·52	Ukkasiksalik.	28th July.
56·33	Nain.	28th July.
57·30	Okak.	28th July.
58·30	Hebron.	15th August
58·46	Lampson. (Over three-and-a-half degrees of latitude.)	15th August

Cape Chidley is still farther north—in lat. 60° 30'. It is not included in the table, being too far north to have any practical bearing on the question before the Commissioners.

"This is a curious misconception. Mr. Harrisse is doubtless alluding to Prof. Hind as 'the modern explorer,' but neither Prof. Hind nor anyone who borrows his graphic phrase, applies the expression 'living slime' to the salmon and cod, but to the infusoria and other minute organisms with which the Arctic current abounds, and which constitute the food of the immense number of fish in these waters, and the attraction which draws them there. . . . Again, in dwelling upon the amazing quantity of codfish as a crucial indication of the true landfall, Mr. Harrisse has conclusively disproved his main thesis; for the codfish do not arrive at Cape Chidley until August 15th, five days after John Cabot is known to have been in London. In fact, the codfish do not approach any part of Northern Labrador before July 20th." In an appendix to his very useful paper, Dr. Dawson gives full particulars of the arrival of the codfish[1] at various points along the coast, taken from the evidence given by Prof. Hind before the Fishery Commission of the Treaty of Washington, which met at Halifax in 1877.

Simultaneously with the establishment of a more decided opinion, that in the absence of precise information each person must be left to form his or her own opinion as to the exact spot for the landfall, it has lately been a matter of frequent remark that a consensus of opinion exists to the effect that the greatest reliance should be placed upon the valuable map constructed by La Cosa. This famous map affords positive proof—all sufficient, even if there were no written records in existence—that the land found by John Cabot was part of the continent of

[1] *Ante*, p. 291.

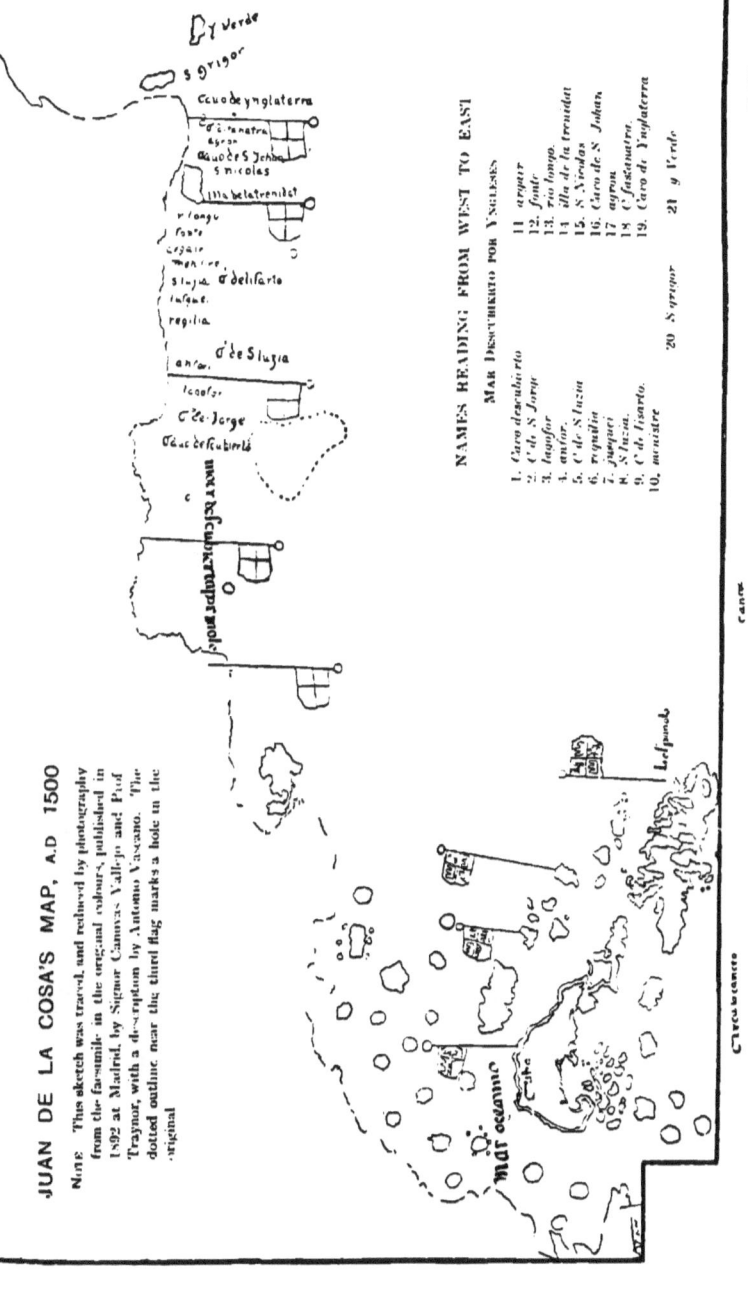

North America. La Cosa's map is headed as follows: "Juan de la Cosa la fizo en el puerto de S : ma^a en año de 1500:—Juan de la Cosa executed it at the Port of Sancta Maria in the year 1500." Upon the map is a quaint representation of St. Christopher carrying the Christ-child across the waters. "As St. Christopher is reported to have received that name because he carried Christ over the deep water with great danger to himself, whence came the name of Christopher, and as he carried over people whom no other would have carried, so Admiral Christophorus Colonus [Columbus], imploring the assistance of Christ in that dangerous voyage, went over safely himself and his company, that those Indian nations might become citizens and inhabitants of the Church triumphant in heaven." (*Histoire del S. D. Fernando Colombo*, cap. i.)[1]

Juan de la Cosa was born about the year 1460, at Santoña, a seaport in the north of Spain. Christopher Columbus started upon his first voyage of discovery on August 3, 1492, and one of his three caravels, the *Santa Maria* or *Capitana*, was the property of Juan de la Cosa, who was a man of considerable nautical experience. La Cosa commanded her, with an experienced navigator, Sancho Ruiz, as the pilot. Upon this caravel, which was the largest of the three, Columbus hoisted his flag. The other caravels were respectively named the *Niña* and the *Pinta*.

[1] The legend as to St. Christopher states that after he was baptized by the Bishop of Antioch he went to live in a desert. In the neighbourhood was a dangerous stream, and he is said to have rendered great help to his fellow-men by carrying them across the stream on his back. One day he proffered his services to a little child whom he carried across the water. It turned out that the little child was Christ!—hence the designation, Christophorus, the Christ-bearer. The vignette was evidently intended by La Cosa to represent Christopher Columbus carrying the Christ-child to the aborigines.

In connection with the proceedings of Columbus, after his discovery of land, it may be briefly related that after visiting four islands (the Bahamas) he landed upon the island of Cuba, which he firmly believed to be a portion of the mainland of the continent of Asia! Subsequently he discovered the island of Hayti, which he named Española, or Hispanolia—Spanish land. On December 25, 1492, the flagship, La Cosa's vessel, struck upon a sandbank and became a wreck. Thereupon Columbus determined to return to Spain in the *Niña*, and amongst those who returned with him appears the name of Juan de la Cosa, of Santoña, the master and owner of the ill-fated *Santa Maria*. Columbus, as everybody knows, got back to Spain safely, and he proudly announced to their Catholick Majesties Ferdinand and Isabella that he had discovered a direct oceanic path to the Indies! Hence the origin of the term "West Indies" as applied to some of the American Islands. The second expedition of Columbus, which consisted of fourteen caravels and three carracks, that is, vessels of a larger kind, and about 1500 persons in all, started on the twenty-fifth of September 1493. Juan de la Cosa, who was an adroit map-constructor, joined the expedition for the express purpose of making charts, etc. Among the company were several cavaliers of good family, including Juan Ponce de Leon, who at a later date became recognised—probably without good reason—as the discoverer of Florida; and Alonso de Ojeda, of whom more will be said hereafter.

In the course of his (Columbus's) explorations among the islands, it seems to have dawned upon his mind that the position assigned to Cipango

(Japan) by Toscanelli in his chart might not, after all, be quite correct. Columbus never went far enough during this expedition to enable him to perceive that Cuba was an island; he fully believed, to the end of his days, that it formed part of the mainland of Asia. The natives of Cuba intimated to Columbus that "the next country to the west of themselves was named 'Mangon,' and it was inhabited by people with tails, which they carefully hid by wearing loose robes of cloth. This information seemed decisive to Columbus. Evidently this Mangon was Mangi, the province in which was the city of Zaiton, the province just south of Cathay. And as for the tailed men, the book of Mandeville had a story of some naked savages in eastern Asia who spoke of their more civilised neighbours as wearing clothes in order to cover up some bodily peculiarity or defect. Could there be any doubt that the Spanish caravels had come at length to the coast of opulent Mangi?" During this voyage Columbus procured a notarial declaration from all concerned in this expedition (including La Cosa), to the effect that they all fully believed that they had discovered a part of the coast of Asia, and that, if any of the adventurers should thereafter declare anything to the contrary, he should have his tongue slit. Columbus returned to Spain from this expedition in June 1496. His third voyage commenced on May 30, 1498, and he returned to Spain in 1500 as a prisoner, loaded with fetters of iron.[1]

[1] On his fourth and last voyage he set sail from Cadiz on the 11th May 1502, and on the 7th November 1504 he anchored in the little port of San Lucar de Barrancada, 12 leagues from Seville. He died on the 20th May 1506 at Valladolid.

It will be observed that John Cabot had succeeded in landing upon the continent of North America about eleven months before Columbus started upon his third expedition, in the course of which he (Columbus) sighted a portion of the continent of South America.

[1] We have seen that John Cabot returned to Bristol from the land discovered by him in August 1497, and thereupon it was arranged that in the following year an expedition should start for the purpose of colonising the newly-discovered land. By letters-patent, dated the 3rd February 1498, John Cabot was authorised to take a number of ships for the purpose of going to the land and islands ("ad terram et insulas") found by him. On or about the 25th of July 1498, the senior Spanish ambassador in England, Dr. Puebla, wrote to the Court of Spain that an expedition, consisting of five armed ships, had actually sailed. It may be assumed, therefore, that between Easter 1498[1] and July of that year, John Cabot started upon his second voyage, under the authority of the letters-patent. ‖ In a despatch from the Spanish prothonotary,[2] Don Pedro de Ayala, it is again stated that the expedition consisted of five vessels, which carried provisions for one year. In a MS. Chronicle,[3] which is yet extant, the statement as to the number of vessels receives confirmation. Then comes an announcement that one of the five vessels, in which one Friar Buil[4] went, had returned to Ireland in great

---

[1] See document now published for the first time, *ante*, p. 131.
[2] *Ante*, p. 162.   [3] *Ante*, p. 245.
[4] Sir Clements Markham is of opinion that this Friar is not the same man as Bernardo Boyl, who was specially appointed by the Pope

distress, the vessel being much damaged. It may be assumed that the other vessels continued the voyage.

In 1499, Alonso Ojeda, who has been described as one of those "aristocratic young men, hot-blooded, and feather-headed hidalgos whom the surrender of Granada had left without an occupation . . . a daredevil of unrivalled muscular strength, full of energy and fanfaronade, and not without generous qualities but with very little soundness of judgment or character,"[1] obtained permission to fit out an expedition of discovery, and he at once secured La Cosa as a chief pilot.[2] Amerigo Vespucci,[3] the titular discoverer of America, was one of the "useful companions" connected with this expedition, which put to sea in May 1499. Hererra, the historian, under a misapprehension both as to Cabot and Columbus, put forward a claim on behalf of La Cosa to the effect that he, rather than Vespucci, was the true discoverer of the mainland of America, which discovery, he contended, was made during this voyage. But we now know that Cabot discovered the mainland of North America in June 1497, and that Columbus discovered the coast of Venezuela in 1498, on his third voyage. Referring to this

---

to go out with Columbus. The evidence is insufficient to identify the Friar Buil. Sir Clements thinks that "*Buil*" is a Spanish corruption of some English name.

[1] Fiske, vol. i. p. 463.

[2] After his return to Spain in 1496, La Cosa seems to have resumed his position as a shipowner. It is worthy of remark, as showing the great advantage which La Cosa possessed for making maps, that he had in his possession, before the commencement of this voyage, a copy of a map made by Columbus as to his previous discoveries.

[3] The circumstances connected with Amerigo Vespucci (Americus Vespucius) might perhaps with advantage be dilated upon did space permit. It is pretty clear, however, that the continent of North America should be called Cabotia, in honour of the discoverer.

voyage, Navarette, a Spanish historian, in his work *Collection de los viages y Descubrimientos*, etc., tomo iii. p. 41, states that it is certain that Ojeda (Hojeda) in his first voyage found some Englishmen in the immediate vicinity of Coquibacoa. ("Lo cierto es que Hojeda en su primer viage nallo a ciertos ingleses por las immediaciones de Coquibacoa"). Now the historian, unfortunately, does not give his authority, and, therefore, we are somewhat puzzled as to the source whence he derived his information. Ojeda may or may not have met with some Englishmen, and he may have met with them not at Coquibacoa but at some other point on his return voyage.[1] The statement made by Navarette, although not supported by evidence, so far as we can at present gather, must not be lightly dismissed. It is exceedingly important, having regard to the fact that it was just after his return from this voyage that La Cosa completed his map showing the extent of the English discoveries. And it is certainly significant that nothing more was ever heard, so far as we can ascertain, of John Cabot and his co-adventurers.[2] The only information, and meagre enough

[1] Ojeda's first expedition sailed, *via* the Cape Verde Islands, in a direction which brought them in view of the Coast of Brazil. They got back to Maracaibo and to Cape de la Vela. It is quite clear that from the last-mentioned Cape, Ojeda, with a portion of the expedition, went towards Hispaniola.

[2] Biddle, writing in 1831 with reference to Ojeda, hazards a conjecture that "that fiery and daring adventurer would have regarded the rival party as impudent trespassers on the dominions of the King of Spain, and as setting at defiance the papal bull. A man who gravely quotes this instrument in his manifesto to the poor Indians as sufficient authority for subjugating them, would hardly have exacted less deference to it from Christians." It should be added that Ojeda, who was a man of great natural courage and of tremendous energy, was convicted and heavily fined for trespassing upon Portuguese land in the course of a subsequent voyage.

it is, from which we may gather any idea as to what became of John Cabot is contained in a letter relating to the Corte Real voyages. ¶ In the "Documents relating to the voyages of Gaspar Corte Real" published at the end of Sir Clements R. Markham's work, *The Journal of Christopher Columbus*, we learn that Gaspar Corte Real in the year 1500, under licence of the King of Portugal, sailed from the island of Terceira with two ships, armed at his own cost, and after making explorations returned safely to Lisbon. In his second expedition, the ship in which he went never returned, and his brother Miguel Corte Real went in search of him, with three ships, armed at his own cost. Two of the ships returned to Portugal without finding Gaspar, but the ship in which his brother Miguel sailed was never afterwards heard of. In a letter from Pietro Pasqualigo to the Seigneury of Venice, the writer relates that some of the adventurers brought back with them to Portugal "a piece of a broken sword, gilded, which was certainly made in Italy. A native boy had two silver rings in his ears, which without doubt seems to have been manufactured at Venice. This made me believe that it was mainland, because it is not possible that a ship could ever have reached that place without having been heard of."[1] Sir Clements Markham says that "these must have been relics of the expedition of John Cabot in 1498."[2]

[1] It was fully believed that Columbus had discovered mainland. Cabot's voyages were unknown to the Portuguese, and their historians have been very slow to admit that the voyages ever took place.
[2] In Mr. Henry Harrisse's work on the voyages of the Cortereals will be found a facsimile of the western portion (3 feet 5¾ inches in width by 3 feet 2½ in height, the original colours being given) of

The agreement with Ojeda for the second voyage, says Biddle, is found to enjoin a continuation of his examination of the region he had discovered on the former voyage, and which seemed to run east and west, as it must lead towards (Hacia), the place where it was known the English were making discoveries. He is directed to set up marks as he proceeds with the Royal Arms, so that it might be known he had taken possession for Spain, and the English be thereby prevented from making discoveries in that direction (Navarette, tom. iii. p. 86). "Item: que vaes ò sigais aquella costa que discubristes que se corre leste —vuest, segun paroce, per razon que va hácia la parte donde se ha sabido que descubrian los Ingleses ó vais poniendo las marcas con las armas de SS. A. A. ó con otras señales quescan conocidas, cuales vos pareciere porque se conozca como vos habes descubierto aquella tierra, para

what is known as the Cantino map. The original is in the Biblioteca Estense at Modena. It is beyond doubt that the map was constructed for Alberto Cantino, in Portugal, about the year 1502. Cantino was the representative of the Duke of Ferrara. Did space permit, a great deal of interesting information might be given as to the bearing of the Cortereal voyages on the respective claims of Portugal, Spain, and England. In some respects the map gives confirmation to the genuineness of the La Cosa map. The Cantino map clearly proves that the art of map-making had made great progress. The constructor of the map has produced a beautiful example of his skill. The continents are coloured green, the islands are portrayed in blues and reds. The tropics are shown in red, the Equator in gold, and the papal line of demarcation in blue. The land of Brazil is decorated with representations of tall trees in green, gold, and brown, while other representations of the rich vegetation are coloured in different shades of blue. Brazil was named "The Land of Parrots," and on the map are three delicately coloured representations of paraquets. The north-western portion of the map sets forth twenty inscriptions, seven being the names of capes, one the name of a river, another of an island, a third of a lake, and so on.

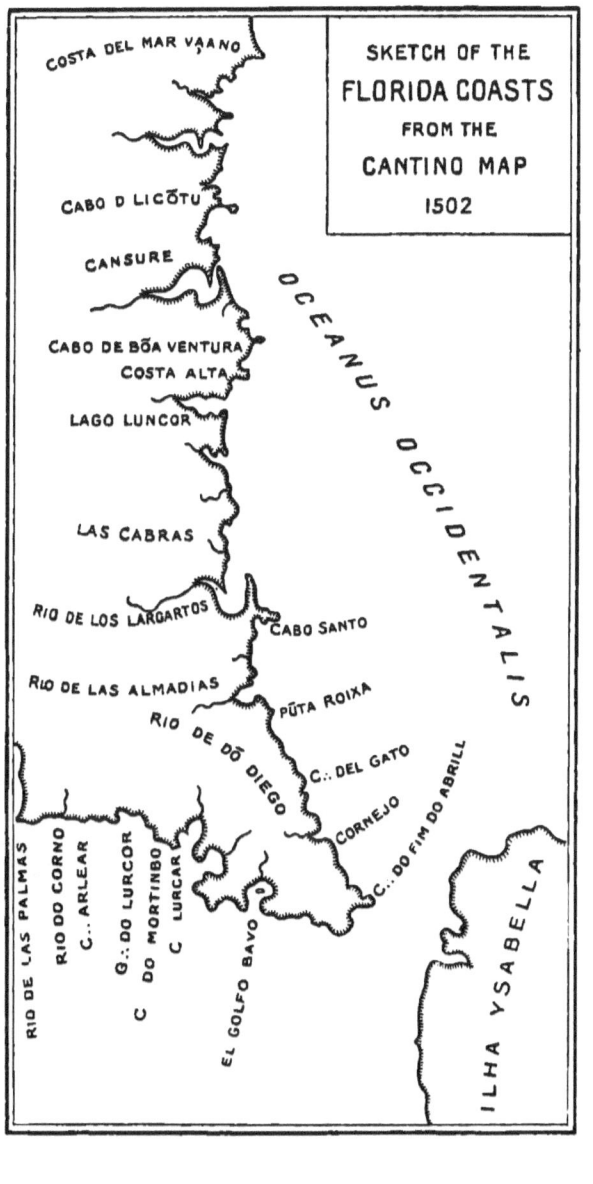

que atages el descubrir des los Ingleses por aquella via."

A grant of land was made to Ojeda, in consideration prospectively of his active exertions to prosecute discoveries and to check those of the English (Navarette, tom. iii. p. 88.) "Para que labrees, é faques labrar, é vos aprovecheis é podais aprovechar de alli, para lo que habees de descubrir é en la costa de la tierra firme para el atajo de los Ingleses."

Apart from these meagre and unsatisfactory references to the presence of the English, from which it seems pretty clear that the Cabot expedition of 1498 reached some part of the mainland now called America, all authentic information on the subject comes abruptly to an end. In all probability the knowledge of the movements of the English had become known to La Cosa, and it may be that his map contains the result of the progress of the Cabot expedition in 1498. But this is not absolutely certain. The map, however, is almost certain to contain information of a reliable character. Again, and yet again, we are irresistibly driven to ask—Did John Cabot and his expedition, or any persons connected therewith—other than the Friar and those associated with him, who were driven back by stress of weather—ever return to England? Numerous ideas have been hazarded.[1] But is it not

[1] "But we do not know when they returned to England, nay, whether John Cabot survived the expedition, or where it went. Our only information is that Lancelot Thirkill, who owned or commanded one of the ships, was in London, June 6th, 1501. At that date he repaid a loan of £20 made to him by Henry VII. Mr. Desimoni justly presumes that it may have been the one of March 2nd, 1498, received from the King while fitting out a ship for the voyage" (Harrisse, pp. 134, 135). The reference given by Harrisse to the MS.

most probable that the absence of all information as to the return of John Cabot's expeditions is due to the fact that they all perished? If Ojeda really met with them it is pretty clear that he would have had very little doubt as to the course to be adopted; it may be considered certain that he would have felt justified in exterminating men who, according to his view of the papal bull, were incurring the wrath of the Church, and had placed themselves in the position of excommunicated persons. Of course there may not be the slightest ground for such a suggestion, but it is not to be regarded as an impossible solution of the mystery. Then, we must also remember, quite apart from the possibility of Ojeda having met with the English adventurers, that the natives had a nasty habit of making short work of the intruders on their land. Here, again, we are merely plunging ourselves into a mass of conjectures from which it is not possible to extract any real informa-

in which the supposed entry of repayment is given is incorrect. The following entry, which is taken from the B.M. Add. MS. 21,480, folio 76*b*, refers to two future payments for the livery [of seisin], that is, the actual delivery of certain lands. These amounts have no connection whatever with the payments (*ante*, pp. 154, 155) to Thirkill by Henry VII.; in fact, it is not at all certain that the sums paid by the king were loans in the true meaning of the word. "Prest-money" means a payment for impressment, and it is highly probable, although it is not a certainty, that the king impressed or requisitioned Thirkill's ships. On the 6th June 1501, "Lancelot Thirkell Thomas Par Walt. Strickland and Thomas Mydelton ar boundē in 1/ obliḡ [obligation] to pay at Whitsontyde next coming xxli and that day twelve moneth xl marcs for lyverye of Flemyngs lands." In the absence of any distinct contemporary statement that Thirkill actually sailed from Bristol in 1498, the question must be relegated to the realm of probabilities. And even if we consider that the probabilities are in favour of Thirkill's having joined in the expedition, we are at once met with another probability, namely, that he may have joined the ship in which the Friar returned! Directly you commence to wander from actual facts, you are never sure as to your ultimate destination.

tion. We can only say that the men who endured the toils of the ocean, and who risked everything with a view to colonise the newly-discovered lands, must be placed among those who have helped towards the advancement and glory of England, and —sad to relate—their fate is quite unknown. But while we are bound to express our regret that we have nothing, or very little, to guide us as to the fate of the pioneer of English colonisation, it is satisfactory to be assured that, after the lapse of centuries, in the year 1897, the quater-centenary of John Cabot's great achievement, the men of England on the one side of the Atlantic will join with their kith and kin on the other to celebrate duly this important historical episode. And, as a matter of yet greater satisfaction, we must recognise the fact that by almost unanimous consent the name of John Cabot will for evermore be allowed a niche in a prominent position in the Temple of Fame.

APPENDIX A

Plato's Story of the Lost Island of Atlantis

Critias : "Then listen, Socrates, to a strange tale, which is, however, certainly true, as Solon, who was the wisest of the seven sages, declared. He was a relative and great friend of my great-grandfather, Dropidas, as he himself says in several of his poems; and Dropidas told Critias, my grandfather, who remembered, and told us, that there were of old great and marvellous actions of the Athenians, which have passed into oblivion through time and the destruction of the human race—and one in particular, which was the greatest of them all, the recital of which will be a suitable testimony of our gratitude to you." . . .

Socrates : "Very good; and what is this ancient famous action of which Critias spoke, not as a mere legend, but as a veritable action of the Athenian State, which Solon recounted?"

Critias: "I will tell an Old-World story which I heard from an aged man; for Critias was, as he said, at that time nearly ninety years of age, and I was about ten years of age. Now the day was that day of the Apaturia which is called the registration of youth; at which, according to custom, our parents gave prizes for recitations, and the poems of several poets were recited by us boys, and many of us sung the poems of Solon, which were new at the time. One of our tribe, either because this was his real opinion, or because he thought that he would please Critias, said that, in his judgment, Solon was not only the wisest of men but the noblest of poets. The old man, I well remember, brightened up at this, and said, smiling: 'Yes, Amynander, if Solon had only, like other poets, made poetry the business of his life, and had completed the tale which he brought with him from Egypt, and had not been compelled, by reason of the factions and troubles which he found stirring in this country when he came home, to attend to other matters,—in my opinion he would have been as famous as Homer, or Hesiod, or any poet.'"

"And what was that poem about, Critias?" said the person who addressed him.

"About the greatest action which the Athenians ever did, and which ought to have been most famous, but which, through the lapse of time and the destructions of the actors, has not come down to us."

"Tell us," said the other, "the whole story, and how and from whom Solon heard this veritable tradition." He replied: "At the head of the Egyptian Delta, where the river Nile divides, there is a certain district which is called the district of Sais, and the great city of the district is also called Sais, and is the city from which Amasis the king was sprung. And the citizens have a deity who is their foundress: she is called in the Egyptian tongue

Neith, which is asserted by them to be the same whom the Hellenes called Athene. Now, the citizens of this city are great lovers of the Athenians, and say that they are in some way related to them. Thither came Solon, who was received by them with great honour; and he asked the priests, who were most skilled in such matters, about antiquity, and made the discovery that neither he nor any other Hellene knew anything worth mentioning about the times of old. On one occasion, when he was drawing them on to speak of antiquity, he began to tell about the most ancient things in our part of the world—about Phoroneus, who is called 'the first,' and about Niobe; and, after the Deluge, to tell of the lives of Deucalion and Pyrrha; and he traced the genealogy of their descendants, and attempted to reckon how many years old were the events of which he was speaking, and to give the dates. Thereupon, one of the priests, who was of very great age, said: 'O Solon, Solon,—you Hellenes are but children, and there is never an old man who is an Hellene.' Solon, hearing this, said: 'What do you mean?' 'I mean to say,' he replied, 'that in mind you are all young; there is no old opinion handed down among you by ancient tradition, nor any science which is hoary with age. And I will tell you the reason of this: there have been, and there will be again, many destructions of mankind arising out of many causes. There is a story which even you have preserved, that once upon a time Phaëthon, the son of Helios, having yoked the steeds in his father's chariot, because he was not able to drive them in the path of his father, burnt up all that was upon the earth, and was himself destroyed by a thunderbolt. Now, this has the form of a myth, but really signifies a declination of the bodies moving around the earth and in the heavens, and a great conflagration of things upon the earth recurring at long intervals of time; when this happens, those who live upon the mountains and in dry and lofty places are more liable to destruction than those who dwell by rivers or on the seashore; and from this calamity the Nile, who is our never-failing saviour, saves and delivers us. When, on the other hand, the gods purge the earth with a deluge of water, among you herdsmen and shepherds on the mountains are the survivors, whereas those of you who live in cities are carried by the rivers into the sea; but in this country neither at that time nor at any other does the water come from above on the fields, having always a tendency to come up from below, for which reason the things preserved here are said to be the oldest. The fact is, that wherever the extremity of winter frost or of summer sun does not prevent, the human race is always increasing at times, and at other times diminishing in numbers. And whatever happened either in your country or in ours, or in any other region of which we are informed—if any action which is noble or great, or in any other way remarkable, has taken place, all that has been written down of old, and is preserved in our temples; whereas you and other nations are just being provided with letters and the other things which States require; and then, at the usual period, the stream from heaven descends like a pestilence, and leaves only those of you who are destitute of letters and education; and thus you have to begin all over again as children, and know nothing of what happened in ancient times, either among us or among yourselves. As for those genealogies of yours which you have recounted to us, Solon, they are no better than the tales of children; for, in the first place, you remember one deluge only, whereas there were many of them; and, in the next place, you do not know that there dwells in your land the fairest and noblest race of men which ever lived, of whom you and your whole city are but a seed or remnant. And this was unknown to you, because for many generations the survivors of that destruction died and made no sign. For there was a time, Solon, before that great deluge of all, when the city which now is Athens was first in war, and was preeminent for the excellence of her laws, and is said to have performed the noblest deeds, and to have had the fairest constitution of any which tradition tells, under the face of heaven.' Solon marvelled at this, and earnestly requested the priest to inform him exactly and in order about these former citizens. 'You are welcome to hear about them, Solon,' said the priest,—' both for your own sake and for that of the city; and, above all, for the sake of the goddess who is the common patron and protector and educator of both our cities. She founded your city a thousand years before ours, receiving from the Earth and Hephxstus the seed of your race, and then she founded ours, the constitution of which is set down in our sacred registers as eight thousand years old. As touching the citizens of nine thousand years ago, I will briefly inform you of their laws and of the noblest of their actions; and the exact particulars of the whole we will hereafter go through at our leisure in the sacred registers themselves. If you compare these very laws with your own, you will find that many of ours are the counterpart of yours, as they were in the olden times. In the first place, there is the caste of priests, which is separated from all the others; next, there are the artificers, who exercise their several crafts by themselves, and without admixture of any other; and also there is the class of shepherds and that of hunters, as well as that of husbandmen; and you will observe, too, that the warriors in Egypt are separated from all the other classes, and are commanded by the law only to engage in war; moreover, the weapons with which they are equipped are shields and spears, and this the goddess taught first among you, and then in Asiatic countries, and we among the Asiatics first adopted. Then, as to wisdom, do you observe what care the law took from the very first, searching out and contemplating the whole order of things down to prophecy and medicine (the latter with a view to health); and out of these divine elements drawing what was needful for human life, and adding every sort of knowledge which was connected with them. All this order and arrangement the goddess first imparted to you when establishing your city; and she chose the spot of earth in which you were born, because she saw that the happy temperament of the seasons in that land would produce the wisest of men. Wherefore the goddess, who was a lover both of war and of wisdom, selected, and first of all settled, that spot which was the most likely to produce men likest herself. And there you dwelt, having such laws as these and still better ones, and excelled all mankind in all virtue, as became the children and disciples of the gods. Many great and wonderful deeds are recorded of your State in our histories; but one of them exceeds all the rest in greatness and valour; for these histories tell of a mighty power which was aggressing wantonly against the whole of Europe and Asia, and to which your city put an end. This power came forth out of the Atlantic Ocean, for in those days the Atlantic was navigable; and there was an island situated in front of the straits which you call the Columns of Heracles;[1] the island was larger than Libya and Asia put together, and was the way to other islands, and from the islands you might pass through the whole of the opposite continent which surrounded the true ocean; for this sea which is within the Straits of Heracles is only a harbour, having a narrow entrance, but that other is a real sea, and the surrounding land may be most truly called a continent. Now, in the island of Atlantis there was a great and wonderful empire, which had rule over the whole island and several others, as well as over parts of the continent; and, besides these, they subjected the parts of Libya within the Columns of Heracles as far as Egypt, and of Europe as far as Tyrrhenia. The vast power thus gathered into one endeavoured to subdue at one blow our country and yours, and the whole of the land which was within the straits; and then, Solon, your country shone forth, in the excellence of her virtue and strength, among all mankind; for she was the first in courage and military skill, and was the leader of the Hellenes. And when the rest fell off from her, being compelled to stand alone, after having undergone the very extremity of danger, she de-

[1] Hercules.

feated and triumphed over the invaders, and preserved from slavery those who were not yet subjected, and freely liberated all the others who dwell within the limits of Heracles. But afterwards there occurred violent earthquakes and floods, and in a single day and night of rain all your warlike men in a body sank unto the earth, and the island of Atlantis in like manner disappeared, and was sunk beneath the sea. And that is the reason why the sea in those parts is impassable and impenetrable, because there is such a quantity of shallow mud in the way; and this was caused by the subsidence of the island.'
. . . But in addition to the gods whom you have mentioned, I would specially invoke Mnemosyne; for all the important part of what I have to tell is dependent on her favour, and if I can recollect and recite enough of what was said by the priests, and brought thither by Solon, I doubt not that I shall satisfy the requirements of this theatre. To that task, then, I will at once address myself. Let me begin by observing, first of all, that nine thousand was the sum of years which had elapsed since the war which was said to have taken place between all those who dwelt outside the Pillars of Heracles and those who dwelt within them : this war I am now to describe. Of the combatants on the one side, the city of Athens was reported to have been the ruler, and to have directed the contest; the combatants on the other side were led by the kings of the islands of Atlantis, which, as I was saying, once had an extent greater than that of Libya and Asia; and, when afterwards sunk by an earthquake, became an impassable barrier of mud to voyagers sailing from hence to the ocean. The progress of the history

will unfold the various tribes of barbarians and Hellenes which then existed, as they successively appear on the scene; but I must begin by describing, first of all, the Athenians as they were in that day, and their enemies who fought with them; and I shall have to tell of the power and form of government of both of them. Let us give the precedence to Athens. . . . Many great deluges have taken place during the nine thousand years, for that is the number of years which have elapsed since the time of which I am speaking; and in all the ages and changes of things there has never been any settlement of the earth flowing down from the mountains, as in other places, which is worth speaking of; it has always been carried round in a circle and disappeared in the depths below. The consequence is that, in comparison of what then was, there are remaining in small islets only the bones of the wasted body, as they may be called, all the richer and softer parts of the soil having fallen away, and the mere skeleton of the country being left. . . . And next, if I have not forgotten what I heard when I was a child, I will impart to you the character and origin of their adversaries; for friends should not keep their stories to themselves, but have them in common. Yet, before proceeding further in the narrative, I ought to warn you that you must not be surprised if you should hear Hellenic names given to foreigners. I will tell you the reason of this: Solon, who was intending to use the tale for his poem, made an investigation into the meaning of the names, and found that the early Egyptians, in writing them down, had translated them into their own language, and he recovered the meaning of the several names and retranslated them, and copied them out again in our language. My great-grandfather, Dropidas, had the original writing, which is still in my possession, and was carefully studied by me when I was a child. Therefore, if you hear names such as are used in this country, you must not be surprised, for I have told you the reason of them. The tale, which was of great length, began as follows: 'I have before remarked, in speaking of the allotments of the gods, that they distributed the whole earth into portions differing in extent, and made themselves temples and sacrifices. And Poseidon, receiving for his lot the island of Atlantis, begat children by a mortal woman, and settled them in a part of the island which I will proceed to describe. On the one side toward the sea, and in the centre of the whole island, there was a plain, which is said to have been the fairest of all plains, and very fertile. Near the plain, again, and also in the centre of the island, at a distance of about fifty stadia, there was a mountain, not very high on any side. In this mountain there dwelt one of the earth-born primæval men of that country, whose name was Evenor, and he had a wife Leucippe, and they had an only daughter, who was named Cleito. The maiden was growing up to womanhood when her father and mother died; Poseidon fell in love with her, and had intercourse with her; and, breaking the ground, enclosed the hill in which she dwelt all round, making alternate zones of sea and land, larger and smaller, encircling one another; there were two of land and three of water, which he turned as with a lathe out of the centre of the island, equi-distant every way, so that no man could get to the island, for ships and voyages were not yet heard of. He himself, as he was a god, found no difficulty in making special arrangements for the centre island, bringing two streams of water under the earth, which he caused to ascend as springs, one of warm water and the other of cold, and making every variety of food to spring up abundantly in the earth. He also begat and brought up five pairs of male children, dividing the island of Atlantis into ten portions: he gave to the first-born of the eldest pair his mother's dwelling and the surrounding allotment, which was the largest and best, and made him king over the rest; the others he made princes, and gave them rule over many men and a large territory. And he named them all: the eldest, who was king, he named Atlas, and from him the whole island and the ocean received the name of Atlantic. To his twin brother, who was born after him, and obtained as his lot the extremity of the island towards the Pillars of Heracles, as far as the country which is still called the region of Gades in that part of the world, he gave the name which in the Hellenic language is Eumelus, in the language of the country which is named after him, Gadeirus. Of the second pair of twins, he called one Ampheres and the other Evæmon. To the third pair of twins he gave the name Mneseus to the elder, and Autochthon to the one who followed him. Of the fourth pair of twins, he called the elder Elasippus and the younger Mestor. And of the fifth pair, he gave to the elder the name of Azaes, and to the younger Diaprepes. All these and their descendants were the inhabitants and rulers of divers islands in the open sea; and also, as has been already said, they held sway in the other direction over the country within the Pillars as far as Egypt and Tyrrhenia. Now Atlas had a numerous and honourable family, and his eldest branch always retained the kingdom, which the eldest son handed on to his eldest for many generations; and they had such an amount of wealth as was never before possessed by kings and potentates, and is not likely ever to be again; and they were furnished with everything which they could have, both in city and country. For, because of the greatness of their empire, many things were brought to them from foreign countries, and the island itself provided much of what was required by them for the uses of life. In the first place, they dug out of the earth whatever was to be found there, mineral as well as metal, and that which is now only a name, and was then something more than a name—orichalcum—was dug out of the earth in many parts of the island, and, with the exception of gold, was esteemed the most precious of metals among the men of those days. There was an abundance of wood for carpenters' work, and sufficient maintenance for tame and wild animals. Moreover, there was a great number of elephants in the island; and there was provision for animals of every kind, both for those which live in lakes and marshes and rivers, and also for those which live in mountains and on plains, and therefore for the animal which is the largest and most voracious of them. Also, whatever fragrant things there are in the earth—whether roots, or herbage, or woods, or distilling drops of flowers or fruits—grew and thrived in that land; and again, the cultivated fruit of the earth, both the dry edible fruit and other species of food, which we call by the general name of legumes, and the fruits having a hard rind, affording drinks, and meats, and ointments, and good store of chestnuts, and the like, which may be used to play with, and are fruits which spoil with keeping—and the pleasant kinds of desert which console us after dinner, when we are full and tired of eating—all these that sacred island lying beneath the sun brought forth fair and wondrous in infinite abundance. All these things they received from the earth; and they employed themselves in constructing their temples, and palaces, and harbours, and docks; and they arranged the whole country in the following manner :—First of all, they bridged over the zones of sea which surrounded the ancient metropolis, and made a passage into and out of the royal palace; and then they began to build the palace in the habitation of the god and of their ancestors. This they continued to ornament in successive generations, every king surpassing the one who came before him to the utmost of his power, until they made the building a marvel to behold, for size and for beauty. And, beginning from the sea, they dug a canal three hundred feet in width and one hundred feet in depth, and fifty stadia in length, which they carried through to the outermost zone, making a passage from the sea up to this which became a harbour, and leaving an opening sufficient to enable the largest vessels to find ingress. Moreover, they divided the zones of land which parted the zones of sea, constructing bridges of such a width as would leave a passage for a single trireme to pass out of one into another, and roofed them over; and there was a way underneath for the ships, for the banks of the zones were raised considerably above the water. Now the largest of the zones into which a passage was cut from the sea was three stadia in breadth, and the zone of land which came next of equal breadth; but the next two, as well the zone of water as of land, were two stadia, and the one which surrounded the central island was a stadium only in width. The island in which the palace was situated had a diameter of five stadia. This, and the zones and the bridge, which was the sixth part of a stadium in width, they surrounded by a stone wall, on either side placing towers, and gates on the bridges where the sea passed in. The stone which was used in the work they quarried from underneath the centre island and from underneath the zones, on the outer as well as the inner side. One kind of stone was white, another black, and a third red; and, as they quarried, they at the same time hollowed out docks double within, having roofs formed out of the native rock. Some of their buildings were simple, but in others they put together different stones, which they intermingled for the sake of ornament, to be a natural source of delight. The entire circuit of the wall which went round the outermost one they covered with a coating of brass, and the circuit of the next wall they coated with tin, and the third, which encompassed the citadel, flashed with the rich light of orichalcum. The palaces in the interior of the citadel were constructed in this wise. In the centre was a holy temple dedicated to Cleito and Poseidon, which remained inaccessible, and was surrounded by an enclosure of gold; this was the spot in which they originally begat the race of the ten princes, and thither they annually brought the fruits of the earth in their season from all the ten portions, and performed sacrifices to each of them. Here, too, was Poseidon's own temple, of a stadium in length and half a stadium in width, and of a proportionate height, having a sort of barbaric splendour. All the outside of the temple, with the exception of the pinnacles, they covered with silver, and the pinnacles with gold. In the interior of the temple the roof was of ivory, adorned everywhere with gold and silver and orichalcum; all the other parts of the walls and pillars and floor they lined with orichalcum. In the temple they placed statues of gold; there was the god himself standing in a chariot—the charioteer of six-winged horses—and of such a size that he touched the roof of the building with his head; around him there were a hundred Nereids riding on dolphins, for such was thought to be the number of them in that day. There were also in the interior of the temple other images which had been dedicated by private individuals. And around the temple on the outside were placed statues of gold of all the ten kings and of their wives; and there were many other great offerings, both of kings and of private individuals, coming both from the city itself and the foreign cities over which they held sway. There was an altar, too, which in size and workmanship corresponded to the rest of the work, and there were palaces in like manner which answered to the greatness of the kingdom and the glory of the temple.

"'In the next place, they used fountains both of cold and hot springs; these were very abundant, and both kinds wonderfully adapted to use by reason of the sweetness and excellence of their waters. They constructed buildings about them, and planted suitable trees; also cisterns, some open to the heaven, others, which they roofed over, to be used in winter as warm baths; there were the king's baths, and the baths of private persons, which were kept apart; also separate baths for women, and others again for horses and cattle, and to them they gave as much adornment as was suitable for them.

"'The water which ran off they carried, some to the grove of Poseidon, where were growing all manner of trees of wonderful height and beauty, owing to the excellence of the soil; the remainder was conveyed by aqueducts which passed over the bridges to the outer circles; and there were many temples built and dedicated to many gods; also gardens and places of exercise, some for men, and some set apart for horses, in both of the two islands formed by the zones; and in the centre of the larger of the two there was a race-course of a stadium in width, and in length allowed to extend all round the island, for horses to race in. Also there were guard-houses at intervals for the bodyguard, the more trusted of whom had their duties appointed to them in the lesser zone, which was nearer the Acropolis; while the most trusted of all had houses given them within the citadel, and about the person of the king. The docks were full of triremes and naval stores, and all things were quite ready for use. Enough of the plan of the royal palace. Crossing the outer harbours, which were three in number, you would come to a wall which began at the sea and went all round; this was everywhere distant fifty stadia from the largest zone and harbour, and enclosed the whole, meeting at the mouth of the channel toward the sea. The entire area was densely crowded with habitations, and the canal and the largest of the harbours were full of vessels and merchants coming from all parts, who, from their numbers, kept up a multitudinous sound of human voices and din of all sorts night and day. I have repeated his description of the city and the parks about the ancient palace nearly as he gave them, and now I must endeavour to describe the nature and arrangement of the rest of the country. The whole country was described as being very lofty and precipitous on the side of the sea, but the country immediately about and surrounding the city was a level plain, itself surrounded by mountains which descended toward the sea; it was smooth and even, but of an oblong shape, extending in one direction three thousand stadia, and going up the country from the sea through the centre of the island two thousand stadia; the whole region of the island lies toward the south, and is sheltered from the north. The surrounding mountains he celebrated for their number, and size, and beauty, in which they exceeded all that are now to be seen anywhere; having in them also many wealthy inhabited villages, and rivers, and lakes, and meadows supplying food enough for every animal, wild or tame, and wood of various sorts, abundant for every kind of work. I will now describe the plain, which had been cultivated during many ages by many generations of kings. It was rectangular, and for the most part straight and oblong; and what it wanted of the straight line followed the line of the circular ditch. The depth, and width, and length of this ditch were incredible, and gave the impression that such a work, in addition to so many other works, could hardly have been wrought by the hand of man. But I must say what I have heard. It was excavated to the depth of a hundred feet, and its breadth was a stadium everywhere; it was carried round the whole of the plain, and was ten thousand stadia in length. It received the streams which came down from the mountains, and winding round the plain, and touching the city at various points, was there let off into the sea; these canals were at intervals of a hundred stadia, and by them they brought down the wood from the mountains to the city, and conveyed the fruits of the earth in ships, cutting transverse passages from one canal into another, and to the city. Twice in the year they gathered the fruits of the earth—in winter having the benefit of the rains, and in summer introducing the water of the canals. As to the population, each of the lots in the plain had an appointed chief of men who were fit for military service, and the size of the lot was to be a square of ten stadia each way, and the total number of all the lots was sixty thousand.

"' And of the inhabitants of the mountains and of the rest of the country there was also a vast multitude having leaders, to whom they were assigned according to their dwellings and villages. The leader was required to furnish for the war the sixth portion of a war-chariot, so as to make up a total of ten thousand chariots; also two horses and riders upon them, and a light chariot without a seat, accompanied by a fighting man on foot carrying a small shield, and having a charioteer mounted to guide the horses; also, he was bound to furnish two heavy-armed men, two archers, two slingers, three stone-shooters, and three javelin-men, who were skirmishers, and four sailors to make up a complement of twelve hundred ships. Such was the order of war in the royal city; that of the other nine governments was different in each of them, and would be wearisome to narrate. As to offices and honours, the following was the arrangement from the first :—Each of the ten kings, in his own division and in his own city, had the absolute control of the citizens, and in many cases of the laws, punishing and slaying whomsoever he would.

"'Now, the relations of their governments to one another were regulated by the injunctions of Poseidon, as the law had handed them down. These were inscribed by the first men on a column of orichalcum, which was situated in the middle of the island, at the temple of Poseidon, whither the people were gathered together every fifth and sixth year alternately, thus giving equal honour to the odd and to the even number. And when they were gathered together they consulted about public affairs, and inquired if anyone had transgressed in anything, and passed judgment on him accordingly; and before they passed judgment they gave their pledges to one another in this wise : There were bulls which had the range of the temple of Poseidon; and the ten who were left alone in the temple, after they had offered prayers to the gods that they might take the sacrifices which were acceptable to them, hunted the bulls without weapons, but with staves and nooses; and the bull which they caught they led up to the column. The victim was then struck on the head by them, and slain over the sacred inscription.

"'Now, on the column, besides the law, there was inscribed an oath invoking mighty curses on the disobedient. When, therefore, after offering sacrifice according to their customs, they had burned the limbs of the bull, they mingled a cup and cast in a clot of blood for each of them; the rest of the victim they took to the fire, after having made a purification of the column all round. Then they drew from the cup in golden vessels, and, pouring a libation on the fire, they swore that they would judge according to the laws on the column, and would punish anyone who had previously transgressed; and that for the future they would not, if they could help, transgress any of the inscriptions, and would not command or obey any ruler who commanded them to act otherwise than according to the laws of their father, Poseidon. This was the prayer which each of them offered up for himself and for his family, at the same time drinking, and dedicating the vessel in the temple of the god; and, after spending some necessary time at supper, when darkness came on and the fire about the sacrifice was cool, all of them put on most beautiful azure robes, and, sitting on the ground at night near the embers of the sacrifices on which they had sworn, and extinguishing all the fire about the temple, they received and gave judgment, if any of them had any accusation to bring against anyone; and, when they had given judgment, at daybreak they wrote down their sentences on a golden tablet, and deposited them as memorials with their robes. There were many special laws which the several kings had inscribed about the temples, but the most important was the following:—That they were not to take up arms against one another, and they were all to come to the rescue if anyone in any city attempted to overthrow the royal house. Like their ancestors, they were to deliberate in common about war and other matters, giving the supremacy to the family of Atlas; and the king was not to have the power of life and death over any of his kinsmen, unless he had the assent of the majority of the ten kings.

"'Such was the vast power which the god settled in the lost island of Atlantis; and this he afterwards directed against our land on the following pretext, as traditions tell :—For many generations, as long as the divine nature lasted in them, they were obedient to the laws, and well-affectioned toward the gods, who were their kinsmen ; for they possessed true and in every way great spirits, preaching gentleness and wisdom in the various chances of life, and in their intercourse with one another. They despised everything but virtue, not caring for their present state of life, and thinking lightly on the possession of gold and other property, which seemed only a burden to them; neither were they intoxicated with luxury, nor did wealth deprive them of their self-control, but they were sober, and saw clearly that all these goods are increased by virtuous friendship with one another, and that by excessive zeal for them, and honour of them, the good of them is lost, and friendship perishes with them.

"'By such reflections, and by the continuance in them of a divine nature, all that which we have described, waxed, and increased in them; but when this divine portion began to fade away in them, and became diluted too often, and with too much of the mortal admixture, and the human nature got the upper-hand, then they, being unable to bear their fortune, became unseemly, and to him who had an eye to see, they began to appear base and had lost the fairest of their precious gifts; but to those who had no eye to see the true happiness, they still appeared glorious and blessed at the very time when they were filled with unrighteous avarice and power. Zeus, the god of gods, who rules with law, and is able to see into such things, perceiving that an honourable race was in a most wretched state, and wanting to inflict punishment on them, that they might be chastened and improved, *collected all the gods into his most holy habitation*, which, being placed in the centre of the world, sees all things that partake of generation, and when he had called them together he spake as follows:'"—

[Here Plato's story abruptly ends.]

APPENDIX B

THE LATIN TEXT OF THE BULL OF POPE ALEXANDER VI., DATED 4TH DAY OF MAY 1493.

"ALEXANDER, Episcopus, servus servorum Dei, Charissimo in Christo filio Ferdinando Regi, et Charissimæ in Christo filiæ Elizabeth Reginæ Castellæ, Legionis, Aragonum, Siciliæ, et Granatæ, illustribus, salutem et Apostolicam benedictionem. Inter cætera Divinæ majestati beneplacita opera et cordis nostri desiderabilia illud profecto potisimum existit, ut fides Catholica et Christiana religio nostris præsertim temporibus exaltetur, ac ubilibet amplietur ac dilatetur, animarunq' salus procuretur, ac barbaræ nationes deprimantur, et ad fidem ipsam reducantur. Unde cum ad hanc sacram Petri sedem, Divina favente clementia (meritis licet imparibus), evocati fueremus, cognoscentes vos tanquam veros Catholicos Reges et Principes, quales semper fuisse novimus, et a vobis præclare gesta, toti pœne orbi notissima demonstrant, nedum id exoptare, sed omni conatu, studio, et diligentia, nullis laboribus, nullis impensis, nullisq' parcendo periculis, etiam proprium sanguinem effundendo efficere, ac omnem animum vestrum, omnesq' conatus ad hoc jam dudum dedicasse, quemadmodum recuperatio regni Granatæ a tyrannis de Sarracenorum hodiernis temporibus per vos, cum tanta Divini nominis gloria facta, testatur. Digne ducimur non immerito et debemus illa vobis etiam sponte, et favorabiliter concedere, per quæ hujusmodi sanctum ac laudabile ab immortali Deo acceptum propositum, in dies ferventiori animo ad ipsius Dei honorem et imperii Christiani propagationem prosequi valeatis.

"Sane accepimus quod vos dudum animum proposueratis aliquas insulas et terras firmas remotas et incognitas, ac per alios hactenus non repertas quærere et invenire, ut illarum incolas et habitatores ad colendum redemptorem nostrum et fidem catholicam profitendum reduceretis, hactenus in expugnatione et recuperatione ipsius regni Granatæ plurimum occupati, hujusmodi sanctum et laudabile propositum vestrum ad optatum finem perducere nequivistis ; Sed tamen, sicut Domino placuit, regno prædicto recuperato, volentes desiderium vestrum adimplere, dilectum filium Christoforum Colonum, virum utiq' dignum et plurimum commendatum ac tanto negotio aptum, cum navigiis et hominibus ad similia instructis, non sine maximis laboribus ac periculis, et expensis destinatis ut terras firmas et insulas remotas et incognitas, hujusmodi per mare, ubi hactenus navigatum non fuerat, diligenter inquireret.

"Qui tandem (Divino auxilio facta extrema diligentia in mare Oceano navigantes) certas insulas remotissimas et etiam terras firmas, quæ per alios hactenus repertæ non fuerant, invenerunt. In quibus plurimæ gentes pacifice viventes, et (ut asseritur) nudi incedentes, nec carnibus vescentes, inhabitant: Et ut præfati nuncii vestri possunt opinari, gentes ipsæ in insulis et terris prædictis habitantes, credunt unum Deum Creatorem in Cœlis esse, ac ad fidem Catholicam amplexandum et bonis moribus imbuendum satis apti videntur : Spesque habetur, quod si erudirentur, nomen Salvatoris Domini nostri Jesu Christi in terris et insulis prædictis facile induceretur. Ac præfatus Christoforus in una ex principalibus insulis prædictis, jam unam turrim satis munitam, in qua certos Christianos qui secum iuerant, in custodiam et ut alias insulas ac terras firmas remotas et incognitas inquirerent posuit, construi et ædificari fecit.

"In quibus quidem Insulis et terris jam repertis aurum, aromata, et aliæ quamplurimæ res præciosæ diversi generis et diversæ qualitatis reperiunter.

"Unde omnibus diligenter et præsertim fidei Catholicæ exaltatione et dilatatione (prout decet Catholicus Reges et Principes) consideratis, more progenitorum vestrorum claræ memoriæ Regum, terras firmas et insulas prædictas, illarumq' incolas et habitatores vobis Divina favente clementia subiicere et ad fidem Catholicam reducere proposuistis. Nos itaque hujusmodi vestrum sanctum et laudabile propositum plurimum in Domino commendantes, ac cupientes, ut illud ad debitum finem perducatur, et ipsum nomen Salvatoris nostri in partibus illis inducatur, hortamur vos quamplurimum in Domino, et per sacri lauacri susceptionem, qua mandatis Apostolicis obligati estis, et per viscera misericordiæ Domini nostri Jesu Christi attente requirimus, ut cum expeditionem hujusmodi omnino prosequi et assumere prona mente orthodoxæ fidei zelo intendatis, populos, in hujusmodi insulis et terris degentes, ad Christianam religionem suscipiendum inducere velitis et debeatis, nec pericula nec labores ullo unquam tempore vos deterreant, firma spe fiduciaq' conceptis, quod Deus omnipotens conatus vestros fœliciter prosequetur.

"Et ut tanti negotij provintiam Apostolicæ gratiæ largitate donati, liberius et audacius assumatis, motu proprio non ad vestram vel alterius pro vobis super hoc nobis oblatæ petitionis instantiam, sed de nostra mera liberalitate, et ex certa scientia, ac de Apostolicæ potestatis plenitudine, omnes insulas et terras firmas inventas et inveniendas, detectas et detegendas versus Occidentem et Miridiem, fabricando et construendo unam lineam a Polo Arctico, scilicet septemtrione, ad polo Antarcticum, scilicet Meridiem (sive terræ firmæ et insulæ inventæ et inveniendæ sint versus Indiam aut versus aliam quamcunq' partem), quæ linea distet a qualibet insularum quæ vulgariter nuncupantur de los Azores et Cabo Verde, centum leucis versus Occidentem et Meridiem. Itaque omnes Insulæ et terræ firmæ repertæ et repeciendæ, detectæ et detegendæ a præfata linea versis Occidentem et Miridiem quæ per alium Regem aut Principem Christianum non fuerint actualiter possessæ, usq' ad diem nativitatis Domini nostri Jesu Christi proxime præteritum, a quo incipit annus præsens millesimus Quadringentessimus Nonagessimus tercus, quando fuerunt per nuncios et capitaneos vestros inventæ aliquæ prædictarum Insularum, Auctoritate omnipotentis Dei nobis in beato Petro concessa, ac vicariatus Jesu Christi qua fungimur in terris, cum omnibus illarum dominijs, civitatibus, castris, locis, et villis, iuribusque et jurisdictionibus ac pertinentijs universis, vobis heredibusque et successoribus vestris (Castellæ et Legionis regibus) in perpetuum tenore præsentium donamus, concedimus et assignamus : Vosque et hæredes ac successores præfatos illarum Dominos cum plena, libera, et omnimoda potestate, autoritate, et jurisdictione, facimus, constituimus, et deputamus.

"Decernentes nihilo minus per hujusmodi donationem, concessionem, et assignationem nostram, nullo Christiano Principi qui actualiter præfatas Insulas et terras firmas possederit usq' ad prædictum diem nativitatis Domini nostri Jesu Christi ius quæsitum, sublatum intelligi posse aut auferri debere. Et insuper mandamus vobis in virtutæ sanctæ obedientiæ (ut sicut pollicemini et non dubitamus pro vestra maxima devotione et regia magnanimitate vos esse facturos), ad terras firmas et Insulas prædictas, viros probos et Deum timentes, doctos, peritos, et expertos ad instruendum incolas et habitatores præfatos in fide Catholica et bonis moribus imbuendum, destinare debeatis, omnem debitam diligentiam in præmissis adhibentes.

"Ac quibuscunq' personis, cuiuscunq' dignitatis, etiam imperialis et regalis, status, gradus, ordinis vel conditionis, sub excommunicationis latæ sententiæ pœna quam eo ipso, si contra fecerint, incurrant, districtius inhibemus ne ad Insulas et terras firmas inventas et inveniendas detectas et detegendas versus Occidentem et Meridiem, fabricando et construendo lineam a Polo Arctico ad polum Antarcticum, sive terræ firmæ et Insulæ inventæ et inveniendæ sint versus Indiam aut versus aliam quamcunq' partem, quæ linea distet a qualibet Insularum quæ vulgariter nuncupantur de los Azores y Cabo Verde centum leucis versus Occidentem et Meridiem ut præfertur, pro mercibus habendis, vel quavis alia causa accedere præsumat absq' vestra ac heredum et successorum vestrorum prædictorum licentia speciali.

"Non obstantibus constitutionibus et ordinationibus Apostolicis, cæterisq' contrariis quibiscunq': in illo, a quo imperia et dominationes ac bona cuncta procedunt: Confidentes, quod dirigente Domino actus vestros, si hujusmodi sanctum et laudabile propositum prosequamini, brevi tempore cum fœlicitate et gloria totius populi Christiani, vestri labores et conatus exitum fœlicissimum consequentur.

"Verum quia difficile foret præsentes literas ad singula quæque loca in quibus expediens fuerit deferri, volumus, ac motu et scientia similibus decernimus, quod illarum transsumptis manu publici Notarii inderogati subscriptis et sigillo alicuius personæ in ecclesiastica dignitate constitutæ, seu curiæ ecclesiasticæ munitis, ea prorsus fides in judicio, et extra ac alias ubilibet adhibeatur, quæ præsentibus adhiberetur, si essent exhibitæ vel ostensæ. Nulli ergo omnino hominum liceat hanc paginam nostræ commendationis, hortationis, requisitionis, donationis, concessionis, assignationis, constitutionis, deputationis, decreti, mandati, inhibitionis et voluntatis infringere, vel ei ausu temerario contraire.

"Si quis autem hoc attentare præsumpserit, indignationem, omnipotentis Dei, ac Beatorum Petri et Pauli Apostolorum ejus se noverit in cursurum. Datum Romæ apud sanctum Petrum: Anno incarnationis dominicæ millesimo quadringentesimo nonagesimo tertio, quarto nonas Maii: Pontificatus nostri anno primo."

APPENDIX C

"BRISTOL"

"VIEW of the account of Arthur Kemys and Richard A. Meryk, collectors of the customs and subsidies of the king in the port of the town of Bristol, and in all the ports and places to the said port adjacent, to wit, of such customs and subsidies of the king there from the feast of St. Michael the Archangel, 13 Henry VII., until the feast of Easter happening on the 15th day of April then next following, to wit, for the moiety of one year and fifteen days, as below.

"The same charge themselves gratis with £554, 18s. 5½d. of the customs and subsidies of divers merchandises of divers merchants Jews and aliens, as well those brought to the said ports and places as those taken away from the same, and there customed (custumat) within the time of this view, as contained in 4 sections (quaternis) of parchment of the said collectors of particulars thereof shown and examined upon this view, and by the oath of the said collectors.

"Sum of the receipts, £554, 18s. 5½d.; whereof is respited to the said collectors, 72s. 4d., for their fees for the said time of this view, according to the rate of 10 marks yearly between them, as is allowed in divers preceding accounts. And 100s. paid by them to Quintius (Quintino) Poulet, keeper of the king's library, for his fee of £10 a year, granted to him by the king, that now is by letters-patent during his life, to be paid at two terms of the year, to be paid out of the customs and subsidies accruing to the king in the said port of Bristol, to wit, for the term of Easter happening within the time of this view, by an acquittance of the said Quintius thereof shown upon this view, and remaining in the possession of the said collectors. And £10 paid by them to George Herbert, for his annuity of £20 a year, granted to him by the king by letters-patent, to be paid at two terms of the year out of customs and subsidies forthcoming and growing in the said port of Bristol; to wit, for the term of the Annunciation of the B. V. M. happening within the time of the said view, by an acquittance of the said George thereof shown upon this view and remaining in the possession of the said collectors. And £10 by them paid to John Calbot, a Venetian, late of the said town of Bristol, for his annuity of £20 a year, granted to him by the said lord the king by his letters-patent, to be taken at two terms of the year out of the customs and subsidies forthcoming and growing in the said port of the town of Bristol, to wit, for the term of the Annunciation of the Blessed Virgin Mary happening within the time of this view, by an acquittance of the said John, to be shown thereof upon this view, and remaining in the possession of the said collectors. And £400, by them paid for two tallies, into the receipt of the exchequer of the lord the king, levied for the household of the king, whereof one tally was levied on the

29th January, and the other on the 30th of January, in the said 13th year, each tally containing £200, shown upon this view, and remaining in the possession of the said collectors.

"Sum of respites, £428, 12s. 4d.

"And they owe £126, 6s. 1½d. Whereof is respited to the said collectors, £9, 2s. 6d., paid by them to Robert Marleton one of the king's serjeants-at-arms, for the exercise and occupation of the said office, at 12d. a day, granted to him by the said king by letters-patent for the term of his life, to be taken yearly out of the customs and subsidies of the said port of Bristol by the hands of the customers or collectors of the same, to wit, for the term of Easter happening within the time of this view, by an acquittance of the said Robert. And they owe £117, 3s. 7½d., whereof is respited to the said collectors £6, 13s. 4d., by them paid to John Karre for his annuity of 20 marks by the year, granted to him by the said king, to hold and take yearly during the pleasure of the said king out of the customs and subsidies growing within his port of Bristol by the hands of the customers there for the time being, at the feasts of Easter and Michaelmas, by equal portions, to wit, for the said feast of Easter happening within the time of this view by an acquittance of the said John Karre, shown upon this view, and remaining in the possession of the said collectors. And 33s. 4d., by them paid to John Lawrence for his annuity of 66s. 8d. yearly, to him granted by the said king for the term of his life, out of the customs and subsidies of the town of Bristol and of Gadecombe, by the hands of the customers or other occupiers of the port of the said king for the time being, to be paid at the feasts of Easter and Michaelmas by equal portions, to wit, for the said feast of Easter happening within the said time of this view, by an acquittance of the said John Lawrence, shown upon this view and remaining in the possession of the said collectors.

"And they owe £108, 16s. 11$\frac{1}{2}$d."

INDEX

AFRICA, 3, 4, 10.
Africa, circumnavigation of, 3, 4, 30.
Alexander VI., Pope of Rome, 62, 64.
Alexandria, 76, 125.
Alliacus, Petrus, 28.
Alma, Don Fernando, 48-50.
Almazan, 163.
America, name of, 297.
America, North, 34, 70, 71, 92, 116, 257.
American Islands, 8.
Amerigo (Vespucci), [Americus Vespucius], the titular discoverer of America, 297.
Amoo, land of the, 3.
Anspach, L. A., *History of Newfoundland* by, 105.
Antilia, Island of, 31, 43, 44, 45, 47, 55.
Antilles. See Antilia.
Arabian Gulf, 4.
Arabs, belief of, as to the "Fortunate Islands," 35.
Aristotle, 6, 8, 27, 47.
Arnold, Matthew, lines on St. Brandon, 55.
Arômata-Akron, 2.
Arran Islands, 41.
Ashehurst, Thomas, 184.
Asia, 5, 6, 20, 127.
Astrolabe, 90.
Atlantic Island, 10, 11, 40.
Atlantic Ocean, 8, 9-13, 27, 28, 32.
Atlantis, the island of, 10-12.
Atlantis, Plato's story of, 10-12, 305-326.
Atlas, 11.
Augustine, Bishop of Hippo, 79.
Avezac. See D'Avezac.

Avon (Bristol), river, 59.
Ayala, Pedro de, 59, 101, 141, 151, 160, 163, 267, 280, 296.
Azores, 38, 46, 47, 67.

BACCALAOS, 169, 172, 173, 176, 186-188, 193, 194, 205, 261-265.
Backe, the, Bristol, 134.
Bacon, Roger, 27, 28.
Baker, E. E., 121, 122.
Baffin's Bay, 256.
Bahr-al-Zulmat, 8.
Baldwin Street, Bristol, 133.
Balsam Land. See Punt.
Barrett's *History of Bristol*, 115, 118, 121.
Bassarion, Cardinal, 89.
Befinn, 41.
Behaim, Martin, 29.
Behaim's globe, 55.
Belle Isle, 285, 288.
Belle Isle, Strait of, 288.
Bergenroth, G. A., 163.
Bibliothèque, Nationale, Paris, 276.
Biddle, Richard, 31, 298, 300.
Bimini, 271.
Blanc Sablon, 288.
Blest, Isles of the, 35, 36, 39.
Bojador, Cape, 61, 85.
Boranden, San. See Brandon, Saint.
Bosworth, Battle of, 134.
Botoner, W. See Worcestre, W.
Boyl, Friar. See Buil.
Bracie, Insula de, 38.
Bradley, Thomas, 155.
Brandon, Island of St. See Brandon, St.

Brandon, St., 31, 44, 54–58, 75.
Brasil, 31, 39, 41–43, 55, 58, 59, 107, 109.
Brasil or O'Brasil or O'Brazile. See Brasil.
Brasile. See Brasil.
Brasille. See Brasil.
Brazi, Isle of, 38.
Brazil or Brasil, origin of the name, 42, 43.
Brazil wood, 42, 43.
Brendan. See Brandon.
Brendon. See Brandon.
Breton, Cape, 180, 280, 282, 283.
Breton, Cape, Island of, 282.
Bristol, account of the collectors of customs, 333–336.
Bristol Bridge, 133.
Bristol, Cabot's pension payable out of the customs and subsidies of, 128, 129, 131.
Bristol (England), 33, 34, 58, 60, 97, 99, 101, 106, 107, 134, 135, 139, 140, 146–150, 160, 162, 178–181, 184, 205, 207, 244, 245, 248, 252, 254, 267, 296.
Bristol Harbour, 13.
Bristol, History of. See Barrett.
Bristol, men of, their belief in the existence of the mythical islands, 33.
Bristol, merchants of, discovery of North America by, 116.
Bristol, port of, 128, 129, 133.
Bristol, rise of the tide at, 140.
Bristol River, 13, 14.
Bristol, sailors of, on board the *Matthew*, 115.
Bristowe. See Bristol.
Brittia, Island of, 39.
Brooke, family of (Bristol), 129, 130.
Brown, Rawdon, 139, 143, 144.
Brown, Sir Wolston, 210.
Buil, Friar, 161, 162, 296.
Bull, Papal, 60–69, 71, 99, 327–332.
Burgundian, a, on board the *Matthew*, 147, 150, 285.

CABOT, John, as to the flag of St. Mark, 15; reference to, 30; of Genoese origin, but a naturalised Venetian, 67, 70; copy entry of grant of citizenship of Venice, 70; sailed from Bristol in 1497, and succeeded in discovering North America, 70; the effect of Cabot's discovery referred to, 70, 71; references to, 73, 74; as to his belief that he would find the lands of the Grand Khan, and the probability of his belief in the existence of the mythical islands of "St. Brandon," of "Brasil," and of the "Seven Cities," 74–78; Cabot's ideas compared with those of Columbus, 77, 78; as to Toscanelli's theory, 79; the relegation of Cabot's achievement to obscurity, 91; pride of the citizens of Bristol in Cabot's triumph, 92, 93; petition of Cabot and his three sons to King Henry VII. for a grant of letters-patent, 94; copy (in Latin) of letters-patent, 96, 97; translation of letters-patent, 97–100; references to Cabot's negotiations with the king, 100; reference to Cabot's probable settlement in Bristol, 105; reference to a supposed relic of Cabot's voyage, 109, 110; reference by Ruy Gonzales de Puebla to Cabot, 110, 111; reference to the delay which elapsed between the grant of the letters-patent and Cabot's embarkation, 113, 114; references to the sailing of John Cabot in the *Matthew* of Bristol, 115; references to Cabot's discovery, 115; references to a MS. Chronicle containing an entry as to Cabot's discovery, 115–122; Rev. M. Harvey's reference to Cabot's voyage, 123, 124; John Cabot's arrival at Court to announce his discovery to the king, 124; Tarducci's reference thereto, 125, 126; references to the gift of £10 by the king to Cabot, and of the grant of an annuity of £20 per annum, together with the present value of the gift and of the annuity, 126, 127; copy grant of £20 per year by King Henry VII. to Cabot, 128; copy warrant for

INDEX 339

payment of the annuity, 129; copy entry as to the actual payment of the annuity, 131; copy letter written by Lorenzo Pasqualigo as to Cabot's discovery, 138; extract from a despatch of Raimondo de Soncino, 143; copy of the second despatch of Raimondo de Soncino, 145; copy petition of John Cabot for a grant of letters-patent for a voyage of colonisation, 156; copy (in English) of the letters-patent granted to Cabot, 156, 157; copy (in Latin) of the letters-patent, 158, 159; extract from a despatch from Dr. Puebla, 159; copy despatch from Pedro de Ayala, 160; extract from a MS. Chronicle as to Cabot's departure, 164; Cabot's fate enshrouded in mystery, 165; the equipper of the two voyages of 1497 and 1498, 167; Hakluyt's reference to John Cabot, 254; references to Hakluyt's mention of John Cabot's name, 257-259; Biddle's references to John Cabot, 259; Hakluyt's reference to the name of John Cabot in the letters-patent of 1498, 260; John Cabot's name on inscriptions on the so-called Sebastian Cabot's map, 261, 262, 264-266; d'Avezac's references to Cabot, 266, 268; as to the comparative agency of John and Sebastian Cabot, 277; references to the landfall of John Cabot in 1497, the map of Juan de la Cosa, 278-280; the proceedings of the Royal Society of Canada as to the landfall, the theory of H. Harrisse compared with that of Dr. Dawson as to the landfall, 278-292; the La Cosa map, and the date and place of the birth of La Cosa, 293; the legend of St. Christopher, 293; reference to Alonso Ojeda, 297, 298; references to La Cosa, Ojeda, and the presence of Englishmen at Coquibacoa, 298; relics of Cabot's expedition, 299; Ojeda directed to prevent further English discoveries, 300, 301; conjectures as to the fate of Cabot's expedition of 1498, 301-303.

Caboto, Giovanni. See Cabot, John.

Caboote. See Cabot.

Cabot, Jean. See Cabot, John.

Cabot, Sebastian, name in petition for grant of letters-patent, 94; name in the letters-patent of 1497, 96, 98; Sebastian's accounts of his voyages referred to, 153; as to whether Sebastian sailed with his father in 1497, 155, 156; Biddle's work on Sebastian Cabot, 165; Sebastian visits Spain and accepts employment under the Spanish Government, 167; Peter Martyr's account of Sebastian's alleged discovery, 169-173; arguments as to the probabilities connected with Martyr's account, 173-183; Steven's remarks on Martyr's statements, 184; references to Ramusio's account of Sebastian's alleged discovery, 184, 185; the statement of Ramusio and that given by Robert Thorne referred to, 184, 185; Ramusio's account referred to, 186; Dr. Dawson's comments, 187, 188; Dr. Justin Winsor's comments, 188, 189; Antonio Galvão's account of Sebastian's alleged discovery, 190; Gomara's account of Sebastian's alleged discovery, 193; Giovanni Battista Ramusio's references to Sebastian's alleged discovery, 195; the Mantuan Gentleman's statement as to the alleged discovery, 197-203; arguments as to Ramusio's statements, 203-208; questions raised by the accounts of the alleged discovery by the various historians, 208, 209; Sebastian's negotiations with King Henry VIII., 210-212; references to Magellan's circumnavigation of the globe, 212; Sebastian's intrigues with Venice, 214-241; grant of a pension to, 232; Harrisse's comments on Sebastian's alleged discovery, 244; Hakluyt's references to Sebastian

Cabot, 251; Fabian's Chronicle, 251, 252; John Stow's account, 253; Hakluyt's account, 254; Harrisse's notes, 255; Biddle's references, 258-260; legends on the so-called Sebastian Cabot map, 261-266; d'Avezac's reference to the so-called Cabot map, 267, 268; Kohl's references to the so-called Cabot map, 269-273; Harrisse's references thereto, 273; Dr. Justin Winsor's references thereto, 275; R. H. Major's explanation as to the date 1494 in the legend on the Cabot map, 276; remarks on the Cabot map, 277.
Cabot, Lewis, 94, 96, 98.
Cabot, Sanctus, 94, 96, 98.
Cabot voyage, supposed relics of, 109, 299.
Cabotia, the continent of North America should be so called in honour of the discoverer, 297.
Cabral, Goncalo, 48.
Calboto (see Cabot, John), 131, 132.
Calf, Henry, 57.
Canadian (Cabot Celebration) Committee, 280.
Canary Islands, 35, 36, 47.
Canynges, William, merchant of Bristol, 107-109.
Cantino, Alberto, 299, 300.
Cape Bojador, 61, 85.
Cape Guardafui, 1.
Cape de Verde Islands, 46.
Cape of England, on La Cosa's map, 279.
Cape of Good Hope, 3, 4, 86.
Carolina, on the Cabot map, 272.
Carter, John, 155.
Carthage, 4.
Carthaginians, 5.
Carribean Sea, 71.
Catalan map, 39.
Cathay (China), 22, 26, 50, 75, 82.
Catherine of Aragon, 112.
Celtic, old, romances, 39, 40, 41.
Chatterton, the boy poet of Bristol, 109.
Chidley, Cape, 286-288, 290-292.
China, 19, 20, 26.
Chinese, 17, 38.

Chipangu. See Cipangu.
Christian, King of Denmark, 106.
Christopher, St., the legend of, 293.
Chronicle, MS. (in Barrett's possession), containing an entry of the discovery by Bristol men in the *Matthew*, 115.
Chronicle, MS. (formerly in the possession of the Fust family), containing an entry of the discovery "by the merchants of Bristowe," 116; facts relating to, 116-122.
Chronicle, in Cottonian MSS., 245.
Chronicle, Fabian, 253.
Cibola, seven cities of, 51, 52.
Cipangu, 19, 24, 75, 76, 82, 295.
Cochin China, 26.
Cog-Anne, a Bristol ship, 112.
Collona, Stragliano, 226.
Colonus. See Columbus.
Columbus, Bartholomew, 86, 103-105.
Columbus, Christopher, 1, 6-9, 30, 33, 38, 61, 62, 65, 66, 74, 76-80, 83, 103, 111.
Columbus, Ferdinand, 8, 45.
Constantinople, 14-16, 61, 88, 89.
Contarini, Gaspar, Venetian ambassador to Spain, 214, 219, 234, 236, 237, 239, 241-243.
Contarini, Marc-Antonio, 182.
Coquibacoa, 297.
Corpus Christi College, Cambridge, 59.
Correa, Pedro, 45.
Cortereal, Gaspar and Miguel, voyages of, 299, 300.
Cosa, Juan de la, map of, 278; map discovered by Humboldt in 1832, 279; Cavo de Ynglaterra (Cape of England), 279; Mar descubierta por ingleses (sea discovered by the English), 279; map based on John Cabot's own map, 280; inscription on the map as to its construction in the year 1500, 293; birthplace of La Cosa, 293; La Cosa with Columbus in his first voyage of discovery, 293; La Cosa with Columbus in his second voyage, 294; La Cosa with Amerigo Vespucci in his voyage of 1499, 297; the completion of La Cosa's map, 278.

Cow, Dun, 108.
Cow-whale, rib of, 109, 110.
Crete, 6.
Cuba, 76, 77, 273, 295.
Cyprus, 7.

DALLAWAY'S *Antiquities of Bristol*, 56, 57.
Dandolo, Venetian Admiral, 18.
Danish King, 106.
Darius, 5.
D'Avezac, M., 178, 197, 267, 268, 275.
Dawson, Dr. S. E., of Ottawa, 149, 152, 153, 205-207, 255, 256, 279, 280, 283, 284, 287.
Deane, Charles, 273.
Deir-el-Bahari, 1.
Demons, Isle of, 31.
Demogorgon, the spirit of the ocean, 169, 173.
Denmark, 106.
Diaz, Bartholomew, 4.
Dictionary of Bristol, 110.
Diodorus, 3.
Donnelly, Ignatius, 10.
Druid, the, of Skerr, 39, 40.

EASTERN potentates, Courts of, 14.
Eden, Garden of, 38.
Eden, Richard, 170, 171, 177-180.
Edward IV., King of England, 102.
Egypt, priests of, 10, 11.
Egypt, Queen of, 1.
Egyptian Empire, 3.
Egyptian King. See Necôs.
Egyptian Nile, 5.
Egyptians, 1, 3.
Eldorado, 34.
Elizabeth, of the York family, Queen of England, 102.
Elizabeth, Queen, 133.
Elliot, Hugh, 184.
Elysian isles, 35.
Elysian plains or fields, 35, 36, 38.
Elysium, 36.
England, Cape of, in La Cosa's map, 279.
Erythræan Sea, 4.
Estevánico, 51, 52.
Europe, 5, 6, 19.

Europé, 6.
Europus, 6.

FABIAN, Robert, 250, 252-254, 259.
Falstaff, Sir John, 57.
Ferdinand and Isabella of Spain, 8, 64, 76, 101, 110, 112, 113, 141, 151, 159, 160, 163, 203.
Fernandez, Francisco, 184.
Fernandez, João, 184.
Fiske, John, 51, 52, 77, 115.
Fleming, Sandford, 115.
Florida, 250.
Florence, 89.
Florentines, 29.
Fluyt, John, 57.
Fortunate Islands, 35-37.
Fox, F. F., of Bristol, 130.
Francis I., King of France, 111.
Fray, Marco, 52.
Fuju, 23.
Fust, family of, 115-122.
Fust MS. Chronicle, 115-122.

GALVÃO, Antonio, 153, 190.
Gama, de, 3.
Garnett, Dr. R., C.B., 121, 122.
Gascony, 167.
Genoa, 86.
Genoese, 29.
Genoese merchants, 112, 113.
George, William, of Bristol, 122.
Gibraltar, Strait of, 10.
Gomara, Francisco, Lopez de, 153, 193.
Gonzales, João, 184.
Gothic kings of Spain, 44.
Goths, 87.
Grand Khan, 13, 14, 17-24, 28, 33, 74-78, 138, 140, 141.
Grant, Rev. Father, as to coins found in the Bristol River, 13.
Greek provinces, 15.
Green, Isle of, 39.
Guadalquavir, 213.
Guardafui, Cape, 1.
Guinea coast, 29.
Guyenne, map of, 167.

HAKLUYT, Richard, 103, 246-263, 275.
Hanno, 5.

Index

Hannu, 2.
Harrisse, Henry, of Paris, 83, 196, 212, 255, 261, 273, 283-287.
Harvey, Rev. Dr. (of St. John's, Newfoundland), 71, 85, 123.
Hebrews, early belief of, 11.
Henry, Prince, of Portugal, 28, 48, 49, 61, 62, 84, 102, 107, 112-114.
Henry VII., of England, 60, 70, 94-97, 100-102, 104, 105, 112-114, 124-132, 135, 136, 140, 143, 144, 148, 154, 156, 158, 159, 161, 164, 176, 181, 191, 193, 202, 245, 251, 253, 254, 266.
Henry VIII., of England, 182,185,210.
Hercules, Pillars of, 4, 10, 36.
Herodotus, 3-6.
Herrera, 297.
Hesperian Islands, 32, 37.
Hoby, Sir Philip, 232.
Homer, 34.
Hudson's Strait, 287, 290.
Humboldt, Friedrich, 36, 79, 90, 272.

IBERIA, 9.
Imago Mundi, 8.
India, 6, 9, 62.
Indian Ocean, 3.
Indies, East, 63.
Indies, West (American Islands), 294.
Isle of Antilia. See Antilia.
Isle of Brazil. See Brazil.
Isle of the Blest. See Blest.
Isle of Green. See Green.
Isle of St. Brandon. See Brandon.
Isle of San Borandon. See Brandon.
Isle of Seven Cities. See Seven Cities.

JAPAN, 19, 24, 43, 76.
Jay, John, of Bristol, 58, 108, 109.

KEFA, 2.
Kemys, Arthur, 129-133, 136, 333.
Kêphene, 2.
Khan, Grand. See Grand Khan.
Khatai, 33.
Kochhaff, Nathaniel, 263.
Kohl, J. G., 268-273.

LABRADOR, 292.
Lathrop, L., 71.

Leon, Juan Ponce de, 32, 294.
Lok, Michael, 249.
Ludovico, Mr., nephew of Toscanelli, 84.
Lybia, 3.
Lybius, 6.

MAGELLAN, the navigator, 212, 213, 216.
Major, R. H., 263, 265, 266, 276.
Mantuan Gentleman, 181, 197-204.
Manzi (or Mangi), 24, 82.
Mare Mortuum, 8.
Mare Tenebrosum, 8.
Marino, Hieronimo (the Ragusan), 214-240.
Mark, St., Church of, at Venice, 15.
Mark, St., Flag of, 15, 70.
Mark, St., Patron of Venice, 15, 141.
Markham, Sir Clements R., K.C.B., 160, 192, 299.
Martin, A. T., as to coins found in the Bristol river, 14.
Martinez, Fernando, 80.
Martyr, Peter, 33, 167-169, 171-182, 186, 188, 190, 195, 204, 205, 207, 208, 241.
Matthew, the, a ship of Bristol, 71 92, 114-116, 123, 124, 128, 155, 207.
Maundeville, Sir John, 27.
Mediterranean, 4, 86.
Meryk, Richard (or A'Meryk), 129-133, 136, 333.

NAVARETTE, 8.
Necôs, King of Egypt, 3, 4.
Neptune, 12-14.
Newfoundland, 274.
"New found land," 184, 210.
Nicholas V., Pope of Rome, 62, 214.
Niña, a ship, 293.
Non, Cape, 62.
North-west passage to the Indies, search after, 105, 185, 189, 202, 212, 216.
Nova Scotia Coast, 273, 281.

OCEANUS, 6.
Odericus, Friar, 26.
Ojeda, Alonzo de, 294, 297, 298, 300-302.
Ophir, 2, 29.

INDEX

PAPAL, Bull. See Bull.
Pasqualigo, Alvise and Francesco, 138.
Pasqualigo, Lorenzo, 138, 141.
Penn, Sir William, 108, 109.
Penn, William, 108.
Phœnicians, 1-4, 14.
Pinta, a ship, 293.
Pigott-Smyth, J. H., 118-122.
Plato, 10-12.
Plato's story of Atlantis, 10-12, 305-326.
Pliny, 36.
Polo, Andrea, 16.
Polo, Maffio, 16.
Polo, Marco, 17-26, 39, 75.
Polo, Nicolo, 16.
Portugal, 212, 299.
Portuguese, 3, 47, 61, 63, 85, 187, 188, 201, 298, 299.
Poseidon, 12.
Prester John, 33.
Procopius, 39.
Ptolemy, Claudius, 74, 104, 265, 266.
Puebla, Ruy Gonzales, 110-113.
Punt, 1, 2.

QUARITCH, B., 249.
Quinsay, City of, 82.

RACE, Cape, 279.
Rameses II., 3.
Ramusio, Giovanni Battista,
Redcliff, St. Mary, Church of (Bristol), 107-110.
Red Sea, 3.
Renaissance, period of the, 86-91.
Roman Empire, 87.
Rowley, John, 133.
Rowley, William, 133.
Rowlie, described by Chatterton, 109, 133.

SAGRES, 29.
Santa Maria, the flagship of Columbus, 293, 294
Sargossa Sea, 9.
Satanaxio or Satanatio, 31.
Sesostris, 3.
Seven Cities, Island of, 31, 43-53.

Seville, 167, 184, 199, 201, 216, 217, 226, 240.
Sforza, Ludovico, Duke of Milan, 143, 145, 152.
Solon, 10, 11.
Soncino, Raimondo, 100, 125, 142-145, 152.
Spain, 9, 28, 34, 44, 45, 71, 74, 84, 141, 151, 167, 175, 176, 210, 211, 212, 214, 268, 269, 270, 300.
Spaniards, 99, 201, 205, 211.
Stow, John, 252-255, 257-260.
Strabo, 9, 27, 34, 35.
Sturmye, Robert, of Bristol, 112.
Syria, 15.

TARDUCCI, Francesco, 142, 165, 176, 196, 255.
Thebes, 3.
Thirkill, Lancelot, 154, 155.
Thomas, John, 184.
Thorne, Nicholas, 184.
Thorne, Robert, 184.
Times Newspaper, 71.
Toby Chronicle. See Fust Chronicle.
Tolzey Court, of Bristol, Old book of, 129, 130.
Tordesillas, Treaty of, 63, 268.
Toscanelli, Paolo, 55, 79, 80-84.

VENETIANS, 16.
Venice, 15, 177, 178, 179, 180, 182, 204, 211, 216, 218, 225-241, 299.
Verde, Cape de, 62, 63, 67.
Vespucci. See Amerigo.
Vincent, Cape, 30.

WARDE, Richard, 186.
William of Worcester. See Worcestre, William.
Winsor, Justin, 275.
Worcestre Family, 57.
Worcestre, William, 57.
Wynkfeld, Sir Robert, 211.

YULE, Sir Henry, his edition of the book of Marco Polo, 20.

ZAYTON, 23, 24, 81.